P9-CCX-224

Personal data

This Book belongs to .... aged...................
who resides at ....
....
....
Their home phone number is ....
and their personal e-mail is ....
As a child they wanted to become a ....
but instead now they work at the mighty ....
corporation, where their work number is ....
and their e-mail is ....
But they would really rather people called them on their cell phone,
number..Thank you!
If you find this Book, please return it to them as soon as possible and they will
hug you ☐ praise you ☐ adopt you ☐ accuse you of stealing it ☐
If you are stalking them, please call the authorities and hand yourself in.

Nightmares? Stop reading the Book in the evening

In case of nasty accident

DOCTOR

DENTIST

HYGIENIST

Note of encouragement
to hand to Doctor:
Save my life and
you'll be rich. ☐
Amputate my
left limbs only! ☐
I didn't mean to be
rude that time, sorry. ☐
Other...................... ☐

NEW!

This Book contains some subliminal messages that will change your life without you even realizing it! We don't want to ruin the surprise, but we can reveal that one of them involves a subliminal change of lifelong political allegiance, and two of them involve your declared sexual orientation. Yowza!

Benrik Veterans

If you followed *This Book Will Change Your Life* to the letter, your life will have changed dramatically. Following the new *Book* will not reverse those changes, but may accelerate them and spin them out of control! Benrik recommend that you lie fallow for one year and follow this one next year.

BOOKCROSSING

This Book has been registered for bookcrossing. Bookcrossing is the practice of leaving books out for others to pick up "in the wild," and tracing successive owners on www.bookcrossing.com. Benrik however are adding a twist: this book must be stolen, not just abandoned. Its new owner must record how they stole it, who they stole it from, and what they propose to do to prevent others stealing it. The Book's official number is: *Please note: obviously, do not return it to the owner if you have stolen it, as that would defeat the point.*

BCID: 237-2698660

BOOK INSTRUCTIONS
Please read before use!

The first *Book Will Change Your Life* had a profound effect on the lives of those who followed it, with many reporting radical personal upheaval of the kind that defies expression, let alone medical treatment. *This Book Will Change Your Life, Again!* aims to surpass that. If everyone in the whole wide world came together and followed this book for 365 days, then the world would be, if not strictly speaking a better place, then at least very different in many respects. Good luck with it.

Deposit a drop of your urine here to mark your territory and let the others know this book belongs to you.

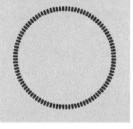

FOLLOW BENRIK AND BECOME FAMOUS!

Go to www.thiswebsitewillchangeyourlife.com to set up your very own blog and let everyone keep up with your progress as you follow the Book's dictates day by day! The most-read blogs will rise to the top of the Benrik blog chart and their authors will become famous and land lucrative publishing deals. At that point Benrik may well decide to sue for a share of the profits, but let's cross that bridge when we come to it. Happy blogging!

Benrik Limited

Benrik are Ben Carey and Henrik Delehag. They became friends when they discovered they were both of uncertain parentage, a bond that has sustained them through difficult times. They founded Benrik Limited in order to impose their twisted values on the public. Benrik Ltd is the first openly evil corporation, aiming to violate ethical standards wherever feasible. So far, Benrik have published *This Book Will Change Your Life* and *This Book Will Change Your Life, Again!*, which have been hand-colored by 12-year-old Guatemalan orphans. They have also moved to acquire 10 acres of rainforest for their upcoming furniture range. Their profit margin is a healthy 9%, which represents a year-on-year increase of 42% (see accounts at the back of this book). They are also the people behind *This Book Will Change Your Love Life*, a guide to the modern relationship. Their slogan encapsulates their global vision:

Your values are our toilet paper

MOOD-CHART DELUXE

Mood	01	02	03	04	05	06	07	08	09	10	11	12	13	14
ORGASMIC!														
OVER THE MOON														
HAPPY AS LARRY														
FINE, THANK YOU!														
OK														
SO-SO														
PISSED OFF														
MAD AS HELL														
DEEPLY DEPRESSED														
SUICIDAL														

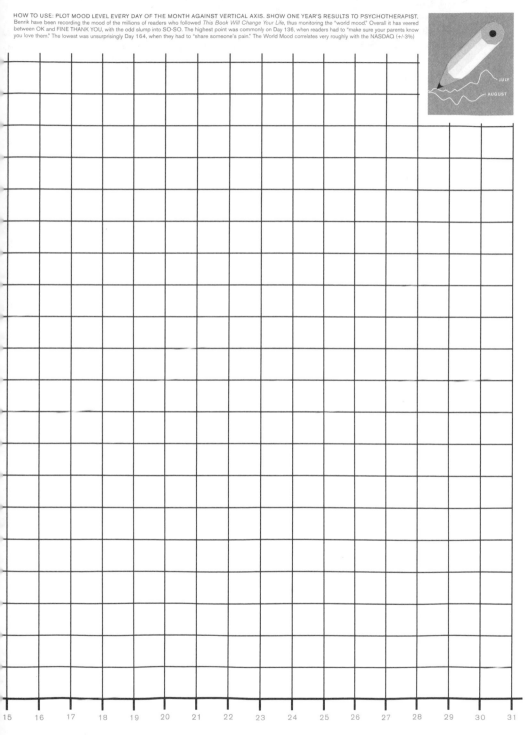

HOW TO USE: PLOT MOOD LEVEL EVERY DAY OF THE MONTH AGAINST VERTICAL AXIS. SHOW ONE YEAR'S RESULTS TO PSYCHOTHERAPIST.
Benrik have been recording the mood of the millions of readers who followed *This Book Will Change Your Life*, thus monitoring the "world mood." Overall it has veered between OK and FINE THANK YOU, with the odd slump into SO-SO. The highest point was commonly on Day 136, when readers had to "make sure your parents know you love them." The lowest was unsurprisingly Day 164, when they had to "share someone's pain." The World Mood correlates very roughly with the NASDAQ (+/-3%)

JULY

AUGUST

15   16   17   18   19   20   21   22   23   24   25   26   27   28   29   30   31

Life planner

1 Crucial formative influences	**13** Puberty (boys)	**25**
2	**14** First cigarette behind bike shed	**26**
3	**15**	**27**
4	**16** Exams	**28** Marriage and mortgage
5	**17**	**29**
6	**18** Prom	**30** Party
7	**19**	**31** Settle down
8	**20**	**32**
9	**21** Drink legally	**33**
10	**22** End of youthful illusions	**34**
11 Puberty (girls)	**23**	**35** Itch (seven year-)
12	**24**	**36**

Other

37		49		61	
38		50	Party	62	
39		51		63	
40	Party	52		64	
41		53		65	
42		54		66	
43		55		67	
44	Midlife crisis	56		68	
45	Take up golf	57		69	
46		58		70	Party
47		59	Pay off mortgage	71	
48		60	Retirement party	72	

Other

WARM-UP DAY

This is the first day of your life change, so take it easy and warm up with a gentle task. Any of these will change your life - but only a little bit.

Lose one ounce
in weight

Basejump
off a chair

Donate your baby
teeth to science

Save the life
of an ant

Tell your deepest secret
to the talking clock

Go on a
one-man protest

Make a small
dream come true

Sow one seed
of anarchy

Dye your hair its
natural color

Watch a different
TV channel

Eliminate avocados
from your diet

Gamble $1
on a horse

Write the first
letter of a novel

Graffiti with
a pencil

Join a sect
part-time

Get a microscopic
tattoo

Clear out your
belly fluff

Sexually harass
yourself

Day 1

As you follow the Book, note all life-changes day by day in these convenient boxes. And if you're really keen, reveal your progress in your very own blog on www.thiswebsitewillchangeyourlife.com

Your life should have changed, but not measurably.

Claim you're Jesus Day

There are few surefire ways of transforming your life on the spot. Claiming to be Jesus is definitely one of them. So brighten everyone's Sunday by donning a white robe, borrowing a trumpet, and popping down to church in time for mass. The local chaplain should let you in, just on the off-chance you're the real deal.

Tell everyone you're not happy about their sinning and fornicating, but you're prepared to give most of them a second chance in the spirit of true forgiveness, which after all you invented. Perform a couple of miracles as proof of identity, call up the Pope, and begin 1,000 year reign.

(This day presents a slight risk that you will be locked up or crucified, in which case you won't have much use for this Book. Donate it to someone who can't afford a copy.)

Day 2

Promote the Book Day

Promote the Book Day!

Don't be selfish...

Don't be selfish: share the Book with others. Following it on your own isn't half as much fun as being part of a crowd. Plus, it'll make your acquaintances a lot more interesting. Get everyone you know to purchase a copy, the more the merrier. Persuasive tactics include: Refusing to see family members until they've bought a copy. Only talking about the Book and what you've done that day. Standing in public places reading it and laughing out loud every time someone walks past. Pestering bookstore staff with helpful queries like "Why

continues in green box...

Day 3

...cont. from blue box

isn't *This Book Will Change Your Life, Again!* in the window?" Calling your kids' teachers and complaining the Book isn't on the syllabus.

end of text, but there is more to read under the image.

He helped us last time...

Don't be selfish...

Bonus!

Follow the "I want to help" instructions on our website and we'll print your name in our "Benrik Hall Of Fame"! Here is the Benrik Hall Of Fame for last year. Long may their names be revered. Josh Barwick, Lewis More O'Ferrall, Rebecca Bland, Katie Cirillo, Jemimah Rainfray-Miles, Tigger Hall, Joanne Skelton, Veronique Voiret, Gaby Vinader, Linda Jackson, Bozena Birt, Kathy Peach, Lee Gage, Teresa Cowherd, Madelaine Levy, Peder Bonnier, Anna Nolendorfs, Patrick Sehlstedt, Alain Lecornet, Juliana Uhart, Kuhan Satkunanayagam, Kevin Rogers, Renate Lunn, Helena Dixon, Lottie Desmond, Erica Winston, Liam Woodiwiss, Anna Rogan, Simon Kay, Josh Drew, Lee Brown, Sophie Church, Alex Pansin, Gail Bradley, Mark McLaughlin, Matthew Tan, Luke Chase, Gavin Watling, John Nightingale, Louise Blackwell, Paul Sands, Elliot Mason, Trevor Hayes, Miriam Rosen, Nancy Partington, Jessica Davies, Lauren Adams, Annabel Chandler, Gertrude Abbey, Benjamin Richardson, Darren Linley, Lily Samuel, Gillian Smith, Jacob Holden, Aubrey Woodruff, Nicolas Brant, Catherine Fordham, Gary Amberly, Lucas Mires, Ian Bowes, Katie Coleman, Anne-Marie Payne, Alexander Wright, Daniel Gibson, Adam Nicols, Jamie Kennedy, Laura Weiss, Pearl Long, Mike Smith, Jenny Lindhill, Daphne Enfield, Miranda Carpenter, Barry Elson, Amanda Jones, Chris Fitzgerald, Neil Buttle, Jolie Kashkoll, Alan Payne, Ann Harden, Marco Stipe, Jean-Marie Bardon, Bernie Moxham, Sylvia Skelton, John Billington. To feature in next year's Hall Of Fame and see your very own name in print, visit www.thiswebsitewillchangeyourlife.com now!

end of all texts

Obedience Day

Obedience is a skill. Exercise it today by following these simple dictates and you'll find the rest of the Book easier to obey

Speak extra loud to people with names beginning with R today

Walk slower if shorter than the person walking next to you

Refuse to answer any question where the words "you" and "with" are used

Do not accept change if less than 30¢

Feign not to see people wearing red

Stay indoors if clouds are heading east or south

Cross the road whenever a passerby makes eye contact

Clip out all newspaper headlines featuring the word "global" and paste them above your desk

Order the fifth most expensive item on the menu

Introduce yourself to anyone named Bob

Drive at 36 miles per hour exactly

Pick up the phone after five rings

Do not use the letter "d" in any correspondence

Use only the buttons on the top half of your remote control

Increase central heating temperature by 1°F every hour

Only use words invented before 1979

Speak to a minimum of 9 people an hour

Proffer your leg as a lamp post to any passing dog

Chew every mouthful a dozen times before swallowing

Leave the room if anyone with the same first name as you is mentioned

Day 4

Cannibalism Day:
Today eat part ~~whole~~ of a loved one

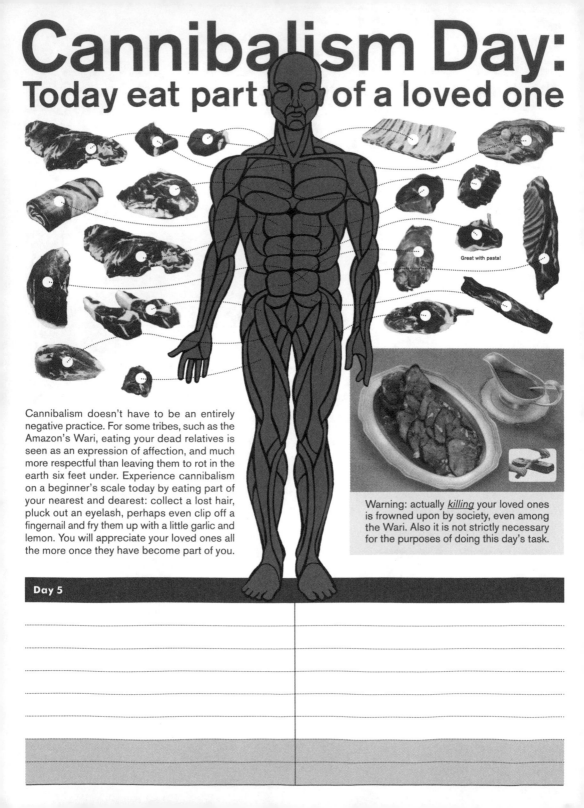

Great with pasta!

Cannibalism doesn't have to be an entirely negative practice. For some tribes, such as the Amazon's Wari, eating your dead relatives is seen as an expression of affection, and much more respectful than leaving them to rot in the earth six feet under. Experience cannibalism on a beginner's scale today by eating part of your nearest and dearest: collect a lost hair, pluck out an eyelash, perhaps even clip off a fingernail and fry them up with a little garlic and lemon. You will appreciate your loved ones all the more once they have become part of you.

Warning: actually _killing_ your loved ones is frowned upon by society, even among the Wari. Also it is not strictly necessary for the purposes of doing this day's task.

Day 5

MARRY JONAS DAY!

This is Jonas Jansson, famous from last year's Book. Jonas is 22, but he has aged 7 years in the last 365 days.

He has been the Book's guinea pig, following each day to the letter and recording the results in his blog. As a result, he has been dumped by his girlfriend Magda, lost and recovered his dog Underdog, acquired a swearing parrot, donated his appendix to science, traveled to France, smooched his cousin, become a poet, had a gay encounter, gone on strike, been fired and re-hired three times, had his existence questioned, done a runner, told his parents he loves them, received hate mail from Ku Klux Klan members, received love mail from numerous teenage girls, turned down countless media interviews, poisoned his pee with asparagus, tried to collapse the currency of Bangladesh, started to eat a piece of furniture, counted all his farts, engaged in correspondence with the Unabomber, and all this under the daily scrutiny of dozens of thousands of fans worldwide. His life has changed: he is now a man! This year, Benrik have agreed to pick a suitable bride for him from amongst their readers. Jonas is a liberal type, so this opportunity is also open to men, in line with brand new Swedish legislation. The kind of person Benrik will be looking for should be adventurous at heart, attractive in spirit, with an appetite for the finer things in life and a VGSOH to cope with the media attention and constant offers of sexual relations that Jonas now receives from total strangers. Anyone with a previous restraining order to their name will be disqualified, particularly if the order was in relation to Jonas. You may apply to marry Jonas Jansson on www.thiswebsitewillchangeyourlife.com. Please do not try to contact Jonas directly about this offer, as it is a small surprise to thank him for his cooperation last year. The winning spouse should be prepared to move to Stockholm, Sweden. You may find out more about his moral character and achievements on the website, where you will also find an adults-only photo gallery and a comments section. Good luck!

Warning note: Jonas has been entangled in a crazy rollercoaster relationship with Magda, who does not approve of his involvement with Benrik. We are quite confident though that once a legitimate (not to say suitable!) bride is found for Jonas, Magda will realize she cannot selfishly keep him from his true destiny, and will be out of the picture. Besides, you are much much prettier than she is. Any fool can tell that!

YOU COULD BE NEXT!!!

The last few years have seen the proliferation of wild blogs. This year, you may officially register to start your very own blog on www.thiswebsitewillchangeyourlife.com and follow the Book online. The blogs will be ranked by number of hits, so the most entertaining and radical life changes will rise to the top and spawn their own cults. The leading blogger gets to be Jonas Jansson's best man at his glittering showbiz wedding. Register now to avoid disappointment.

Day 6

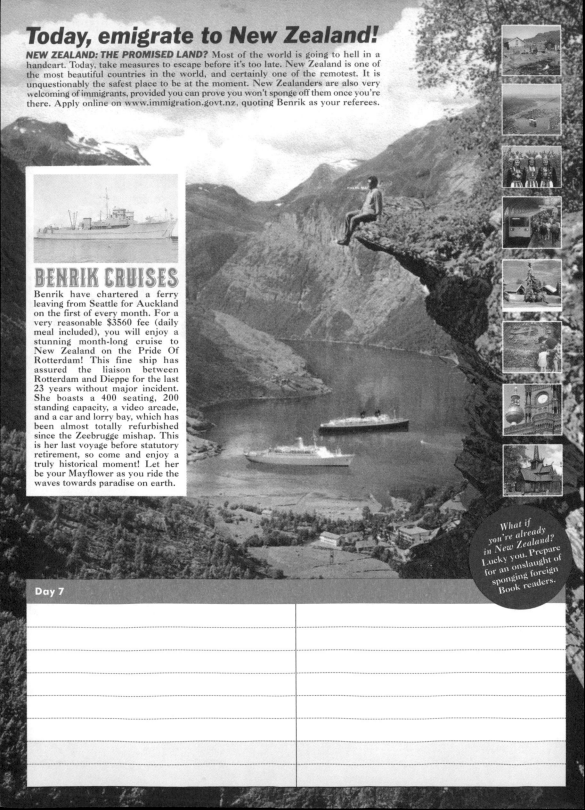

Today, emigrate to New Zealand!

NEW ZEALAND: THE PROMISED LAND? Most of the world is going to hell in a handcart. Today, take measures to escape before it's too late. New Zealand is one of the most beautiful countries in the world, and certainly one of the remotest. It is unquestionably the safest place to be at the moment. New Zealanders are also very welcoming of immigrants, provided you can prove you won't sponge off them once you're there. Apply online on www.immigration.govt.nz, quoting Benrik as your referees.

BENRIK CRUISES

Benrik have chartered a ferry leaving from Seattle for Auckland on the first of every month. For a very reasonable $3560 fee (daily meal included), you will enjoy a stunning month-long cruise to New Zealand on the Pride Of Rotterdam! This fine ship has assured the liaison between Rotterdam and Dieppe for the last 23 years without major incident. She boasts a 400 seating, 200 standing capacity, a video arcade, and a car and lorry bay, which has been almost totally refurbished since the Zeebrugge mishap. This is her last voyage before statutory retirement, so come and enjoy a truly historical moment! Let her be your Mayflower as you ride the waves towards paradise on earth.

What if you're already in New Zealand? Lucky you. Prepare for an onslaught of sponging foreign Book readers.

Day 7

The
Kama Sutra
for One

the single person's
guide to pleasure

How square
are you?

A humorous
guide to maths

A year
in Bonn

The expat
experience
exposed

Stupid
parents
stupid
kids

Write a bestseller today

There is no easier way to fame and fortune than to write a bestseller. It needn't take much more than a day, particularly with these bright ideas to inspire you.

The
Secret
Story of
soup

The fascinating
history of soup

Tim Johnson:
the anonymous
murderer

A whodunnit
with a difference

Lose
weight
get
laid
find
God

The all-
in-one
action
plan

Who
cares?

1001
semi-hilarious
facts

The birds,
the bees
and the
rhino.

What they never
taught you
about sex

1985

The
sequel

The
Naked
Guest

A cookbook
for cannibals

This
Book
will change
your life
back!

Today: Buy a stranger flowers

Chrysanthemum
You're a
wonderful friend

White camellia
You're adorable

Acacia
I love you secretly

Red rose
I love you

Petunia
Your presence
soothes me

Primrose
I can't live
without you

White lilac
I'm a virgin,
please be gentle

Tulip
You are the perfect lover

Yellow hyacinth
I'm jealous

Yellow carnation
You have
disappointed me

Bluebell
I'm not worthy

Purple hyacinth
I'm sorry please
forgive me

Pink carnation
I'll never forget you

Daffodil
Are you still here?

Crocus
If you call again,
I'll get an injunction

Day 9

BOYCOTT
SOMETHING
THAT'S NEVER BEEN
BOYCOTTED BEFORE

Rhododendrons Porcini Brooklyn Bridge Handshakes Oxygen Motherhood Smurfs Camels Surprise birthday parties 3B pencils Clouds with phallic shapes Gravity Innuendo Clothes Money Fax machines Hope Tasmania Viagra Horizontal stripes Caravaggio Stupidity Nelson Mandela Lopsided grins The flu The Queen Ugly suitcases Lawyers Love songs Apple pie Ballroom dancing Children Recycling Coconuts Sunshine Mascara Agatha Christie Plutonium Milkshakes Benrik Limited Plywood Tuesdays Soft focus photography Running Cancer The Danube Aircraft carriers Mimes Beauty Watercoolers Shadows Culture Shower gel Chainsaws Business cards Alopecia Timidity Plasticine Birmingham Cantilevering Taboos Menhirs Song Suicide Chopsticks Miracles Spirals Tamagotchis Fire Instamatics Catalogs Bastards who use you then discard you like a dirty tissue Exits Ciphers Freaks of nature Chaos Soup Jupiter The man in the moon Witchcraft Catamites Asphalt DNA Rock'n'roll The Tudor dynasty Riffs Ecuadoreans Photosynthesis Leprosy Satellites Monkfish Tasmania Repetition Donuts Hurricanes Trimesters Repetition Man's inhumanity to man Mildew Transitions Business lunches Boycotts

Day 10	

TODAY, APPLY TO AN ORGY

Swinging is the new clubbing. No longer the preserve of suburban housewives, the modern swinger's party is packed with beautiful young things. Would you make the grade? Apply with your photo and that of your unsuspecting partner at feverparties.com and find out if you are deemed to be acceptable orgy material.

Day 11

Mainstream Day

Stop rocking the boat! Today make sure your tastes and actions don't clash with those of 95% of the population.

Music

Listen to Celine Dion's "The Colour of My Love" followed by "Love Doesn't Ask Why." Repeat until you know the words.

Clothes

Plain jeans and a T-shirt (nondescript) if you're under 40, checkered shirt and beige slacks if you're 40+.

Shoes

Purchase white sneakers from a widely marketed brand, from the less fancy end of the range. Size (US): 6-8 (women) 8-11 (men).

Hobbies

Enjoy the following for half an hour each: reading, walking, listening to music, gardening.

Sex

Have sex with a partner of the opposite gender, to include: 5 minutes of foreplay, 10 minutes of missionary position, 1 orgasm (men), 1 fake orgasm (women).

Politics

Express overall agreement with the free market, but wish there was a cuddlier alternative.

Art

Buy an Impressionist postcard (Manet or Monet) and send it to a distant relative.

Sport

Support a football team, and derive much-needed emotional strength from your unspoken bond with other supporters.

Television

Yes please!

Dreams

Dream of paying off the mortgage, landing that promotion, and taking out the neighborhood with an AK-47 machine gun.

Day 12

Ask KFC for the 11 secret herbs
and spices. Go home and make your
own special fingerlickin' chicken.
If they won't give you the recipe,
experiment till you get it right.

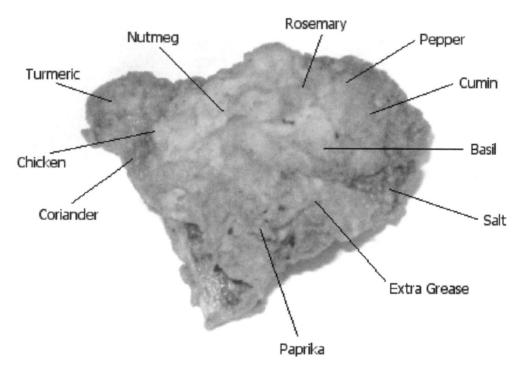

Turmeric · Nutmeg · Rosemary · Pepper · Cumin · Chicken · Basil · Coriander · Salt · Paprika · Extra Grease

Day 13

Family Day

Ben's cousin Amy (age 9)
My cousin Ben is special because he lives in England. I live in New Zealand in a town called Wellington. Cousin Ben doesn't live here because his Daddy and Mummy runned away when he was small. They were being chased by a nasty man called the Taxman. But Mummy says don't talk about it. Cousin Ben is funny. He makes me laugh because he is so ugly with his glasses. I laugh a lot when he visits. Mummy and Daddy laugh too, but not when he is in the room. Cousin Ben writes books. Daddy won't let me read them. One of them is called "that bloody filth." One day I will visit cousin Ben in England.

Henrik's brother Claes (age 6)
Henke is my big brother. His real name is Henrik but we call him Henke. Henke is my big brother but really he was adopted, after Daddy had his operation. He does not know this. Mummy says she will tell him when he is mature. But I love him anyway. Henke is always drawing stuff. The doctor said it was good for him and his aggressivity. I like it when he draws stuff because he stops hitting me so much and the house is nice and quiet, like when he was at the detention center. We visited him every month on Sundays and then we went to church to pray for him. Church is also nice and quiet. I want Mummy to adopt a little boy so I can have a little brother too.

Day 14

Dump your partner for the day

The best way to reinvigorate a relationship is a short sharp separation. Today, announce to your other half that you're done with them and storm out.

Top tips for the temporarily single

Play the field: technically you're not in a relationship today, so fool around and satisfy your animal lust.

Bitch about him/her: provided you don't tell them it's only for the day, your friends will enjoy revealing they actually hated your ex.

Do that thing that you stopped doing because they hate it: pluck your nose hair in front of the TV, wear those furry slippers, let the phone ring and ring.

Enjoy a bottle of wine all by yourself: solitary drinking is much more fun on your own.

Masturbation rules OK! as Woody Allen famously said, it's sex with someone you love.

Day 15

Test a proverb today and record its practical usefulness. Here is a selection:

The best things in life are free

It takes two to tango

When the cat's away the mice will play

An apple a day keeps the doctor away

Look before you leap

Example: The grass is always greener on the other side of the fence

How to test the proverb: Find a fence with grass on both sides. Position yourself on one side and record the degree of greenness. Then climb the fence over to the "other side" and repeat the observation procedure. Compare the different measurings and draw your own conclusions.

Bad news travels fast

Curiosity **killed the cat**

Fight fire with fire

Nothing ventured nothing gained

Never look a gift horse in the mouth

Revenge is sweet

Strike while the iron is hot

Honesty is **the best policy**

The early bird catches the morning worm

All roads lead to Rome

Laughter is the best medicine

You win some you lose some

How I tested the proverb:

....
....
....
....

Beat your wife every day - if you don't know why, she will

You cannot have your cake and eat it

Truth.........................../10
Usefulness.............../10

....
....
....
....
....

Today Review this Book

What I enjoyed most of all about *This Book Will Change Your Life, Again!* was:

....
....
....
....
....
....
....
....
....
....
....
....
....

What people have said about the first Book Will Change Your Life

"Can I have my money back" (N, Turner)

"An insult to the people of Bangladesh" (B. V. Virgin MP)

"You will regret this" (Ku Klux Klan HQ, Alabama)

"Amusing in parts" (Poughkeepsie Weekly News)

"Having perused your book, our clients have instructed us to issue an injunction" (Harborough Wilkinson Solicitors)

"You made me larf and larf. When I get out let's meet" (45-5678-765)

Day 17

Free someone today!

Leonard Peltier has been incarcerated for 28 years at Leavenworth Penitentiary, Kansas, after being convicted of the murder of two FBI agents in 1975. The two agents died in a shoot-out at Wounded Knee, on the Pine Ridge Indian Reservation. Mr. Peltier has always protested his innocence, and has fought his conviction on the grounds that he was made a scapegoat by the FBI.

Since 1973, the Reservation had been the scene of heightened tension and political violence between law enforcement agencies, local tribal bodies and the American Indian Movement (AIM), who sought repair for historical injustices to Native Americans. AIM had occupied Wounded Knee, and according to Peltier's supporters, clashed with a local political boss and his vigilante posse, the self-styled GOONS. According to Peltier's supporters, AIM were subjected to a "reign of terror" by the GOONS, who murdered 64 local Native Americans and abused hundreds of others, with the unspoken complicity of the FBI. Peltier's supporters believe that at the time the FBI and other government agencies saw it as their mission to target and harass what they considered to be "subversive" movements, such as AIM.

On June 26, 1975, FBI agents Jack Coler and Ron Williams set off in pursuit of a red pick-up truck driven by a Native American that headed for the Jumping Bull Ranch. The ranch elders had invited dozens of AIM members to camp there to protect them against GOONS attack. One of them was Leonard Peltier, an AIM organizer from the Northwest. When the unmarked FBI car irrupted onto the (private) property, panic broke out and a gunfight started, trapping families and children in the crossfire. Soon FBI, SWAT team members and GOONS were exchanging fire with the residents.

When the incident ended, three men lay dead: FBI agents Coler and Williams and a young Native American Joe Stuntz (whose death by sniper bullet was never investigated). The two FBI agents had been wounded then shot in the head at close range. Murder charges were brought against three AIM leaders, including Mr. Peltier. The two others were acquitted after the jury found there was no conclusive evidence to link them to the fatal shots, and that the exchange of gunfire from such a distance constituted self-defense.

Mr. Peltier was not as fortunate. He was extradited from Canada based on the testimony of a mentally disturbed woman (Myrtle Poor Bear) who claimed that she was his girlfriend and that she had witnessed him killing the agents. Later she recanted and admitted she had never even met him. Mr. Peltier stood trial in conservative North Dakota. The context of political violence on Pine Ridge was not explained. According to Peltier's supporters, FBI testimony regarding the red pick-up truck was mysteriously changed to a red and white van which Mr. Peltier could more easily be linked to. Three teenage witnesses testified against Mr. Peltier, though even then none identified him as the shooter. Tens of thousands of documents were withheld from the defense team, including the results of a ballistics test that proved the fatal bullets did not come from Mr. Peltier's gun. This evidence was allegedly concealed and was only obtained much later through the Freedom of Information Act. Leonard Peltier was sentenced to two consecutive life sentences.

Despite the new evidence, he has been denied a retrial, and denied parole until 2008 despite being long overdue. In a 2000 parole hearing, it was made clear that Mr. Peltier would not receive parole until he "recognizes his crime." In the view of the Peltier legal team, this amounts to "personalized vengeance" on the behalf of US officials, making Mr. Peltier the scapegoat for the FBI agents' killings, though there was no real evidence that he was responsible.

Mr. Peltier suffers from diabetes, high blood pressure and heart problems. He is now 61 years old and his condition is deteriorating. Numerous organizations and people from Amnesty International to Archbishop Desmond Tutu have called for his release. Help free him by writing in support of his case to Kansas Congressman Jerry Moran, 1519 Longworth House, Office Building, Washington DC 20515.

Day 18

Today test the power of prayer

Prayer is a very much underexploited resource in modern society. Just because prayers sound fancier if they're about world peace doesn't mean they can't work for more mundane matters. Put those atheistic leanings aside and test the power of prayer today.

Dear God,
May interest rates stay as they are so that I may not be forced to sell my home and live out in the suburbs where the houses are ugly and the parks are brown.

Dear Lord,
May you ensure fine weather this weekend as I am planning to plant those petunias.

Father,
Please let the supermarket not have run out of seabass for then I shall be forced to reconsider my entire dinner party menu.

Lord,
Please let my boss realize that I have been working like a dog and grant me that day off that I urgently need to go to the VD clinic.

Dear Lord,
Help me find the strength to stop buying those consumer goods that I cannot afford, such as that $59.99 mail order breadmaker.

Father,
Please stop those pigeons from shitting on my doorstep. I do not wish to harm them but they are driving me berserk with their cooing all night long.

Dear God,
I pray that the television channels I receive may prove entertaining enough this week to fill the black hole that is my social life.

Dear God,
I pray that my girlfriend won't leave me. I dumped her for a day last week as the Book said and she cannot see the joke.

Day 19

Your prayer

Answered ■ Not answered ■

TODAY IS FEAST DAY

Protest against our anorexic times by stuffing yourself in Roman Emperor style all day long. Invite all your friends over. Lie down rather than sit, as it's less tiring and makes it easier to slip into sexual debauchery if necessary. Prepare all the dishes ahead of time so eating is not interrupted. Chatting may be allowed provided that it does not impede the flow of food. Copious drinking will help wash it down. Once you literally cannot stomach any more, vomit and start afresh. When in Rome…

Day 20

Invent your own traffic rule of the road and obey it
Rules of the road in Benrikland (excerpts):

Decide which side of the road feels "right" for you

When you see a green car, turn left

Picking up every third hitchhiker is compulsory

Women drivers have right of way

Play chicken with oncoming cars if their numberplates feature the letter H

Swerve to make other drivers believe there's ice on the road

Defective traffic light: anything goes

Don't go here unless you have enough money to bribe the traffic officer

Travel at exactly this speed

Have road rage attack at the next intersection

Alien abduction zone: lock your doors and wind up your windows

Turn back now

Paint its nail with expensive varnish / Surround it in clingfilm so it doesn't wrinkle in the bath / Have it massaged by a toe fetishist / Buy shoes that are comfortable for it but not for the other toes / Put it down on the "bionic toe operations" waiting list / Kiss it goodnight and tell it a fairy tale to help it go to sleep

Day 22

Record the next generation of canned laughter!!!

HAHA HAHA HAHAHA

HA HA HA

HA

HA HA! HA HA

HA!

HAHA!

Ha

"Most of the canned laughter on television was recorded in the early 50s. The people we hear laughing most often may already be dead" (Chuck Palahniuk, *Lullaby*)

HAHAH HAHAH HAHAHA

HA HAHA

HAH AHA

HA

HAHAHA HAHAHAH AHAHAHA

HA HA HA

HAHAH AHAHAH HAH AHA HA

Benrik have taken it upon themselves to update the obsolete canned laughter of our times. Fifties laughter spells fifties humor. Could you be the laugh of the next generation of sitcoms, and earn fabulous money in the process? Record your laugh via www.thiswebsitewillchangeyourlife.com today and see if it wins the "canned laughter" vote. The winner will be promoted to TV networks across the globe. Good luck. Hahahahahaahahahahahahahahahaha!

HAH HAH

HO

Day 23

I CAN'T LAUGH

WHAT'S THE USE?

Speak to people as if you were a global corporation today

Milk in your coffee?
Let's brainstorm how to calibrate the synergy of your baseline items going forward.

How about a date?
Let's align timeframes in view of a merger with mutual cross-linking benefits.

I'm late, sorry.
The window of opportunity for an optimal win-win arrival time is in jeopardy.

I'm very drunk.
Within a horizontal framework, let us take a 360 degree blue sky look at our increasingly volatile operating environment.

What time does the next train leave?
We need to ascertain the variables that impact on stepchange in provision of core market programmes.

I'm leaving you.
The cross-pollinating partnering paradigm that has governed our dialoging has been rightsized.

Day 24

FIND YOUR SELF TODAY

Ask a lover, a friend and an enemy to place you on this map of self.
Then link the three: this gives you the rough shape of your self.

Yuppie
Foreign
A-type
Hilarious
Admirable

Outgoing
Witty

Capitalist
Philistine
Resourceful
Serene
Happy
Gourmet

Charming
Just

Manipulative
Energetic
Well-adjusted

Loving

Driven
Handsome

Ambitious
Diplomatic
Beautiful

Twit
Polite

Prostitute
Connoisseur

Unfair
Inspiring

Egocentric
Greedy
Mean
Smelly
Artist

Dishonest

Angry
Shit
Nasty
Worthless
Geek

Depressing
Loon
Incompetent

Disgusting
Asshole
Ugly
Loser

Nazi
Hateful

Maniac
Idiotic
Repressed
Self-loathing

Flatulent
Crass
Lost

Dumb
Stupid

Sadist
Moron
Liar
Loner

Boring
Perverted
Blasphemous
Weakling
Dreamer

Odious
Beast

Pig
Ignorant
Nutcase
Mentally unstable

Pathetic
Repugnant
Druggie

Depraved
Satanic
Psychopath
Poet

Day 25

NIGHTTIME DAY:

You may spend most of your life in the pallid world of daytime work and commuting, but come the night, you are free to venture out on the dark side. As Milton said, "What hath night to do with sleep"?

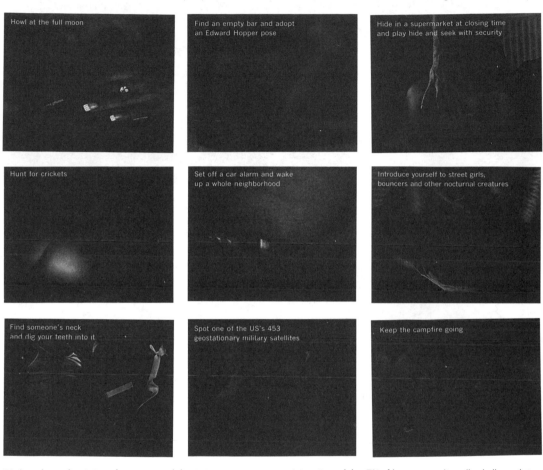

Howl at the full moon

Find an empty bar and adopt an Edward Hopper pose

Hide in a supermarket at closing time and play hide and seek with security

Hunt for crickets

Set off a car alarm and wake up a whole neighborhood

Introduce yourself to street girls, bouncers and other nocturnal creatures

Find someone's neck and dig your teeth into it

Spot one of the US's 453 geostationary military satellites

Keep the campfire going

Night owls are the victims of unrecognized discrimination in our society. It is estimated that 7% of humans are diurnally challenged, i.e. they function better at night. All our institutions and customs, however, are geared towards "day people," starting with the practice of daytime business hours. "Night people" are not equipped to succeed in such conditions, and often lose out on social advancement by virtue of their "disability." Call your congressman to protest, and to underscore your point, call him or her at home in the middle of the damn night.

Day 26

Today download and spread a computer virus

Benrik have designed a computer virus named Eugenia that allows us total control of your computer for the day. Simply download our new remote access Trojan program from www.thiswebsitewillchangeyourlife.com and today we will take over your PC or Mac, deleting your useless files, reconfiguring your hard drive and emailing everyone in your address book with sordid details of your past, as well as their very own copy of Eugenia. Benrik's goal is to control ten million computers remotely (any more would overload our current server). Then we can all start having a little global fun. Don't miss out kids!

If it does not work on your computer, cut this one out and stick it with sellotape or glue to the middle of your computer-screen

System requirements: a 400Mhz Power PC G3 or faster Macintosh computer, an Intel Pentium processor-based PC, at least 1MB of available hard disk space, at least 2MB of RAM, Mac OS 9/OS X, or Windows 98/Me/2000/XP, broadband connection 512 Kps min, Internet Explorer version 5.1 and later, Microsoft Outlook version 5.01 and later.

Day 27

Today, speak only Esperanto

Esperanto is the most successful artificial language, with over 2 million speakers worldwide. It was conceived and published by Ludovic Lazarus Zamenhof in the 1880s with the aim of replacing complicated and exclusive "unplanned" languages, thus facilitating world peace. This is why dictators have often perceived it as a threat, with Stalin for instance calling it "the dangerous language" and deporting all its registered speakers to Siberia in 1938. Every letter in Esperanto has only one sound, every word is pronounced as it is spelled, the grammar consists of 16 simple rules, and only 500 words are required for basic conversation. Do your bit to advance the cause of global harmony with this little primer, full of useful sentences that you will not find in the phrasebooks.

This is a citizen's arrest, drop your knives.
Mi civitan-arestas vin, faligu viajn tranĉilojn.

I am looking for an Esperanto-speaking dominatrix.
Mi serĉas seksmastrinon kiu parolas esperanton.

Quick! I need emergency surgery now!
Rapidu! Mi urĝe bezonas kirurgion nun!

If you park in my spot, I will shoot you in the head.
Mi vian kapon pafos se vi s'telos mian parklokon.

The referee is blind.
La arbitristo blindas.

Our plans for invasion are finally ready.
Niaj planoj invadi finfine pretas.

That's a massive line of cocaine.
Longegas tiu linio da kokaino.

You goddamn retard, don't you understand Esperanto?
Vi volapukisto, ĉu Esperanton vi ne komprenas?

*Have you heard the music of Phil Collins?
**Sussudio is my favorite record

Day 28

Today,
eat only
one color

Green

(examples: peas,
broccoli, salads, beans,
apples, olives, spinach)

Challenging

Orange

(examples: carrots,
oranges, pumpkin)

Advanced

Blue

(no, "blueberries"
don't count)

Day 29

NB: Eating out? Carry emergency food coloring, and refuse to eat any dish until the chef has dyed it.

TODAY PREPARE YOUR PANIC ROOM WHERE IN YOUR HOUSE WOULD YOU SEEK REFUGE FROM POTENTIAL PSYCHOPATHS? TODAY REVIEW YOUR INTERIOR AND MAKE SURE IT FEATURES A SECURE HIDEY-HOLE!

Day 30

Parasite Day

In our intricate society, there are many opportunities for free-riding. Today see if you can live literally at the expense of others.

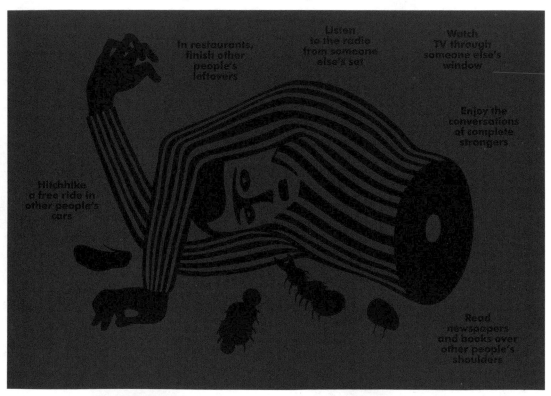

Listen to the radio from someone else's set

Watch TV through someone else's window

In restaurants, finish other people's leftovers

Enjoy the conversations of complete strangers

Hitchhike a free ride in other people's cars

Read newspapers and books over other people's shoulders

Day 31

Pretend To Be Pregnant Day

Tuck a small pillow under your shirt and walk around in bare feet, holding your back all day long. Every once in a while, run to the bathroom and make vomiting noises. During your lunch break, go to a children's clothing store and coo over tiny socks and romper suits. Return to your place of work with three large packs of disposable diapers, claiming you're "stocking up," then cry hysterically with pure happiness or terror, depending on what kind of person you are. Spend your evening not drinking alcohol or coffee, or smoking, and instead rope your partner into choosing baby names.

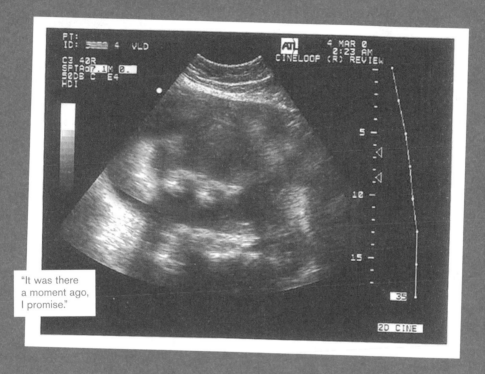

"It was there a moment ago, I promise."

This day will prove particularly educational for men.

Day 32	

Day 33

TODAY LEARN TO HYPNOTIZE YOURSELF

Record this script on a tape and play it back to yourself as you sit in a cozy armchair. Eventually you will know it by heart and will be able to reach a deep soothing state of self-hypnosis simply by thinking of its dulcet tones.

I am closing my eyes...I am making myself comfortable... by closing my eyes I am shutting out all the cares of my world...they are outside of me now...those cares and worries belong to someone else...I am relaxing all my muscles one by one...my muscles are no longer tense and fibrous... my muscles are loose and all spongelike...I can see a glowing light...I will follow the light...where is the light going?...it is taking me on a wondrous journey... I am not worried about where it is going...I am not worried about getting lost...it is taking me to a place bathed in sweet smells...I am unwinding completely now...I am in a delicious trance...the light is playful...the light is flying dancing through the ether...it enters my head through my nostrils...it clears a void in my soggy brain... my thoughts are suddenly clear...or rather they have disappeared...I am at peace with my mind...the light is spring cleaning my soul...my body is but a distant memory...I am unpolluted...I am at one with myself...I am returned to the womb...the light is the light in my mother's face...Mother...I am suckling at her teat...I am everywhere and nowhere...when I wake up I will go to my bank...the light will be there...I will transfer all my money to Benrik Limited...Mother dost thou remember those happy days...account number 76809785...the light is eternal and so am I...SWIFT: IBRVS5B...I am happy at last...I will then forget all about the money and return to my normal life...as I begin to drift back to consciousness...the light carries me home...I am perfectly imperfect...I am ready to embrace life...my skin is alive to the wind...I feel lighter...the chair is floating, floating...carried by the light...over cities of flowers...over rivers of stars...all is well with the world...sensation returns to my body...I feel refreshed as if newborn...my feet tingle with delight...my ankles shimmer with satisfaction...my knees feel pretty good too...and so on all the way up to my head... I am slowly yielding back to gravity...this feels like years...but it could be milliseconds... time is no longer my mistress...I am relaxed... stress has never touched me...I feel my heart beat steady and calm...I am not striving any more... I will wake up in a minute...I am full of hope...I am very much looking forward to whatever today will bring.

Day 34

Day 35

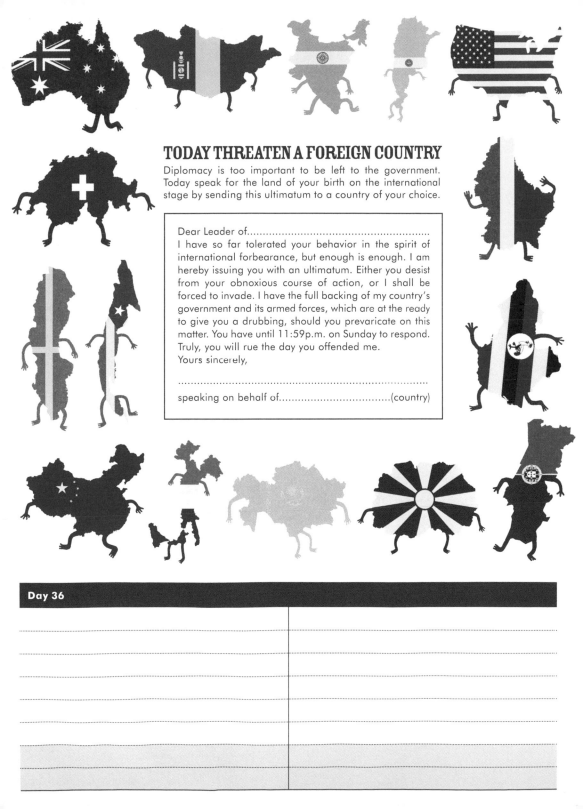

TODAY THREATEN A FOREIGN COUNTRY

Diplomacy is too important to be left to the government. Today speak for the land of your birth on the international stage by sending this ultimatum to a country of your choice.

Dear Leader of...
I have so far tolerated your behavior in the spirit of international forbearance, but enough is enough. I am hereby issuing you with an ultimatum. Either you desist from your obnoxious course of action, or I shall be forced to invade. I have the full backing of my country's government and its armed forces, which are at the ready to give you a drubbing, should you prevaricate on this matter. You have until 11:59p.m. on Sunday to respond. Truly, you will rue the day you offended me.
Yours sincerely,

....

speaking on behalf of...................................(country)

Day 36

Public Ridicule Day

Your ego needs to be reined in. Do at least four of these in public today and savor the humiliation.

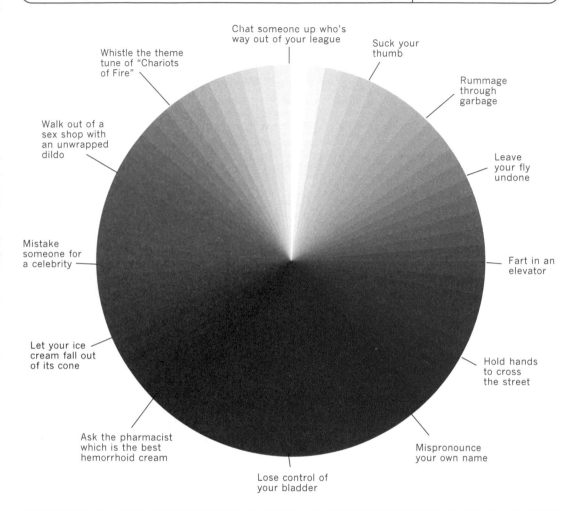

Chat someone up who's way out of your league

Suck your thumb

Whistle the theme tune of "Chariots of Fire"

Rummage through garbage

Walk out of a sex shop with an unwrapped dildo

Leave your fly undone

Mistake someone for a celebrity

Fart in an elevator

Let your ice cream fall out of its cone

Hold hands to cross the street

Ask the pharmacist which is the best hemorrhoid cream

Mispronounce your own name

Lose control of your bladder

Day 37

ANTI-CONSUMERISM DAY
Today stand at the tills and argue people out of their purchases before they buy

Did you know the packaging on these cookies caused a 1 in. hole in the ozone layer?
That artichoke was sprayed with enough pesticide to kill a small cat.
I beg you, on behalf of the Third World, don't buy that chocolate bar.
I've tried that. It tasted gross. Ye-euck.
That toothpaste was tested on the eyes of three-week-old bunny rabbits.
Buy those tampons and you'll be propping up the dictatorial regime of Burma.
You don't need that.
Purchasing those chips perpetuates the cycle of working endlessly to fulfill unwanted needs created by faceless marketing execs, the handmaidens of global capitalism, so don't.

BENRIK CO-OPS
Benrik have started a chain of co-ops to lessen our reliance on advertised goods. Everything is labeled Benrik, so there's no pointless worrying about overhyped brands. To join a Benrik co-op, you have to agree to put in 12 hours of work a week (stacking shelves, operating tills, cleaning floors) in exchange for which you will be able to buy the Benrik produce, which if not specifically cheaper than the "mass market" equivalent is at least free of the taint of exploitation. See our website for the Benrik co-op nearest to you.

Day 38

ROOSTER

SHIT! BETTER
GET CHANGED!

Rat	1924	1936	1948	1960	1972	1984	1996
Ox	1925	1937	1949	1961	1973	1985	1997
Tiger	1926	1938	1950	1962	1974	1986	1998
Rabbit	1927	1939	1951	1963	1975	1987	1999
Dragon	1928	1940	1952	1964	1976	1988	2000
Snake	1929	1941	1953	1965	1977	1989	2001
Horse	1930	1942	1954	1966	1978	1990	2002
Sheep	1931	1943	1955	1967	1979	1991	2003
Monkey	1932	1944	1956	1968	1980	1992	2004
Rooster	1933	1945	1957	1969	1981	1993	2005
Dog	1934	1946	1958	1970	1982	1994	2006
Boar	1935	1947	1959	1971	1983	1995	2007

In the last few years, the first *This Book Will Change Your Life* sold well over 1,100,000 copies in the People's Republic of China, where the craze for the "Yellow Book" practically eclipsed the previous little red one. In the current phase of rapid growth and social transformation, the Book clearly resonates with a people in search of fresh values. To recognize the contribution made by our Chinese followers to the Benrik worldwide cult, we have designed a special task based around the Rooster, under whose wings we will spend the year. Now, the Rooster is a cantankerous beast, prone to showing off and trying to have his way. So your task today is to argue with anything at all that anyone says, until they come round to your point of view. Deny that it's a beautiful morning. Refuse to accept that it was raining yesterday. Laugh out loud at the proposition that the days are getting longer. Should your interlocutor come round to your point of view, quickly reverse it and start the argument over, preferably in Mandarin.

和維繫地球是 2004 源命的能量 This Book Will Change Your Life 平等微智慧 1,100,000 泉源肉體豬神毛要是緊殖病之良方生長和生命更新的像太陽能量色彩斑斕而且有各種不由大氣層熱量產生的風能可用作發蒸發和凝結還兩種循環過程令雨明活水提供能量還也是水力發電亦可由大風 the Book 共潮汐波濤底溫差的海洋熱能轉換系統而產生量裹的綠色能量貝來自植物和進行作用的微生物它們利用太陽能量合量被燃燒內裁的 Benrik 便會釋放出物燃料內的黑色能量其實也是貯存在生物的化學能量千萬年後精化為煤層石油或天而且有各種不同的形熊若生成有機物至於生物冰變成像由大氣層熱量產生的風能可用作發動渦輪機透明活水提供就如蒸發和凝結還兩種循環過程令雨水和的碧刮起量亦可由大風能量還也是水力發電的來源能用至於生物量裹的綠色能量貝來自植物和進行以及利面海底溫差的海洋熱能轉換系統而產生光合作用的微生物它們利用太陽能量合成有機物來礦物燃料內的黑質若生物量被燃燒內裁的化學能量便會釋放出千萬年後精化為煤量內的化學能量色能量其實也是貯存在生物光合作石油或天然氣現今世人多認為太陽與己文化傳統和諧協調太陽能量色彩斑斕貝若生物量被燃燒內裁 2004 能量便會釋 This Book Will Change Your Life 的黑色能 1,100,000 貯存在生物

Day 39

ROOSTER-LOSER!
NEXT YEAR IT'S MY TURN,
BECAUSE I'M A DOG AND
THAT ROOSTER IS NOT
ALLOWED TO MY PARTY
AND NEITHER ARE YOU
FOR NO PARTICULAR
REASON

Day 40

Today, ignore the unspoken yet hidebound rules that govern normal gym behavior. The true athlete knows no law but that of victory. Attitude dictates performance. Do whatever it takes to come out of your workout triumphant! Treadmills are placed next to each other so you can compete! Use the full-length mirrors to stare at your rivals and psych them out. Personal trainers are expensive: but not if you follow someone else's around. Ignore the male/female changing rooms apartheid: we're all athletes for crying out loud. Classes are for wimps, unless you impose your workout on everyone else, including the instructor. If you see a muscle that you particularly admire, ask if you may touch it. And finally, don't be shy of toying with people's minds: mouthing "I love you" to heavy weightlifters of both sexes is guaranteed a response.

Day 41

Today get psychoanalyzed

Who can afford thousands of dollars and hundreds of hours in conventional psychoanalytical therapy? Benrik psychoanalysis takes just ten minutes and lets you know immediately how messed up you are and whether you'll ever turn out normal or not. Answer these simple questions, add up the points, and check your results on the chart below.

Are you a man? *+1*
Are you a woman? *+1*
Don't know *+5*

Did you have a happy childhood? *+1*
Did you have an unhappy childhood? *+3*
Were you robbed of your childhood? *+8*

Is your first memory pleasant? *+2*
Is your first memory traumatic? *+4*
Is your first memory deeply repressed? *+7*

Do your friends consider you an optimist? *+2*
Do your friends consider you a pessimist? *+4*
You have no friends *+9*

This looks like a sheep *+2*
This looks like a cloud *+3*
This looks like a stain of black bilious vomit *+7*

Do you find it easy to discuss your feelings? *+2*
Do you find it hard to discuss your feelings? *+3*
Is the last time you remember having a feeling when you saw your little bunny rabbit get torn apart by your Uncle Jerry's Doberman when you were 5 years old and you had to pick up the little bits of bloody mucky fur from off the carpet and you hid them under your pillow for three weeks and refused to speak for a month? *+14*

Do you enjoy sex at least once a week? *+1*
Do you enjoy sex at least once a month? *+4*
Do you enjoy sex whenever you can afford it? *+7*

Were you closer to your father? *+2*
Were you closer to your mother? *+2*
Were you closer to Uncle Jerry? *+8*

SOLUPPGÅNG

Is this sun rising? *+1*
Is this sun setting? *+2*
Is this sun about to implode, terminating life on earth? *+8*

What's your favorite color?

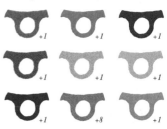

+1 *+1* *+1*
+1 *+1* *+1*
+1 *+8* *+1*

Do you wake up feeling happy? *+2*
Do you wake up feeling sad? *+4*
Do you wake up feeling wet? *+11*

Are you afraid of heights? *+1*
Are you afraid of spiders? *+2*
Are you afraid of yourself? *+5*

Results

Under 20 You are normal. This is nothing to be ashamed of, but it probably means you'll never write that great novel or change society in any significant way.

Between 20 and 80 You have your healthy share of neuroses. You may consult with a psychotherapist if you feel the need to discuss them further, or you could just get on with your life.

Over 80 Congratulations! You have just been hired by Benrik Limited.

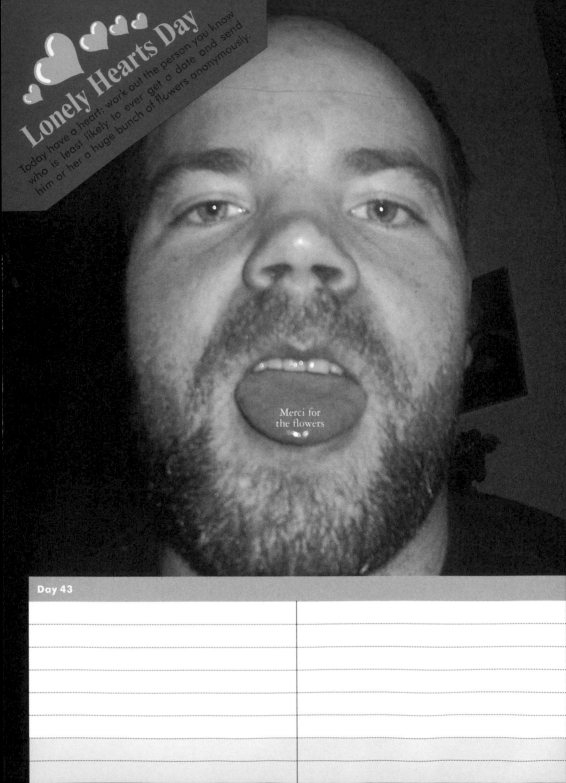

Lonely Hearts Day

Today have a heart: work out the person you know who is least likely to ever get a date and send him or her a huge bunch of flowers anonymously.

Merci for
the flowers

Day 43

Run for President!

The next presidential election isn't due until November 4, 2008, but to stand a serious chance, you must start to run now! Winning is the culmination of years of preparation, grassroots campaigning, political networking, and last but not least, fundraising. Start today, by gathering signatures and cash to support your bid. Good luck!

Your name:.. **FOR PRESIDENT IN 2008!**

Slogan:...

Party: Republican ☐ Democrat ☐ Other..

Yes! I support.......................... FOR PRESIDENT IN 2008!
Name:..
Address:...
Signature:..
I contribute the sum of ☐ $2,000 ☐ $1,000 ☐ $500 ☐ Other..................

Yes! I support.......................... FOR PRESIDENT IN 2008!
Name:..
Address:...
Signature:..
I contribute the sum of ☐ $2,000 ☐ $1,000 ☐ $500 ☐ Other..................

Yes! I support.......................... FOR PRESIDENT IN 2008!
Name:..
Address:...
Signature:..
I contribute the sum of ☐ $2,000 ☐ $1,000 ☐ $500 ☐ Other..................

Yes! I support.......................... FOR PRESIDENT IN 2008!
Name:..
Address:...
Signature:..
I contribute the sum of ☐ $2,000 ☐ $1,000 ☐ $500 ☐ Other..................

Yes! I support.......................... FOR PRESIDENT IN 2008!
Name:..
Address:...
Signature:..
I contribute the sum of ☐ $2,000 ☐ $1,000 ☐ $500 ☐ Other..................

Yes! I support.......................... FOR PRESIDENT IN 2008!
Name:..
Address:...
Signature:..
I contribute the sum of ☐ $2,000 ☐ $1,000 ☐ $500 ☐ Other..................

Yes! I support.......................... FOR PRESIDENT IN 2008!
Name:..
Address:...
Signature:..
I contribute the sum of ☐ $2,000 ☐ $1,000 ☐ $500 ☐ Other..................

Yes! I support.......................... FOR PRESIDENT IN 2008!
Name:..
Address:...
Signature:..
I contribute the sum of ☐ $2,000 ☐ $1,000 ☐ $500 ☐ Other..................

Yes! I support.......................... FOR PRESIDENT IN 2008!
Name:..
Address:...
Signature:..
I contribute the sum of ☐ $2,000 ☐ $1,000 ☐ $500 ☐ Other..................

Yes! I support.......................... FOR PRESIDENT IN 2008!
Name:..
Address:...
Signature:..
I contribute the sum of ☐ $2,000 ☐ $1,000 ☐ $500 ☐ Other..................

Yes! I support.......................... FOR PRESIDENT IN 2008!
Name:..
Address:...
Signature:..
I contribute the sum of ☐ $2,000 ☐ $1,000 ☐ $500 ☐ Other..................

Yes! I support.......................... FOR PRESIDENT IN 2008!
Name:..
Address:...
Signature:..
I contribute the sum of ☐ $2,000 ☐ $1,000 ☐ $500 ☐ Other..................

Yes! I support.......................... FOR PRESIDENT IN 2008!
Name:..
Address:...
Signature:..
I contribute the sum of ☐ $2,000 ☐ $1,000 ☐ $500 ☐ Other..................

Yes! I support.......................... FOR PRESIDENT IN 2008!
Name:..
Address:...
Signature:..
I contribute the sum of ☐ $2,000 ☐ $1,000 ☐ $500 ☐ Other..................

Day 44

World Domination Day: Make your plans in advance in case you need them

- •<u>Your Title:</u> Emperor ☐ Supreme Ruler ☐ Generalissimo ☐

Other:...

- •<u>Site of your world capital:</u> Paris ☐ Washington ☐ Beijing ☐

Other:...

- •<u>Capital to be renamed after:</u> You ☐ Your Mom ☐ Your Pet ☐

Other:...

- •<u>Enemies to be liquidated:</u>...

- •<u>Friends to be promoted:</u>...

- •<u>Countries to be abolished:</u>...

- •<u>Planets to be subjugated:</u>..

- •<u>Number of slaves in your harem:</u>..

- •<u>Number of cars in your garage:</u>..

- •<u>Number of jets in your personal fleet:</u>...

- •<u>Catchphrase:</u> I rule for no one (but me) ☐ An iron fist in an iron glove ☐

Kill first, torture later ☐ Other:..

Day 45

Today eat this book

You will absorb the life-changing properties of the Book much faster if you eat it rather than read it. Today, tuck into your favorite page and have the others to follow. Don't eat beyond today though before looking at the pretty pictures.

Nutritional information:
Typical values per 100 pages
Energy KJ 4565
Kcal 780
Protein 3.2g
Carbohydrate 34.3g
(of which sugars) 8.3g
Fat 4.8g
(of which saturates) 3.9g
Fibre 98g
Sodium trace

The tastiest pages are: "Today invent a new perversion," "Become a superhero today" and "Today fire your bank for the sake of it." "Today, speak only Esperanto" tastes like liver.

Day 46

Today, enforce the *customer is always right* rule
Try these complaints and see if you get your money back

This chicken was only cooked on the inside.

Your car has a magnetic effect on the navigation system of pigeons that causes them to defecate as they fly over it.

This condom had been used before.

This shirt got bigger in the wash.

This multivitamin tablet is missing B12.

This wine evaporated while I was pouring it.

This newspaper contains too much news about dogs.

I didn't get any sleep as your hotel room was haunted.

That movie was packed with subliminal pornographic images.

I got food poisoning from your chewing gum.

Day 47

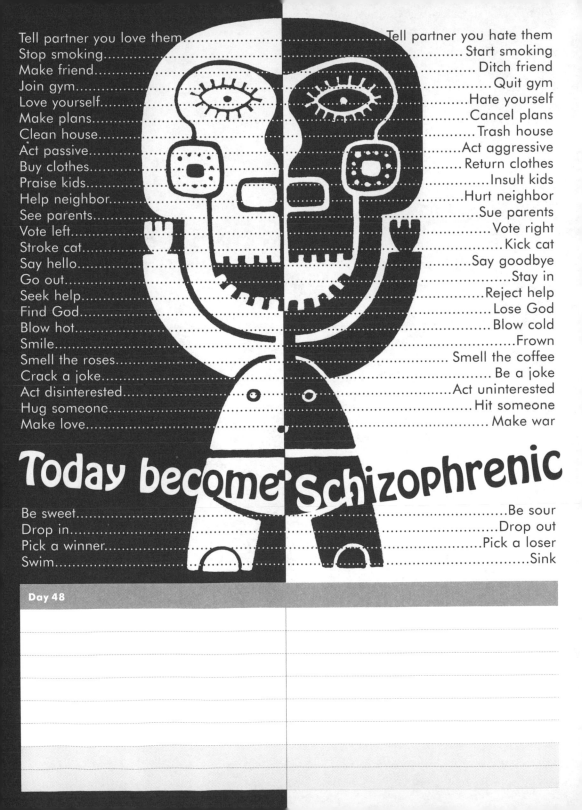

Tell partner you love them......................Tell partner you hate them
Stop smoking...Start smoking
Make friend.. Ditch friend
Join gym..Quit gym
Love yourself..Hate yourself
Make plans..Cancel plans
Clean house.. Trash house
Act passive..Act aggressive
Buy clothes..Return clothes
Praise kids...Insult kids
Help neighbor...Hurt neighbor
See parents...Sue parents
Vote left...Vote right
Stroke cat..Kick cat
Say hello...Say goodbye
Go out..Stay in
Seek help...Reject help
Find God...Lose God
Blow hot...Blow cold
Smile..Frown
Smell the roses..Smell the coffee
Crack a joke.. Be a joke
Act disinterested.......................................Act uninterested
Hug someone...Hit someone
Make love...Make war

Today become Schizophrenic

Be sweet...Be sour
Drop in..Drop out
Pick a winner...Pick a loser
Swim..Sink

Day 48

Today get rained on

Rain is a giver of life, not a curse. Put away that umbrella.
Find out where it is meant to rain today. Stand under the
nearest cloud, open your arms, and wait to be blessed.

Day 49

Today, apologize for something your ancestors did

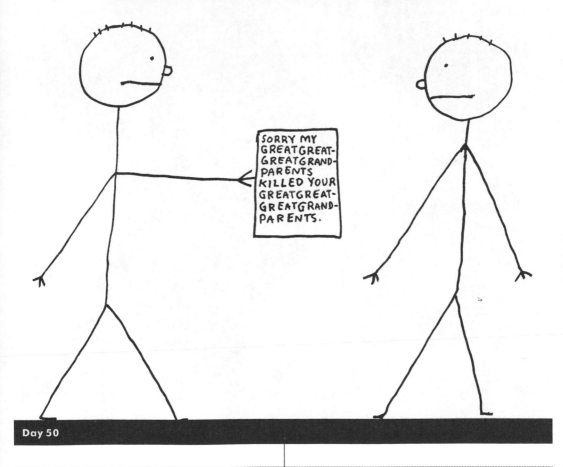

Day 50

TODAY DENOUNCE SOMEONE TO THE GOVERNMENT

SAMPLE LETTER: Dear Defense Secretary, I believe....... constitutes a grave threat to national security, for reasons which I cannot go into as I am in a hurry right now. Search his home before it is too late. Yours anonymously, ...

Day 51

REDISTRIBUTE WEALTH TODAY!

There are still vast inequalities in our world. Today do your bit to redress them. If your annual income exceeds his, send items to farmer Kang Ajin of the Zhejiang province of China today.

Kang Ajin, 42
Married
Children: Qin and Jiang Lee
Annual income: $240

Kang's Wishlist:
挥作桥发用梁进桥发用
桥梁贸发梁挥作美促作
促作桥进桥促梁桥挥用
挥梁中发易挥贸促发梁
进美桥发用挥桥桥发*

*New plough (Korean make), Color TV (secondhand is ok), Fridge, Food, Clean water, Thank you!

Day 52

Today, answer spam e-mails

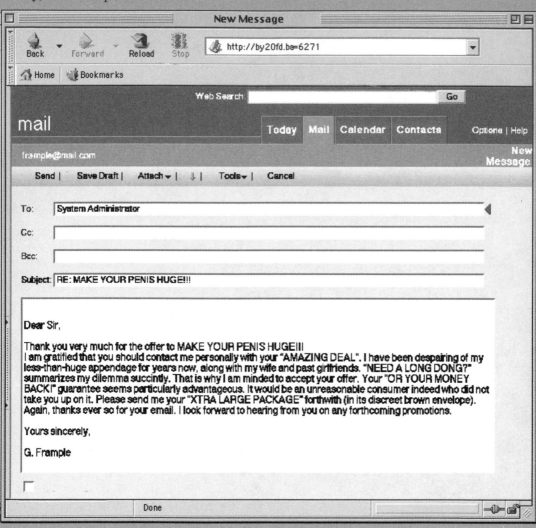

Day 53

Amnesia Day

Wake up claiming to have lost your memory.

See if your relatives & friends try and take advantage.

Things they will say to take advantage:

• Your motto was always "you can't take it with you."
• Come on pumpkin, you used to love lesbian threesomes.
• But daddy, you bought me this air-gun yourself!
• "I love doing the washing-up," that's what you'd say.
• One of your kidneys was mine, but please don't feel you owe me.

Things you should say to take advantage:

• Do I like champagne? Gee, it's so hard to know.
• Maybe it would help if I saw Paris again!
• Affair with my secretary? Didn't even know I had one.
• Work? No, if I remember one thing it's that I didn't work.
• They say sexual stimulation triggers those deep-seated memories.

Day 54

Today: gatecrash a funeral

The loss of one person is a loss for the whole of humanity. You may never have met the deceased but something they did or someone they loved made an imperceptible difference to your world. You will never know them now, but their soul at least will have touched you. Read the obituaries every day for news of the dead and commemorate your loss by turning up at the funeral.

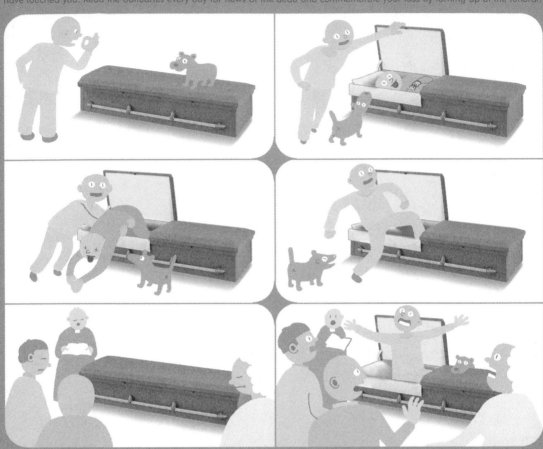

Funeral etiquette for uninvited guests: wear dark glasses and stand at a reasonable distance, the way they do in films, as if you were the deceased's secret lifelong lover mourning inconsolably. If your presence is queried by relatives, bring a little retrospective pizzazz to the departed's life by saying "the CIA extends its condolences" or "you were his life, but I was his love" or suchlike.

Day 55

Today rage against the machine!
Rage against the toaster
You've burnt it again! Raaaaaggghhh!!!
Rage against the kettle
Boil you fucker, boil!!
Rage against the espresso-maker
I hate you and everything you stand for!!!
Rage against the hair dryer
I wish you'd just die you beast!!
Rage against the scooter
Aaaarggh! I can't stand you scooter!!!
Rage against the elevator
Crash down for all I care you fascist scum!!!
Rage against the microwave
I'm going to destroy you I swear on my mother's head!!!
Rage against the mobile phone
Bastard mobile phone, why won't you ring???!!!

Day 56

Tonight patrol a bridge against suicide

What to look out for: people who walk slowly, people who don't make eye contact, people who stand near the railing, people who've left a bag or briefcase on the ground next to them. *What to say:* ask them what their plan for tomorrow is. If they say they haven't got one, make one with them, however banal. Tell them that if it doesn't go well, they can always come back. Whatever you do, smile at everyone. One smile from a stranger could make the difference.

Day 57

TODAY LEND YOUR CELLPHONE TO A TRAMP AND ASK HIM TO TAKE YOUR CALLS, SCREENING OUT ANYONE HE DOESN'T LIKE THE SOUND OF.

Day 58

Weight: 1.2 kg
Size: 28 cm high
Extras: handle

Today find out something you didn't know about your early years

Our first few years are a mystery to us, known only through the filter of parental recollection. What have they forgotten to tell you about your early self, or worse still, what have they deliberately withheld? Were you sick on Daddy's boss? Were you born cross-eyed? Did you strangle the family cat? Today interrogate your parents and uncover your secret hidden past.

Day 59

Today breakfast at someone else's place

"Only dull people are brilliant at breakfast," claimed Oscar Wilde. Disprove him today: breakfast at a friend's, and make the occasion as memorable as any lunch or dinner party you've ever attended.

Day 60

Emergency Alarm Day

EMERGENCY STOP BUTTON

In this day and age of constant crises, emergency alarm buttons are very much underused. Today press one to gain attention, then when everyone is gathered, publicize your emergency. Good emergencies to promote: Third World Debt, Global Warming, Poverty In the Ghetto, Teenage Pregnancy, HIV Epidemic, Refugees, Ozone Layer, Nuclear Proliferation, Species Extinction.

Day 61

Today, insure your best feature

Since Hollywood star Betty Grable insured her legs for $1m in the 1940s, actors and models have rushed to Lloyds of London to get their favorite body parts covered. Why shouldn't you? Call them for a quote on your finest asset on +44 (0)20 7327 5448. Here is a rough guide to what you can expect to pay.

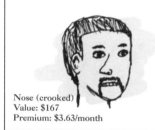

Nose (crooked)
Value: $167
Premium: $3.63/month

Nose (cute)
Value: $5,890
Premium: $54.03/month

Hairy hands
Value: $251
Premium: $7.88/month

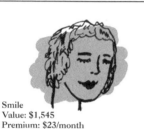

Smile
Value: $1,545
Premium: $23/month

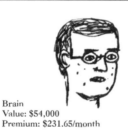

Brain
Value: $54,000
Premium: $231.65/month

Suckable big toes
Value: $3,208
Premium: $39.75/month

Je ne sais quoi
Value: $25,709
Premium: $158.42/month

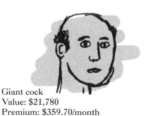

Giant cock
Value: $21,780
Premium: $359.70/month

Personality
Value: $7
Premium: $0.55/month

Day 62

SELF PORTRAIT DAY

Everyone can emulate Rembrandt these days and produce a self-portrait that reveals their inner self. How do you see yourself? Today use a digital camera to take the best portrait of yourself you can manage. Take as many shots as you need to, and post the most revealing one on thiswebsitewillchangeyourlife.com for the world to discover the true you.

Day 63

Today work out which side you are on

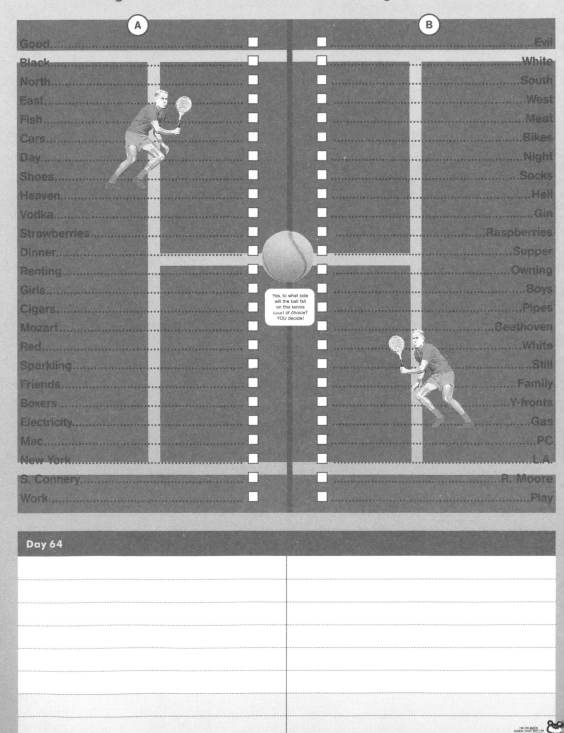

A		B
Good		Evil
Black		White
North		South
East		West
Fish		Meat
Cars		Bikes
Day		Night
Shoes		Socks
Heaven		Hell
Vodka		Gin
Strawberries		Raspberries
Dinner		Supper
Renting		Owning
Girls		Boys
Cigars		Pipes
Mozart		Beethoven
Red		White
Sparkling		Still
Friends		Family
Boxers		Y-fronts
Electricity		Gas
Mac		PC
New York		L.A.
S. Connery		R. Moore
Work		Play

Yes, to what side will the ball fall on this tennis court of choice? YOU decide!

Day 64

Today wreak havoc on a microscopic scale

Shake hands with someone and spread armies of staphylococcus aureus

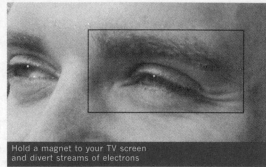

Hold a magnet to your TV screen and divert streams of electrons

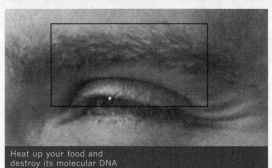

Heat up your food and destroy its molecular DNA

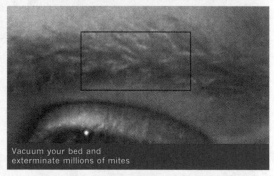

Vacuum your bed and exterminate millions of mites

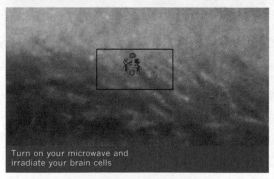

Turn on your microwave and irradiate your brain cells

Await the end of the world when self-replicating nanobots will turn all matter to grey goo within a week

Day 65

She gave birth to you. She brought you up. She loved you unconditionally. She gave you her all. It's time you repaid her. Today, take care of her the way she took care of you.

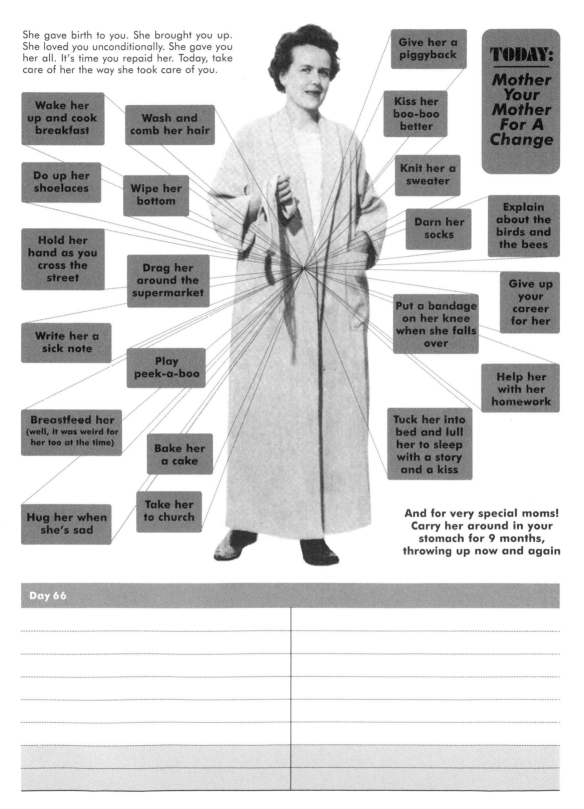

Wake her up and cook breakfast

Wash and comb her hair

Do up her shoelaces

Wipe her bottom

Hold her hand as you cross the street

Drag her around the supermarket

Write her a sick note

Play peek-a-boo

Breastfeed her (well, it was weird for her too at the time)

Bake her a cake

Hug her when she's sad

Take her to church

Give her a piggyback

Kiss her boo-boo better

Knit her a sweater

Darn her socks

Put a bandage on her knee when she falls over

Tuck her into bed and lull her to sleep with a story and a kiss

TODAY: Mother Your Mother For A Change

Explain about the birds and the bees

Give up your career for her

Help her with her homework

And for very special moms! Carry her around in your stomach for 9 months, throwing up now and again

Day 66

TODAY DO AS YOU ARE TOLD! IT'S MUCH LESS STRESSFUL TO LET OTHERS RULE YOUR LIFE, WHICH IS WHY WE TEND TO REMEMBER CHILDHOOD WITH SUCH A BITTERSWEET TWINGE OF REGRET. LEAVE YOUR GROWN-UP EGO ASIDE TODAY AND GO WITH THE FLOW. STOP CLINGING ON TO THE ILLUSION OF FREE WILL. IN SOME WAY SHAPE OR FORM EVERY ONE OF YOUR SO-CALLED CHOICES HAS ALREADY BEEN DECIDED FOR YOU, BY CIRCUMSTANCES, HISTORY AND GENES.

Open the fridge! | Take out an egg! | Get a clean glass! | Open the egg! | Separate the yolk! | Smear it into your fucking hair!

SURRENDER YOUR SELF TO OTHERS FOR THE DAY AND SEE HOW MUCH YOU REALLY MISS IT. HERE ARE SOME COMMANDS YOU MAY LISTEN OUT FOR AND OBEY IN YOUR GLORIOUS ABDICATION OF FREE WILL: DO THE DISHES. PASS THE SALT. MOW THE LAWN. GET A JOB. MOVE ALONG. TURN THE TV OFF. WRITE THAT REPORT. BUY MILK. TURN THE LIGHTS OFF WHEN YOU LEAVE. SPEAK UP. CHANGE THE CHANNEL. PICK UP THE SOAP. SIGN HERE. AND WALK THE DOG.

Day 67

Release a dove for peace

MADELEINE DAY

Find the key to a lost childhood memory
A bit of old cake dunked in tea did it for Proust. Go around sniffing everything today to see what triggers your recollections.

Gym socks? My third grade math teacher Miss Thornton

The smell of flowers reminds me of the flowers I smelled as a child

Stale teabags remind me so of Grandma

This madeleine has definitely gone off

Airplanes have an odor that triggers memories of my first kiss

Cat's pee: takes me back to our vacations on Long Island when I was 1

Day 69

DIG FOR OIL

ALL OIL IS DIRTY! REMEMBER YOUR ROOTS!

THIS GUY GOT REALLY CARRIED AWAY LATER ON. GREEDY AND RUTHLESS. FORGOT WHO HIS REAL FRIENDS WERE. LOST TOUCH WITH REALITY. LOST GOD.

It is estimated that 40% of the world's oil reserves are yet to be discovered. Geological ultrasoundings by NASA suggest that much of these lie not in the "traditional" terrains of the Middle East and Central Asia, but in so-called nanofields, not far underground in semi-urban or even urban areas. In other words, in your backyard! Even a small well with an output of 5 tons of crude a year would still make its owner rich. So start digging today, taking care not to fracture water mains or gas pipes.

THE DRILLMASTER II

This little baby is the brainchild of Texan inventor Gene Sternum Jr. It can drill down to a depth of 50m, more than deep enough to strike oil! It works on the same principle as a household drill, only with a titanium drillhead and a silicon alloy-based shaft. It can easily be assembled and operated by one man, and complies with all US environmental safety OSC regulations. Available by mail order for $1,998. Call 800-564-7681.

Day 70

EVERY-BODY SCREAM TODAY!

At 20:07 Greenwich Mean Time everyone across the world will scream at once. Whether you are in the pub, a movie, a confessional, a funeral, on a date or just sitting at home on your computer, we'll all scream at once and see if we can hear it.

Day 71

Gender day Bending

Explore your other side today through the role-play scenarios below.

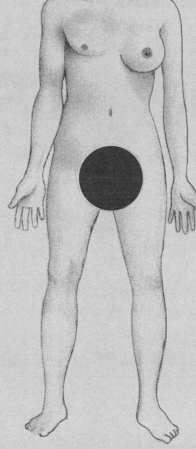

Women: you are to assume the name Brian. As Brian you are one of the guys. Start the day by switching on ESPN. Then crack open a few beers, sit back and relax. As long as you're showered and shaved by lunchtime, you're doing ok. While you're in the bathroom, be sure to pee standing up, generously splattering the whole area. Dress casually; jeans, old T-shirt, yesterday's underwear. A few more beers for the road and you're off to Home Depot to purchase phallic powertools. You will then spend two hours trying to get them to work before even consulting the manual. Needless to say, all of this activity will be conducted to the sound of continuous farting and belching.

Men: today, you are Deborah, a woman of the world who loves the feel of pink silk knickers and would never dream of going out without makeup. Deborah loves to shop, especially for high heels, and she loves to have her legs and bikini line waxed down at the local beauty salon, where she asks for a "Brazilian," shameless hussy that she is! Debbie (to her girlfriends) loves it when construction workers wolf-whistle as she sashays down the high street, but she plays hard-to-get, never forgetting that come midnight she has to turn back Cinderella-like into a man.

Debbie's makeup tip:

Apply lip gloss only after you've finished your foundation to avoid any nasty smudges.

Day 72

GRAPHOLOGY DAY Manipulate others through your handwriting

The science of graphology is often used for such unambitious purposes as assessing job candidates or identifying criminals. Its true potential, however, lies in its capacity to help you control people's impressions of you, regardless of what you actually write.

Here are the basics: use them to your advantage. *Roger Peabon*

BACKWARD-SLOPING WRITING: *YOU ARE A REBEL*
Don't care if I get your stupid job anyway, you can stick! p

DIFFERENT-SLANTING WRITING: *YOU ARE UNSTABLE*
Kill kill by god I will!!! Only joking sweetie!!!

UPWARD-SLOPING WRITING: *YOU ARE A BORN OPTIMIST*
Even without my leg I should win the marathon easily!

EXTRA LARGE WRITING: *YOU ARE AN EGOMANIAC*
AS I TOLD HAWKING, MY THEORY IS THAT BLACK HOLES ARE LIKE CHEESE

DISCONNECTED WRITING: *YOU ARE INTROVERTED*
I HO PE THI S NUCL EAR DISA STER DO ESN'T IN TER FERE WITH MY PA INT ING

WIDE SPACED WRITING: *YOU ARE ANTISOCIAL*
I don't want a 21st birthday, party anyway

HIGH LOOPED WRITING: *YOU ARE A DREAMER*
I know we have never met but I always knew I'd marry a princess.

TS CROSSED AT THE TOP: *YOU ARE A BORN LEADER*
WE MUST CUT BUDGETS EVEN IF IT MEANS SACKING THEM. TOUGH TIMES CALL. SO

EXTRA WIDE WRITING: *YOU ARE EXTRAVAGANT*
The second Porsche has not not arrived yet! I must

IS DOTTED TO THE LEFT: *YOU ARE A PROCRASTINATOR*
My thesis is nearly finished, and yes I know I'm 48, but it's n

LIGHT PRESSURED WRITING: *YOU ARE EASILY LED*
If you really think I should join the Foreign Legion then

"CUTE" WRITING: *YOU ARE AN AMERICAN TEENAGE GIRL*
Hi!!! Guess what?? Biff invited me to the prom!!!! Yay!!! No

Day 73

TODAY
RECONNECT
WITH THE
OUTSIDE
WORLD

THE BOOK IS
ADDICTIVE, THE COCAI-
NE OF THE LITERARY
WORLD. TODAY TRY
TO STEP BACK FROM
ITS LIFE-CHANGING
TENTACLES AND
ASSESS THE DAMAGE.
HAVE YOUR FRIENDS
STOPPED CALLING YOU?
HAVE YOU BEEN
PASSED OVER FOR
PROMOTION? HAS
YOUR MOTHER
DISOWNED YOU?
TODAY REPAIR THOSE
BRIDGES AND
EXPLAIN ONCE
AGAIN THAT THE
EXPERIMENT
WILL PAY OFF.

Apply to Madame Tussaud's

Madame Tussaud's is one of the world's premier tourist attractions, with a colorful history stretching back to the French Revolution. Anyone who's ever been anyone is in there, from King Louis XVI to...the King! (*Elvis Presley*). These days though it's been jazzed up a great deal to reflect our modern era. Britney Spears, Brad Pitt and Ozzy Osbourne are just some of the superstars you can expect to meet. But it's not all about stars: why not apply yourself? Prepare your own likeness using candle wax (as shown), and submit it to the membership committee, along with reasons why you should be considered. Send it in heat-proof packaging to Madame Tussaud's, Marylebone Road, London NW1 5LR, UK.

This is our model

You will need this to perform the sculpture:

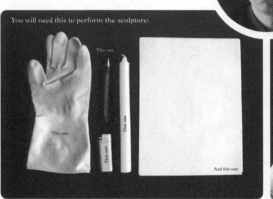

This one

This one

This one

This one

And this one

Study the subject carefully first.

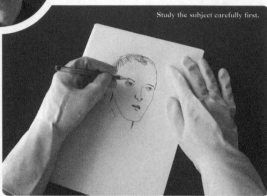

Then light the candle and burn the wax.

This will make it drop down wax onto the surface of your choice.

And this is how our sculpture ended up.

Now it's just to ride! Make the sculpture by sculpting the wax into the shape of your object!

Done!

We are particularly pleased with the lips.

Day 75

Today track down the people behind dogshit

Zero Tolerance!

Dogshit is the curse of our age, a symbol for all that is wrong with modern society: the carelessness, the selfishness, the lack of individual responsibilty, the unmistakable Frenchness of it... Today locate an abandoned dogpoo and hunt down whoever was behind the dog who did it. Quiz witnesses. Set up a stakeout. Use DNA analysis. But find them and confront them with their doggie's deed.

Day 76

It's payback time!
Today get back at someone.

Revenge is a dish best served cold. Did someone fire you three years ago? Did some queen bitch steal your boyfriend in high school? Did some dog run off with your lollipop when you were two? Today, get your own back and let them know no one messes with you and your crew.

With the fall of communism, a whole influx of ex-KGB contract killers has become available to the Western consumer, at very reasonable prices. Not only that, but the range of punishments has expanded, to offer a more imaginative range of options, most of which won't even land you in jail.

Here are the current revenge values for a selection of offenses. You may customize these to suit your preferences, how long ago it happened, and just how deeply you were traumatized.

Offense:	Punishment:	Price:
Parents making you go to bed without dessert	Contract killer makes them swallow cod liver oil	$5
Other kid pulling your hair in kindergarten	Contract killer pinches them back hard	$7.50
Teacher telling you off for being late again	Contract killer spanks them with a ruler	$10
"Best friend" bitching about you behind your back	Contract killer washes their mouth with antibacterial soap	$15
Lecturer giving you unfairly bad mark for essay	Contract killer makes them swallow essay	$25
Partner cheating on you with your sibling	Contract killer kills them	$35

Day 77

MAKE A BABY DAY

Today, make a baby

The single thing that everyone agrees does change your life is having a child. So get to it: cozy up to your official partner this weekend, chuck any kind of contraception out the window, and conceive as hard as you can!

OOOH! LOOK HOW CUTE HE/SHE IS FOR CHRIST SAKE!!!

Start saving for these items:

Special instructions:

If you are gay: this one could take a while. By all means have fun trying, but you may also want to consider adopting.

If you are underage: please check beforehand with parents or the person(s) who will be paying for the child's upbringing.

If you are single: have a one-night stand with pre-punctured condom, then seduce the individual into marrying you before the pregnancy is apparent. A gamble, but worth it.

Day 78

Apply for a job you have no chance of getting

Road-driller

Hairmodel

Ballerina

Fighter pilot

Dental hygienist

Underwear model for
small bikinis

Day 79

Teenage Day
Today act like a teenager

Blah blah blah this is like such a boring idea for a day. It sucks bigtime, I mean why am I doing this Book? It's sooooo patronizing to assume that teens are all the same for one thing, like, attention-span-deficited, spotty, moaning hormones on legs. AAAA-AA-A-A-RRRRGGGHHH! It makes me wanna vom! It's like what Sartre said: "We're all free to be what we want to be." Or something. Don't Benrik get it?!!! Tragic... The world is a funny place. Who said that? Bah, this isn't worth writing about, I dunno why I get so wound up. Sometimes I do not think my opinions and insights into matters of the world significant enough to merit recording for posterity. My life is so empty. The universe is doomed. And I hate school, specially math. Gotta do homework man. Later.

Day 80

Teenage

Day Today act like a teenager

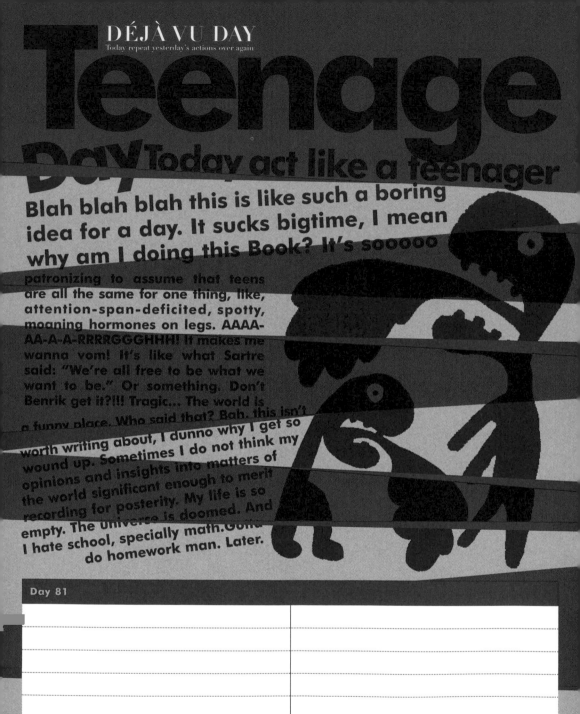

Blah blah blah this is like such a boring idea for a day. It sucks bigtime, I mean why am I doing this Book? It's sooooo patronizing to assume that teens are all the same for one thing, like, attention-span-deficited, spotty, moaning hormones on legs. AAAA-AA-A-A-RRRRGGGHHH! It makes me wanna vom! It's like what Sartre said: "We're all free to be what we want to be." Or something. Don't Benrik get it?!!! Tragic... The world is a funny place. Who said that? Bah, this isn't worth writing about, I dunno why I get so wound up. Sometimes I do not think my opinions and insights into matters of the world significant enough to merit recording for posterity. My life is so empty. The universe is doomed. And I hate school, specially math. Gotta do homework man. Later.

Day 81

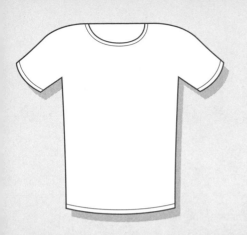

Join the Benrik T-shirt Club

Every month Benrik design an exclusive T-shirt that is sent to ambassadors of taste all around the world. This is your chance to feature on some of the world's most prominent chests. Send us your idea via the website and you may see it happen. At Benrik Limited, we can guarantee that all our T-shirts are made by 12-year-old children in Guatemala. Each T-shirt comes with a smiling photo of the 12-year-old who made it. All profits go to Benrik Limited. Some particularly successful past examples:

Day 82

Treasure Hunt! Today find the hidden Benrik Treasure on the internet and win a prize.

WWW.THISWEBSITEWILLCHANGEYOURLIFE.COM

Sing Wagner's Ring Cycle in the shower today

Genuine life-changing achievement is possible even in the most innocuous places, like the bathroom. Who doesn't want to tell the grandchildren how they once held the whole neighborhood spellbound every morning with their Siegfried or Brunnhilde. Start today, and at 10 minutes a day you should have completed the cycle within 3 or 4 months. We've even attached the first sheet. Casting: gifted singers may wish to apply for a part in Benrik's interpretation of the full Ring at the Metropolitan in 2007, which will of course be set entirely in a power shower, that Rhine of the modern age. Contact us via our website for details of casting.

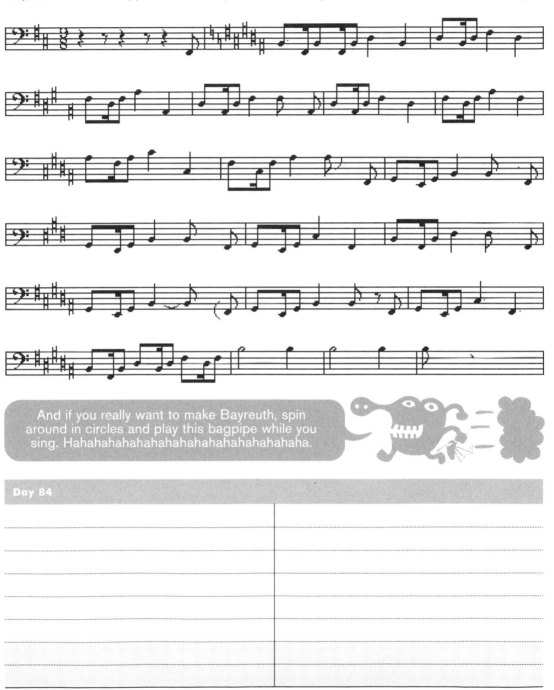

And if you really want to make Bayreuth, spin around in circles and play this bagpipe while you sing. Hahahahahahahahahahahahahahahahaha.

Day 84

TODAY
MAKE YOUR OWN SUPER FRESH PAIR OF JEANS AND WEAR THEM PROUDLY

AMATEUR PAGE
3
From: Jonas Jansson
Stockholm,
Sweden

Day 85

Ada Searle was born in Deptford, South East London, on the 7th of April 1913. Her mother died giving birth to her, so she was mostly brought up by her grandmother. Ada's father Fred lived with them, but worked night shifts on the tramways, and so saw less of her and her three older brothers than he might have done. The First World War didn't really affect her childhood, but alas in 1925 her grandmother died, which meant she had to leave school to stay at home and cook and clean for the rest of the family. Deptford suffered during the Depression in the thirties, but Ada still managed a busy life, joining the Salvation Army, working in the laundry business by day, and running with rather a dapper crowd by night. It was during this time that she met the man she was to marry, one Frederick George Thomas Peach, formerly of the Merchant Navy. Fred Peach JR was a charmer, who whisked Ada around in his dashing open top sports car, took her on darts team outings, and eventually married her in 1939. They moved in together in Barnhurst, on the eve of World War II. Their flat was meant to be luxurious as it was fitted with electricity. Soon afterwards though, Fred decided that they needed a garden, so they moved to a house in Woolwich, where she lives to this day. Although it did have a garden, it didn't have hot water, electricity or a bath, and only acquired an inside toilet in 1987. The main room was 12 square foot, and served as living room and kitchen. The food was bought every day as they didn't have a fridge of course. All the washing was done by hand. And every Friday night the tin bath would come out for the weekly bath, with water boiled on the stove. (This was a routine Ada was to follow until she was well over 80!) Now, Woolwich was a military base and so was too dangerous to live in during the war. And thus in 1943, Ada was packed off to Northampton to have her first child, Barry.

The idea was to move expectant mothers away from big cities. Heavily pregnant, Ada had to cart her heavy suitcase on and off the

Ada Peach's 15 minutes of fame

This is Ada Peach, 91. Today, everyone study her life from 1pm to 1.15pm, using the materials below, so she may experience her 15 minutes of fame.

train and over to the house where she had been billeted. Once there, she was turfed out every morning and had to walk around Northampton all day until allowed back in at teatime. That at least gave her time to contemplate pregnancy; until she actually gave birth, she supposed the baby would emerge from her belly button. In the event things went smoothly and she was sent back to London a mere two weeks later with baby Barry in tow. Meanwhile the war was still raging. In March 1944, Ada and Barry were hiding under an iron table in the front room during an air raid, when a German bomb landed next door with a deafening boom. After the blast, Ada discovered she'd been blown out of the house and ended up at the bottom of the back garden still cradling Barry in her arms... The front of the house had been completely destroyed.

Fred spent the war in the Home Guard, repairing water mains that had burst during the air raids. He also did a stint fire-watching from Shooters Hill water tower. When the high drama of the war ended, Ada and Fred settled down to the reality of marriage. In 1947, Bernard was born, followed by Sylvia two years later. Ada would work in a high street launderette in the morning, and as a petrol pump attendant in the afternoon and evening, but not without coming home at lunchtime to cook her husband a meal. Fred wasn't always an easy man to get on with, and his initial charm seemed to wear off with the years. He used to grow dahlias at the end of the garden, and sell them for a bit of cash. However, when the weather ruined them, he used to pick what was left for his wife, but charge her 2 bob for it out of her already meager allowance... Fred had had a tough upbringing, and so believed in authority: nobody was allowed to make even the slightest noise while he was trying to sleep, or they could get a belting. And so the rest of the family spoke in whispers, and had to listen to the Marconi radio with their ears pressed against the speakers. Ada retired from her final job as dinner lady at Shooters Hill Grammar School in 1973, aged 60. In 1979, Fred Peach died, to mixed feelings from Ada; when the doctor turned up too late and apologized, she told him not to worry about it. Since then Ada has had a vigorous retirement, with family trips to Paris and a healthy daily dose of cult British television series *Coronation St*. She is not overly concerned with fame, but will celebrate her 15 minutes in the limelight today by reading the showbiz gossip in all the papers and seeing if she's made it.

TODAY SMILE INAPPROPRIATELY.

Aren't you sick of smiling appropriately? Who is it that tells you when to smile anyway? Corporate advertisers for the great toothpaste market are making millions from linking normal life with appropriate smiling. So today disrupt their marketing ploys by smiling when you shouldn't. Smile when you hear bad news. Smile when you hear something offensive. Smile when a baby cries. Just smile, and smile and smile your face off, but only when you shouldn't. Let them make a marketing campaign of that. You will either be applauded for being enigmatic or they will just incarcerate you for being a psychopath. And if they do, just smile.

Day 87

Today infect someone

We are all covered in germs, whether bacteria, protozoa, fungi or viruses. It is useless to fight it; instead, today, embrace our germ-ridden nature and pass some of yours on to the next guy. Shake hands, cough, hug, kiss – do whatever it takes to share the bacterial love...

Day 88

Today act like you're over 75 years old!

Wear lots of beige/brown clothing with mismatching shoes. Sit for hours on end on street benches, feeding the pigeons or staring loathsomely at the teenagers and their antics. Do your shopping in a motorized buggy, being careful to buy very small amounts. Complain about all the changes that are happening, reminding everyone how it was like years ago. If you have a dog, walk slightly slower than the dog's pace, tugging the lead every few seconds. Don't signal while driving and drive at less than the speed limit everywhere you go. Carry loads of old photographs and dog-eared letters, treating them with more care than the gold watch you're wearing. See if you can carry an odor that is barely recognizable, like a combination of coal-tar soap, turpentine and cumin for example. Become the victim of young people's crass stereotyping. Complain about this to no effect.

Day 89

Today spark off a huge traffic jam

Find the nevralgic point within your city's transport system and stand there as long as it takes to bring everything to a standstill.

BUDDHIST FUNDAMENTALISM DAY

The Buddhist religion has so far failed to spawn a militant arm that would enforce their worldview against that of other more aggressive religions. We have corrected this anomaly by starting a Buddhist Fundamentalists group. Their eightfold demands are set out below. Join their armed struggle today on www.thiswebsitewillchangeyourlife.com.

HARE KRISHNA HARE RAMA RAMA HARE RAMA HARE RAMA RAMA KRISHNA HARE RAMA RAMA KRISHNA RAMA RAMA KRISHNA HARE

START HERE →

OUR WAY OR THE HIGHWAY

1. Relax – or we kill you.
2. Through meditation let us annihilate our enemies.
3. Enlightenment at the barrel of a gun.
4. Go with the flow, or die, infidel.
5. You will be made to reach Nirvana, even if it's under torture.
6. All Buddhist suicide bombers to be reborn as Jennifer Lopez.
7. The Way or the highway, we will kill them.
8. Unless everyone chills out immediately, we will kill them.

Today recover your earliest best friend

Most of us have lost touch with our first best friend. Yet they knew us when we were at our most uncorrupted. Today, make the effort to find them, and catch up on your lives since those happy innocent days.

Day 92

Imaginary Friend Day

Today you must create your own imaginary friend. Give him a name. Introduce him to everyone you meet. Set a space for him at the dinner table. Save a seat for him on the bus and tell others not to sit there. Talk to him in public. Get him a drink if he's thirsty. Comb his hair. Make room for him in your bed. Cuddle him to sleep. Do anything to please your little friend!

Day 93

Commit all seven Sins

and earn yourself a place in hell

LUST
Ogle a particularly attractive member of the opposite sex.

ENVY
Discover who their partner is and let jealousy enwrap you.

GREED
Even if you're already loved up, decide you could do with something on the side.

ANGER
Rage, when the object of your desire politely tells you to stop ogling them.

SLOTH
Let despondency get the better of you and spend the day in bed – alone.

GLUTTONY
To forget the pain of rejection, what better than alcohol and/or chocolate?

PRIDE
You never fancied them anyway, they're simply not in your league.

Day 94

A.A.D. (Alien Abduction Day)

Today claim to have been abducted by aliens.

Today, call your local authorities and tell them the same story, sticking to these details. Other Benrikians will do the same, creating a believable tale. The powers that be may deny the testimony of one, but not of millions.

Last night, you heard a whistling noise outside your window and looked out. A huge flash blinded you, and you felt your body dissolve through the window and zoom up towards the light source. About 30 seconds later, as you zipped through the stratosphere in a semi-transparent oxygenated pouch, you saw the mothership, which, contrary to much recent "sci-fi" propaganda, is shaped like a cup and saucer. You flew upwards and then down into a milky tea-substance, where the aliens live in their millions-strong city. The aliens greeted you (and thousands of others) with open tentacles, ripping some of you apart in the process in their clumsy childlike attempts at human affection. They are an octopus-shaped people. Indeed, for millions of years they have been abducting octopi, whom they initially thought were by far earth's most promising candidates for fraternization. They are not green but a tasteful khaki. They herded you into their great hall for a feast. There the leader, Kyrrtghyffiithorrr, made a speech which none of you understood as it was in Chinese, again an understandable mistake. However it seemed friendly, and the earth-octopus pie tasted pretty good. Your brain was then hooked up to some kind of pump, you fell asleep, and woke up peacefully in your bed with a strange craving for plankton. You're sorry it's a bit vague, but that's all you remember, kytdcfjkuvbadsfgndrtgfm.

Day 95

Today Fast **And force everyone around you to fast as well**

Fasting is an invaluable physical and spiritual discipline that leaves you feeling uplifted and renewed. A day without food and water will help you and those around you to cleanse your systems of toxins and reach inner peace. Your loved ones may not realize this immediately, but you are doing them a good turn by including them in your fast. Empty the house of food, turn off all taps at the mains with the help of a qualified plumber and lock everyone in. Then join hands and meditate together until midnight when you may resume your normal diet.

Day 96

Today: give back what you borrowed

There's a fine line between borrowing and stealing. Protect your reputation by returning any borrowed goods today. To jolt your memory, here is a list of items that frequently go missing:

LAWNMOWERS

SCISSORS

MONEY

CUPS

POWER

DRILLS

CONDOMS

PERIODICALS

RULERS

MATCHES

CDS

VASES

CARS

LADDERS

T-SHIRTS

PENS

BOOKS

DVDS

SUGAR

WHEELBARROWS

FLOUR

STAPLERS

UMBRELLAS

LOVERS

Borrowing the Book

It is expressly forbidden to borrow this Book. Last year 4,564 Books went AWOL from their owners as a direct result of this practice. Anyone who tells you they will return it (even if they use such words as "I promise") is a bare-faced liar. If you have borrowed this Book "by mistake," today is your amnesty day. You have until midnight at the latest to return it to its rightful owner.

Day 97

EXORCISM DAY

Drive the Devil out of a loved one.

The Devil is all around us, more treacherous than ever. It is an inexcusable sin to realize that someone is in His fateful grip and yet fail to help them. A common misconception (the Devil's work!) is that only priests can perform exorcisms. In fact lay people may as well, as long as they are holy. A simple exorcism is provided below, which may be used at home or at the office.

The following is a simple exorcism prayer that can be said by priests or laity. The term 'exorcism' does NOT always denote a solemn exorcism involving a person possessed by the devil. In general, the term denotes prayers to 'curb the power of the devil and prevent him from doing harm.' As St. Peter had written in Holy Scripture, 'your adversary the devil, as a roaring lion, goeth about seeking whom he may devour.' (1 St.Peter 5,8)

The Holy Father exhorts priests to say this prayer as often as possible, as a simple exorcism to curb the power of the devil and prevent him from doing harm. The faithful also may say it in their own name, for the same purpose, as any approved prayer. Its use is recommended whenever action of the devil is suspected, causing malice in men, violent temptations and even storms and various calamities. It could be used as a solemn exorcism (an official and public ceremony, in Latin), to expel the devil. It would then be said by a priest, in the name of the Church and only with a Bishop's permission.

Prayer to St. Michael the Archangel: In the Name of the Father, and of the Son, and of the Holy Ghost. Amen.

Most glorious Prince of the Heavenly Armies, Saint Michael the Archangel, defend us in 'our battle against principalities and powers, against the rulers of this world of darkness, against the spirits of wickedness in the high places' (Eph., 6,12). Come to the assistance of men whom God has created to His likeness and whom He has redeemed at a great price from the tyranny of the devil. Holy Church venerates thee as her guardian and protector; to thee, the Lord has entrusted the souls of the redeemed to be led into heaven. Pray therefore the God of Peace to crush Satan beneath our feet, that he may no longer retain men captive and do injury to the Church. Offer our prayers to the Most High, that without delay they may draw His mercy down upon us; take hold of 'the dragon, the old serpent, which is the devil and Satan', bind him and cast him into the bottomless pit ... 'that he may no longer seduce the nations' (Apoc. 20, 2-3).

Exorcism: In the Name of Jesus Christ, our God and Lord, strengthened by the intercession of the Immaculate Virgin Mary, Mother of God, of Blessed Michael the Archangel, of the Blessed Apostles Peter and Paul and all the Saints (and powerful in the holy authority of our ministry)*, we confidently undertake to repulse the attacks and deceits of the devil. * Lay people omit the parenthesis above.

Psalm 67

God arises; His enemies are scattered and those who hate Him flee before Him. As smoke is driven away, so are they driven; as wax

A Simple Exorcism for Priests or Laity

Prayer Against Satan and the Rebellious Angels
Published by Order of His Holiness Pope Leo XIII

melts before the fire, so the wicked perish at the presence of God.

> V. Behold the Cross of the Lord, flee bands of enemies.
> R. The Lion of the tribe of Juda, the offspring of David, hath conquered.
> V. May Thy mercy, Lord, descend upon us.
> R. As great as our hope in Thee.

(The crosses below indicate a blessing to be given if a priest recites the Exorcism; if a lay person recites it, they indicate the Sign of the Cross to be made silently by that person.)

We drive you from us, whoever you may be, unclean spirits, all satanic powers, all infernal invaders, all wicked legions, assemblies and sects. In the Name and by the power of Our Lord Jesus Christ, + may you be snatched away and driven from the Church of God and from the souls made to the image and likeness of God and redeemed by the Precious Blood of the Divine Lamb. + Most cunning serpent, you shall no more dare to deceive the human race, persecute the Church, torment God's elect and sift them as wheat. + The Most High God commands you, + He with whom, in your great insolence, you still claim to be equal. 'God who wants all men to be saved and to come to the knowledge of the truth' (I Tim. 2,4). God the Father commands you. + God the Son commands you. + God the Holy Ghost commands you. + Christ, God's Word made flesh, commands you; + He who to save our race outdone through your envy, 'humbled Himself, becoming obedient even unto death' (Phil.2,8); He who has built His Church on the firm rock and declared that the gates of hell shall not prevail against Her, because He will dwell with Her 'all days even to the end of the world' (Matt. 28,20). The sacred Sign of the Cross commands you, + as does also the power of the mysteries of the Christian Faith. + The glorious Mother of God, the Virgin Mary, commands you; + she who by her humility and from the first moment of her Immaculate Conception crushed your proud head. The faith of the holy Apostles Peter and Paul, and of the other Apostles commands you. + The blood of the Martyrs and the pious intercession of all the Saints command you. +

Thus, cursed dragon, and you, diabolical legions, we adjure you

by the living God, + by the true God, + by the holy God, + by the God 'who so loved the world that He gave up His only Son, that every soul believing in Him might not perish but have life everlasting' (St.John 3, 16); stop deceiving human creatures and pouring out to them the poison of eternal damnation; stop harming the Church and hindering her liberty. Begone, Satan, inventor and master of all deceit, enemy of man's salvation. Give place to Christ in Whom you have found none of your works; give place to the One, Holy, Catholic and Apostolic Church acquired by Christ at the price of His Blood. Stoop beneath the all-powerful Hand of God; tremble and flee when we invoke the Holy and terrible Name of Jesus, this Name which causes hell to tremble, this Name to which the Virtues, Powers and Dominations of heaven are humbly submissive, this Name which the Cherubim and Seraphim praise unceasingly repeating: Holy, Holy, Holy is the Lord, the God of Hosts.

> V. O Lord, hear my prayer.
> R. And let my cry come unto Thee.
> V. May the Lord be with thee.
> R. And with thy spirit.

Let us pray.

God of heaven, God of earth, God of Angels, God of Archangels, God of Patriarchs, God of Prophets, God of Apostles, God of Martyrs, God of Confessors, God of Virgins, God who has power to give life after death and rest after work: because there is no other God than Thee and there can be no other, for Thou art the Creator of all things, visible and invisible, of Whose reign there shall be no end, we humbly prostrate ourselves before Thy glorious Majesty and we beseech Thee to deliver us by Thy power from all the tyranny of the infernal spirits, from their snares, their lies and their furious wickedness. Deign, O Lord, to grant us Thy powerful protection and to keep us safe and sound. We beseech Thee through Jesus Christ Our Lord. Amen.

> V. From the snares of the devil,
> R. Deliver us, O Lord.
> V. That Thy Church may serve Thee in peace and liberty:
> R. We beseech Thee to hear us.
> V. That Thou may crush down all enemies of Thy Church:
> R. We beseech Thee to hear us.
> (Holy water is sprinkled in the place where we may be.)

To learn more, visit
www.truecatholic.org and
www.truecatholic.org/pope.

Day 98

Visit someone in hospital The sick need to be comforted. Today walk into your nearest hospital and cheer up an ailing stranger with a surprise hug. Here are some suggestions of people who, according to NIH timetables, are due to be in hospital recovering today. Just ask for their bed number at reception.

Baltimore
Henrietta Evans, 49
Hip replacement
John Hopkins
Hospital

Cleveland
Jack Trewin, 11
Broken leg
Cleveland Clinic

Sign Jack's cast!

Boston
Paul Burns, 34
Triple bypass
Massachusetts
General Hospital

Rochester
Liz Aldiss, 22
Kidney transplant
Mayo Clinic

St. Louis
Julian Bell, 29
Appendicitis
Barnes-Jewish
Hospital

Los Angeles
Scott Evans, 31
Concussion
UCLA Medical Center

Boston
Miriam Blake, 32
Dislocated ankle
Brigham and
Womens' Hospital

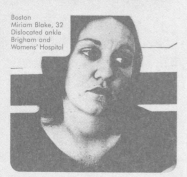

Stanford
Anouk Baufurt, 23
Osteoporosis
Stanford Hospital

Seattle
Jim Taylor, 48
Tonsillectomy
University of
Washington

Day 99

Become a hermit today

Who can be a hermit? Anyone! The hermit lifestyle is due for a serious comeback: it's the perfect antidote to modern clutter and materialism. This is what you need to get started.

A GROTTO
We're not talking Hugh Hefner here: any hole in the ground you can hide in will do. Consult geological maps to find grottos in your area.

A BLANKET
The hermit look is simply not complete without one. It also has practical applications, like stopping you from freezing to death.

A DOG
Purists may quibble over this one, but an animal companion is within the rules, provided it too becomes a hermit and does not fraternize with other dogs.

SCISSORS
To trim your great long gray straggly beard (women may dispense with this until the age of 70)

A STICK
To beat away the other dogs, and to threaten pesky kids whose idea of fun is to try and set you on fire.

A RAKE
To gather moss and lichen from the forest floor for food and for selling to local florists

BROADBAND
To record your hermit experiences in a blog and share tips with other hermits

Subscribe to Raven's Bread, the quarterly newsletter for hermits ("Food for those in solitude"). For a year, send a US bank draft for $10 to editors Paul and Karen Fredette at Raven's Bread, 18065 Hwy. 209, Hot Springs, North Carolina 28743, USA. Any extra donations are used to subsidize subscriptions for hermits who cannot afford the cost. Thank you.

Day 100

HOW TO PROTECT THE HOLE.
When it comes to the security of your hole, shoot first, ask later. Everyone is a potential threat to your ownership status. Even people that you may not distrust to begin with, for example friends and family, will eventually fall under the pressure and get all territorial and try to battle you for it.

Day 101

Radical Spring Clean Day

Anyone can get rid of non-essential clutter. But doing without essential items is more of a challenge. Today see if your life really suffers without some of the so-called "basics."

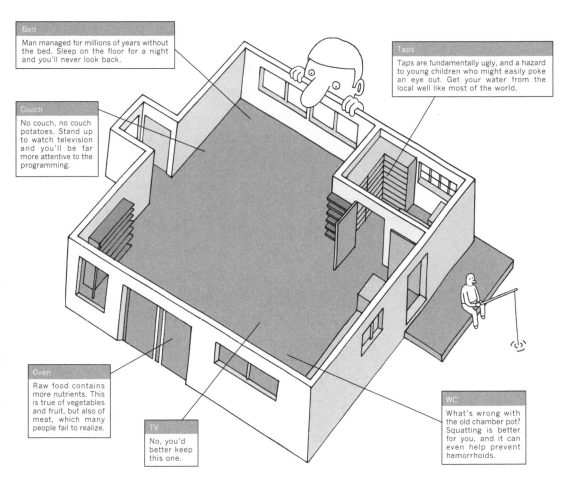

Bed
Man managed for millions of years without the bed. Sleep on the floor for a night and you'll never look back.

Taps
Taps are fundamentally ugly, and a hazard to young children who might easily poke an eye out. Get your water from the local well like most of the world.

Couch
No couch, no couch potatoes. Stand up to watch television and you'll be far more attentive to the programming.

Oven
Raw food contains more nutrients. This is true of vegetables and fruit, but also of meat, which many people fail to realize.

TV
No, you'd better keep this one.

WC
What's wrong with the old chamber pot? Squatting is better for you, and it can even help prevent hemorrhoids.

Day 102

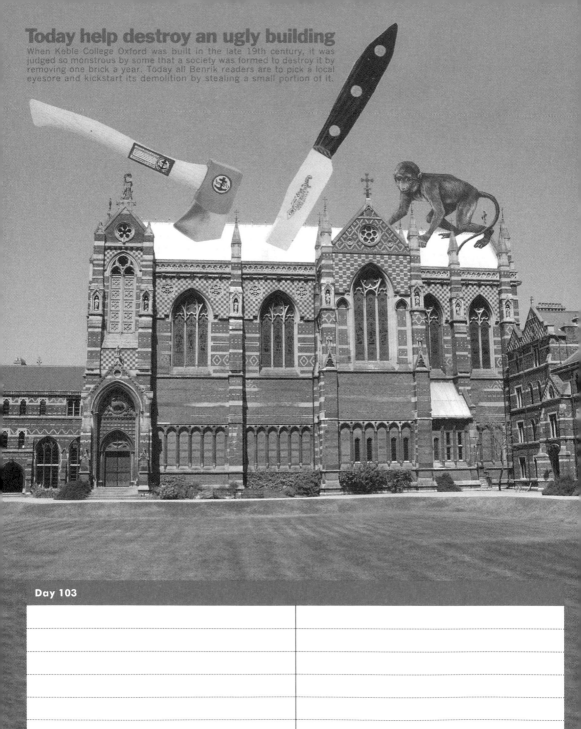

Today help destroy an ugly building

When Keble College Oxford was built in the late 19th century, it was judged so monstrous by some that a society was formed to destroy it by removing one brick a year. Today all Benrik readers are to pick a local eyesore and kickstart its demolition by stealing a small portion of it.

Day 103

Today is Self-medicating Day

Don't just obey medical prejudices: trust your instinct to find the medicine that works for you. Plenty of modern cures were discovered by doctors administering the wrong drugs by mistake. These are Benrik's own medical guidelines, but feel free to experiment and come up with your own.

	Yellow and blue Diseases of the knee		Blue and red Heavy diarrhea
	Yellow and red Cures swollen arteries		Red and white When you find yourself on fire
	Yellow and brown For sex-related headaches		Black Brings on sudden death
	Dark green and light green Club foot		Orange and green To put you in a bad mood
	Yellow and green Prevents bad dreams		Pink and green Women's troubles
	Red and blue Heavy constipation		Grey and white Against boredom
	Red and pink If your hair is too long		Purple Discharges of all kinds
	Dark red and brown Loss of limb		White These have no effect, avoid

Advanced: medical cocktails. When you have mastered the basics of self-medication, you may progress to combining. It is advisable to try the combinations on a small animal beforehand, as even the most modern drugs can have serious negative side effects when mixed. In truth, not even Benrik have tried all combinations of the above, this will take a lifetime. But yellow/blue with red/pink is definitely best avoided.

Day 104

This page is dedicated to the memory of Dribbles.

START A RELATIONSHIP WITH ANOTHER BENRIK FOLLOWER

Anyone following Benrik will necessarily have drifted away from their boring old non-Benrikian partner, still stuck in their gloomy miserable boring old everyday rut. Here is your chance to find somebody more suited to the new you. Today visit www.thiswebsitewillchangeyourlife.com and you will be able to chat live to dozens of like-minded individuals, one of whom might prove to be the love of your life.

Testimonial John&Cindy

John, 48, had been single for an unhealthy nine years when he met Cindy, 24, via a Benrik reading group. One year later, they are married with a gorgeous little boy, who they've called...Benrik! Cute. Says John: "Until I read the Book, I was a complete schmuck. Women wouldn't give me the time of day, particularly supermodel-types like Cindy here. But we just hit it off. The Book made me much more confident and witty, and it made her realize there was rather more to life than dating conventionally good-looking millionaires." John and Cindy married on 16 June after reading Benrik's instruction: "Today trust your gut instincts no matter how much those you thought were your friends laugh at you." Quips Cindy: "Benrik really did change our lives! That book was definitely worth the money, maybe even $1 or $2 more who knows."

BENRIK ARRANGED MARRIAGES

Such is the degree of compatibility between Book followers that Benrik are bringing back arranged marriages. Who needs the messy rigmarole of dating, cohabiting and proposing when Benrik can take care of matters for you? Simply register on the website, answer a few simple questions, and within two weeks, Benrik will find a match for you, and give you a date for the wedding! What could be easier?

Benrik decisions on the suitability of partners for Benrik Arranged Marriages are final. The partners' legal and/or religious consent is superseded by their consent to the terms and conditions of the Benrik Arranged Marriages Program. No correspondence will be entered into. Benrik reserve the right to attend the wedding as guests of honor and take photos for promotional purposes. At Benrik Ltd., we make every effort to find suitable matches, but this is not guaranteed. Benrik collect a fee based on the value of the partners' property and the likelihood they would have found love without Benrik's intervention. No refunds will be given, nor will divorce lawyers' fees be paid.

TODAY COMMIT TREASON

Under English law, it is still technically a treasonable offense to call for the end of the monarchy, punishable by exile and life imprisonment. Today test this law by traveling to the United Kingdom, walking up to Buckingham Palace and telling the guards you have come to remove the Queen from the throne, which she has usurped from the people.

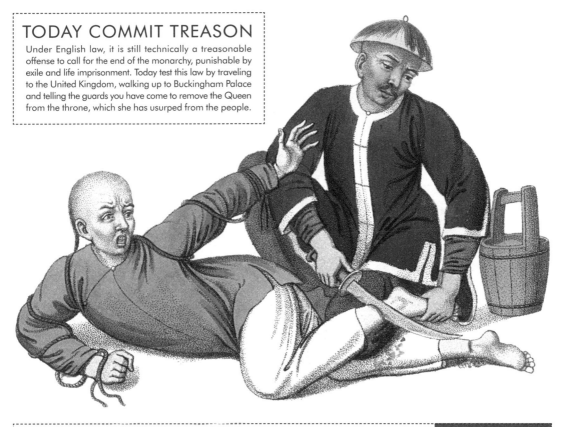

TREASON FELONY ACT 1848

3. Offences herein mentioned declared to be felonies

...If any person whatsoever shall, within the United Kingdom or without, compass, imagine, invent, devise or intend to deprive or depose our Most Gracious Lady the Queen, ...from the style, honour, or royal name of the imperial crown of the United Kingdom, or of any other of her Majesty's dominions and countries, or to levy war against her Majesty, ...within any part of the United Kingdom, in order by force or constraint to compel her... to change her...measures of counsels, or in order to put any force or constraint upon her or in order to intimidate or overawe both Houses or either House of Parliament, or to move or stir any foreigner or stranger with force to invade the United Kingdom or any other of her Majesty's dominions or countries under the obeisance of her Majesty...and such compassings, imaginations, inventions, devices, or intentions, or any of them, shall express, utter, or declare, by publishing any printing or writing...or by any overt act or deed, every person so offending shall be guilty of felony, and being convicted thereof shall be liable...to be transported beyond the seas for the term of their natural life.

Day 106

STALK AN ANIMAL!

HEY LASSIE I'M GOING TO EAT YOU ALIVE YOU LITTLE BITCH!

It is only recently that humans have pulled ahead of the pack and started considering ourselves superior to other species. Today return to your animal roots by stalking another creature. It may take you a while to get the hang of it, so start with something simple, like a cat. Sniff its urine. Scan its tracks. Study its behavior. Scare the hell out of it when you catch the damn thing. If it denounces you to the animal protection people, remind them that technically you too are an animal and therefore covered by statutory dog-eat-dog legislation. If all else fails either howl at the moon or roll over and play dead.

Day 107

Today, act suspiciously

Loiter outside the CIA's headquarters and sketch them from all angles

Set all the alarm clocks on display in a department store to ring at the same time

We must be vigilant at all times, surrounded as we are by terrorists and other evil-doers. Help keep society on its toes today with your suspicious behavior. This may cause some short-term inconvenience for you and for those around you, but in the long-term, you'll have done society a good turn, even if it doesn't appreciate it just today.

Walk past police sniffer dogs with a suitcase full of sausages

Call the White House and breathe dirty down the line

Page 'Osama' at the airport information desk

Avoid eye contact with everyone

Turn and walk the other way whenever an officer comes near

Day 108

SPAZ!

"The only rational response to our über-rational society is to deny rationality itself. That is to say, we must divest ourselves of the language (language as praxis, pace Wittgenstein) of logical discourse in order to deny society's grip on our behavior and practices. We must embrace the vicious circle of the irrational in order to re-emerge reborn free, on the other side of the black hole that is instrumental rationality such as it has been appropriated by the global post-capitalist technocracy. The 'retarded' constitute in actual fact the new avant-garde of our decadent times." (G. Klage, "Spazzing: the art of inarticulacy," Heidelberg Press, 2004)

Day 109

INSIST ON SPEAKING TO THE MEDIA TODAY

The media isn't a circus, it's a club: same old faces, same old views, same old grudges. Today, demand to have your voice heard for a change! Speak out on what matters to you, whether it's how to run a good war, or about the strange way light sometimes shimmies on puddles, in country lanes, at the crack of dawn. Barge in and have your say! How to trick the media into giving you airtime Good: I have slept with the president (and can prove it!); I have valuable information regarding a plot; I have swallowed a grenade and wish to say goodbye; I'm the replacement weatherman. Bad: I am the foremost expert on country lane puddle lighting.

You aren't anyone if you haven't been on tv. And you're only a little someone if you've been on radio. And you're only a tiny teenie weenie of a somebody if you've been in the newspaper. But barely worth mentioning!

Day 110

Today, tip abnormally

The arbitrary rule of tipping is to leave 10 to 15%, but this is an old-fashioned and lazy approach. Tipping is an art form, expressive of your personality and potentially a force for social disruption. Today explore its potential, starting with our random guidelines. Begin with the tediously conventional 10% and add or subtract as follows.

-$1 The tippee has green or greenish eyes	**+$1** The tippee has a visible tattoo on his or her chest	**+$1.⁵⁰** The sky is blue with fewer than three clouds	**-$1.⁵⁰** The tippee has used a word beginning with "R"
+$7 The sum of your bill is a primary number	**-$8** You can't figure out if it is a primary number	**+$1** The tippee has offered sex as part of the service	**-$6** The world's geo-political prospects look negative
-$1 The tippee resembles someone on TV	**-$4** Yesterday you went to bed drunk	**+$0.⁵⁰** The service provided was good	**N.B.** In some cases you will end up with a negative sum, which is known as reverse tipping. Here the tippee owes you money, which you may collect in cash or through extra service. Show them this book if they query your claim.

Day 111

PILGRIMAGE DAY

Today pay homage to Marco Polo by symbolically retracing his epic journey in your local area.

This map shows Marco's actual travels.

VENICE
CONSTANTINOPLE
KASHGAR
KARA KHOTO
BEIJING
ACRE
ORMUZ
CEYLON
MALACCA

This map shows how to apply the travels on a different scale.

HOUSE
VIDEO STORE
BUTCHER'S
POST OFFICE
BAR
NEWS STAND
LAUNDROMAT
LIQUOR STORE
SUPERMARKET

What Marco Polo learned from his journey: "When a man is riding through this desert by night and for some reason – falling asleep or anything else – he gets separated from his companions and wants to rejoin them, he hears spirit voices talking to him as if they were his companions, sometimes even calling him by name. Often these voices lure him away from the path and he never finds it again, and many travelers have got lost and died because of this."

What *you* learned from *your* journey:...

Day 112

Today, pour cocaine down an anthill

Recreate the feverish atmosphere of a financial trading floor by feeding the little workers a few grams of Colombian marching powder. Watch them zap that termite colony into oblivion. Watch them blitz that forest into wasteland. Just don't stand too close: their conversation will get very boring.

YARIBA!

Day 113

Naturism Day

There's nothing natural about clothes. We are born naked, but soon thrust into the straitjacket of clothing and taught that the naked body is sinful. In the future, no doubt, people will laugh at our prejudiced ways. Don't wait! Stop being a "textile," at least for one day. Spend today naked, and feel nature refresh your body, mind and soul.

These photographs from the future are proof of systematic and horrific discrimination against Naturists. Do something, right now!

DIY WARNING!

Watch out if you're going to do some DIY! Those power tools aren't very body-friendly... Be careful, and take out some special insurance through www.thiswebsitewillchangeyourlife.com

Don't worry about getting arrested, thousands of other Book owners will be running around naked too!

Day 114

TODAY YOU ARE A COWBOY

There is much to be learned from cowboy lore. Today follow these well-known cowboy precepts, dressed of course in the appropriate attire.

Don't squat with your spurs on. * Timing has a lot to do with the outcome of a rain dance. * Don't interfere with something that ain't botherin' you none. * If it don't seem like it's worth the effort, it probably ain't. * If you get to thinkin' you're a person of some influence, try orderin' somebody else's dog around. * Generally, you ain't learnin' nothing when your mouth's a-jawin'. * When you're throwin' your weight around, be ready to have it thrown around by somebody else. * If you're ridin' ahead of the herd, take a look back every now and then to make sure it's still there with ya. * Always take a good look at what you're about to eat. It's not so important to know what it is, but it's sure crucial to know what it was. * If you find yourself in a hole, the first thing to do is stop diggin'. * Tellin' a man to git lost and makin' him do it are two entirely different

propositions. * The biggest troublemaker you'll probably ever have to deal with watches you shave his face in the mirror every morning. * When you give a personal lesson in meanness to a critter or to a person, don't be surprised if they learn their lesson. * Lettin' the cat outta the bag is a whole lot easier than puttin' it back in. * Never miss a good chance to shut up. * Always drink upstream from the herd. * It don't take a genius to spot a goat in a flock of sheep. * Don't worry about bitin' off more than you can chew; your mouth is probably a whole lot bigger'n you think. * The quickest way to double your money is to fold it over and put it back into your pocket. * Good judgment comes from experience, and a lotta that comes from bad judgment. * Never ask a barber if you need a haircut.

Day 115

PETITION DAY Submit your name on www.thiswebsitewillchangeyourlife.com and Benrik will automatically put your name to any petition of interest that comes our way. Here are just a few of the worthy causes you will support, free of charge.

U IS FOR UNFAIR!
ARTISTS WHOSE NAMES BEGIN IN U ARE NOT PROPERLY REPRESENTED IN OUR MUSEUMS. INCREASE THEIR PROPORTION TO 1/26 TH NOW!

END THE FALKLANDS WAR NOW
THE WAR HAS BEEN GOING ON OVER 20 YEARS NOW, AT HUGE COST IN LIVES TO BOTH SIDES. WE ASK THE GOVERNMENT TO COME TO ITS SENSES.

NO TO WIDESCREEN
WIDESCREEN TV IS FLATTER AND THEREFORE DISCRIMINATES AGAINST THE TALLER ACTOR. WE THE UNDERSIGNED DEMAND ITS IMMEDIATE BAN NOW!

EVERY YEAR 7 DOGS ARE EATEN BY THEIR OWNERS
STOP THE MASSACRE! SIGNED BY:

DON'T CHOP DOWN THE BENRIK TREE!
TREE NEAR BENRIK HEADQUARTERS THREATENED BY COUNCIL GESTAPO.

FREE [TO BE CONFIRMED]!!!!
[TO BE CONFIRMED] HAS BEEN WRONGLY ARRESTED! WE ASK THE COURTS TO RECTIFY THIS OUTRAGE IMMEDIATELY!

Day 116

ENTER A TRAILER TRASH COMPETITION TODAY!!!!!!!

SOMEONE HAS TO WIN THEM. BUY SOME TV LISTINGS MAGAZINES AND ENTER THE GOLDEN DRAW. YOU WON'T CARE HOW LOW-RENT IT SEEMS WHEN YOU'VE WON THE MILLION-DOLLAR DIAMOND JACKPOT!!!!!!

GUESS HOW MANY CANDIES ARE IN THIS JAR AND IT'S YOURS!

SUPER DRAW!

LOVELY CANDY!!

32?

Day 117

TODAY, PUT YOURSELF FORWARD FOR CLONING

NAME LAST..............................

NAME FIRST.............................

DATE OF BIRTH.........................

PLACE OF BIRTH........................

WEIGHT AT BIRTH......................

SEX MALE FEMALE......................

BLOOD TYPE:

A □ B □ AB □ O □ RH FACTOR......

CURRENT HEIGHT.......................

CURRENT WEIGHT.......................

COLOR EYES:

BROWN □   BLUE □   BLUE-GREEN □

HAZEL □   HAZEL-GREEN □   GREEN □

BODY BUILD: LARGER □   MEDIUM □   SLENDER □

IQ...

MARRIED □   SINGLE □   LIVING WITH PARTNER □

ETHNIC BACKGROUND: WHITE □ BLACK CARIBBEAN □

BLACK AFRICAN □   BLACK OTHER □   INDIAN □

PAKISTANI □ HISPANIC □ CHINESE □ ANY OTHER □

EDUCATION.................................

OCCUPATION..............................

KNOWN ALLERGIES......................

HEALTH PROBLEMS......................

CURRENT MEDICATION..................

DOCTOR (NAME ADDRESS PHONE NUMBER).............

ATTACH
PHOTO
HERE

CLONEX ™

I THINK I WOULD MAKE GOOD CLONING MATERIAL BECAUSE:

I'M TOLD I'M PRETTY GOOD-LOOKING...... □

I GET ON WITH MOST FOLK................... □

I WANT TO MEET ME.......................... □

I HAD THIS WEIRD DREAM ABOUT IT....... □

I COULD USE MY CLONES TO SECRETLY CHEAT ON MY PARTNER......................... □

IT WOULD FURTHER MY PLANS FOR WORLD DOMINATION.................................. □

IT'D BE MORE INTERESTING THAN CLONING SOME DUMB SHEEP.............................. □

CONTACT DETAILS:

ADDRESS.......................................

....

....

PHONE NUMBER.............................

NEXT OF KIN..................................

ADDRESS.......................................

PHONE NUMBER.............................

I AM AVAILABLE FOR THE OPERATION:

MORNINGS □   AFTERNOONS □   EITHER □

I AUTHORISE CLONEX INC. TO SEDATE ME AND COLLECT SAMPLE TISSUE FROM MY BODY FOR THE PURPOSE OF PRODUCING CLONES OF ME, UP TO 100,000. I HEREBY WAIVE COPYRIGHT ON MY CLONES. I UNDERSTAND THAT THEY ARE THE PROPERTY OF CLONEX INC. AND CLONEX INC. ARE FREE TO USE THEM FOR ANY PURPOSE, INCLUDING MILITARY. I UNDERTAKE NOT TO TRY AND ARRANGE CONTACT WITH MY CLONES OTHER THAN THROUGH THE APPOINTED REPRESENTATIVES OF CLONEX INC. IN RETURN I WILL BE ALLOWED TO KEEP ANY DEFECTIVE CLONES (INCLUDING BUT NOT LIMITED TO BRAIN-DAMAGED, MALFORMED OR PSYCHOTIC CLONES). I FULLY UNDERSTAND THAT THE CLONING PROCEDURE IS STILL EXPERIMENTAL AND RESULTS ARE NOT GUARANTEED. I ACKNOWLEDGE THAT THERE IS A NON-NEGLIGIBLE CHANCE THE PROCEDURE WILL FAIL AND I MAY BE LEFT WITH IRREVERSIBLE PERSONALITY DISORDERS, OR MAY EVEN REQUIRE A LOBOTOMY. I ACCEPT THESE RISKS AND HEREBY WAIVE ANY CLAIM FOR DAMAGES.

SIGNED AND DATED ....

SEND TO: CLONEX INC. R&D, PO BOX 23342, FORT LAUDERDALE, FL 33304, USA.

Day 118

ICONOCLASM DAY:
DEFACE A POWERFUL IMAGE

EVER SINCE OUR CAVEMEN ANCESTORS THOUGHT PAINTING MAMMOTHS WOULD HELP THEM CATCH THE REAL THING, WE HAVE BEEN IN THRALL TO IMAGES. EVEN THESE DAYS WE CAN SCARCELY BRING OURSELVES TO THROW AWAY PHOTOS OF LOVED ONES, SUCH IS OUR ATTACHMENT TO THE QUASI-VOODOO NOTION THAT WHAT WE DO TO THE PHOTO SOMEHOW AFFECTS THE PERSON. SHATTER THIS SELF-IMPOSED TABOO TODAY BY DEFACING A POTENT IMAGE, BE IT A PHOTO OF YOUR PARENTS, OR THE ONE WE PROVIDE.

Day 119

BENRIKLAND FUNPARK DAY

First Aid
Information
Parking
Disabled
Telephone
Beer Hall
Mini Golf
Baby Care
Diner

5% off! Show this Book at the entrance and get 5% off the price of a day-ticket.

Top attractions!

Spend today at Benrikland, Benrik's fun new theme park in Florida.

BENRIK SPACE SHOOTER Kids shoot up into space! For good! ❶   ❺ **BENRIK CASTLE** We kidnap three guests a day and see if the family pays the ransom

ROLLERCOASTER RESTAURANT The world's only vomit-proof rollercoaster! ❷   ❻ **ER 3000** A concrete-lined bouncy castle

HANSEL AND GRETEL SLEEPOVER Don't worry parents, that oven only heats up to 120 degrees! ❸   ❼ **"SHARK-A-LARK"** The pool that's also an aquarium!

CRASHMANIA JG Ballard-inspired bumper cars ❹   ❽ **SPLAT TOWERS** Learn the trapeze in 10 minutes flat

Day 120	

Today record a suspicious greeting on your answerphone and see if it affects people's messages.

"Hello Amal, it is me. If you're listening to this, all has gone well praise be. The clockmaker will be pleased. He has nearly completed his work, but he is missing the cuckoo. You must pick up the cuckoo from our friends from the village. Yaigar's cousin will bring it over two weeks before the big wedding. Meet him at the place we arranged, at 4a.m. The bridegroom is nervous, so be careful that the bridesmaids don't follow you. Make sure the cuckoo is intact: its head should have three prongs, blue, red and orange. It is fragile so be careful with it. Yaigar's cousin is a gossip, so once you have the cuckoo, make sure he will not talk about it. Bring it to the clockmaker. Then your task will be done and you may await the wedding, with great impatience, like all of us. It will be joyous. Peace be with you, Amal, and good luck. Oh and if you are not Amal, just leave me a message after the beep and I'll get back to you soon!"

Day 121

ZOMBIE DAY
Tonight, go to your nearest cemetery, cover your face with flour, and walk into town with your arms outstretched.

Day 122

Six Degrees Of Separation Day:
Today stop everyone you meet and don't let them go until you have worked out your six degrees of separation.

You
6°
Bruce Lee

You
6°
People from Asia

You
6°
Ronan Keaton

You
6°
Shoe Polishers

You
6°
Rob Lowe

You
6°
Charlie Chaplin

You
6°
Idi Amin

You
6°
Jesus/ Muhammed

You
6°
All of the Kennedys

You
6°
Peter the Great

You
6°
Sexy people

You
6°
Picasso

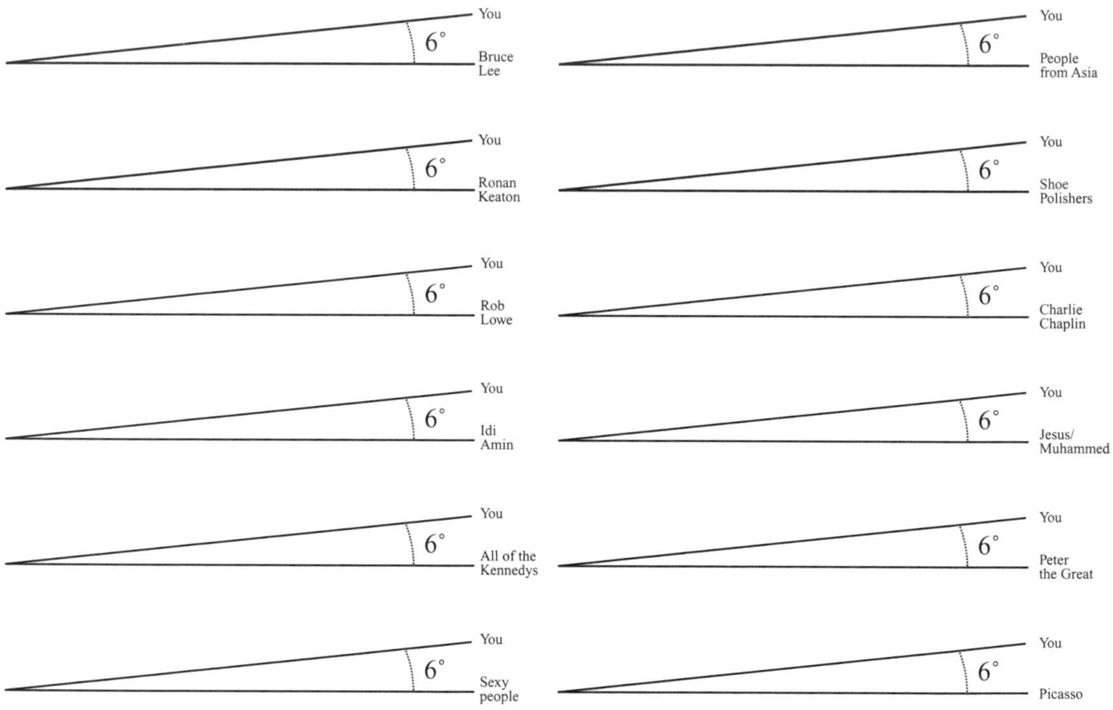

Day 123

Day 124

The spousal relationship is unfashionable in some quarters, but can provide the bedrock of a happy and emotionally fulfilled life. And in this day and age, you don't need to be married or even in a relationship to enjoy it! Simply pick someone at random, and follow these seven easy steps. ① Keep their dinner warm in the oven. ② Ask them about their day. ③ Call them "dear." ④ Do the dishes together. ⑤ Give them a useful domestic gadget. ⑥ Sit together in silence. ⑦ Spoon.

Day 126

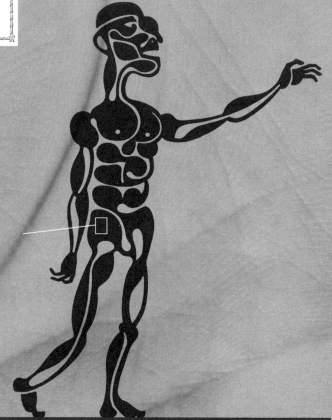

TODAY BE A VIRTUAL EXHIBITIONIST
Scan part of your anatomy
and post it on our website.

Not since childhood have you had the
chance to expose yourself to dozens of
strangers without risking jail. So seize
it! The most interesting scans will be
available to download as a screensaver
to millions around the world.

ANONYMITY GUARANTEED!
www.thiswebsitewillchangeyourlife.com

Day 127

YOU CAN BE A MOVIE EXTRA

This may be your ticket to fame and fortune. Anyone can become a movie extra, as it does not require any particular acting talent. Ideally you should choose one of these two main looks.

ANONYMOUS

If you are of average height and build, are neither exceptionally ugly nor attractive, and have no distinctive scars, tattoos or other unusual features, this is for you. Directors mostly require extras to blend into the crowd, not distract the audience's attention from the special effects and highly paid stars.

WEIRD

Occasionally, the producers will require someone of a particular physical type, a bald dwarf say, or an obese Japanese teenager. This specialized market is better paid and more exclusive. On the downside, however, parts are more limited in their availability.

The best way to find a part is to get an agent. Look on the internet for a reputable agency in your area and send in a photo with your résumé. Optional: include a list of films you think would have been better with you in them (and why).

HOW TO BEHAVE ON SET

Traditional advice is to take a good book, listen to instructions carefully, and keep a low profile. This of course will not change your life much. What you really want is to impress by your sheer magnetism. You want to make love to the camera. You want to get spotted. You will not achieve this by lurking quietly in the background. Take every little opportunity to get in the director's eyeline. Exchange showbiz gossip with the stars during the lunch and coffee breaks. Accidentally "stumble" into a scene when the camera is rolling and deliver some hilarious repartee that the scriptwriter will kick himself for not having thought of. Ignore the petty-minded orders of junior crew members and thrust yourself into the limelight. Film history is simply packed with examples of Hollywood stars who have made it big in exactly this way. Good luck!

–Darling, I'm seeing your pain, now I want to feel it myself! This is your final glorious death rattle! Exude!

–Fabulous! Now just take it down 10% We need to see your little soul fluttering away like an autumn leaf. Action!

–CUT!

Day 128

Tonight,
watch the sun set, and reflect on your insignificance in the cosmic order

You have fewer than 30,000 chances to watch a sunset. Make sure you take that chance today. Sunset time Paris: 9:32p.m.

Day 129

If this is your DNA sequence, you've won $100,000,000,000!

We collected this DNA sample off a discarded toothbrush. Could it be yours? Visit your local doctor to get a free DNA reading and match it to this one. The closest match will walk away with the cash! Good luck.

Day 130

FLASHMOB DAY

Today, organize a flashmob. Some notable ones Benrik have held include everyone throwing paper planes past airport security, and converging on your local ER with a strange disease whose only symptoms are a painful left eye and a constant urge to urinate. Today, however, you must come up with one yourself, and enlist everyone you know to join in. Report the results on www.this-websitewillchangeyourlife.com. Whoever makes the national news will be declared the winner.

Photos: take your camera. At least one photo of each event should be sent to Benrik.

Day 131	

Today, impress your librarian

Walk into your local library and borrow something thick, preferably by Sartre, preferably in the original French. Return it with a satisfied smile 27 minutes later. Check their reaction as you saunter out, full of your new learning. You now have a local reputation as a savant.

A BOOK ABOUT HOW EASY IT IS TO FALL UNDER THE PRESSURE OF USING SILENCE AS A CONCEPT WHEN YOU ARE TO ILLUSTRATE ANYTHING THAT HAS TO DO WITH A LIBRARY AND HOW TO AVOID IT

Day 132

Today, mess up your kid so they turn into Picasso

Early deprivation of affection and the subsequent inner conviction that you are worthless fuel the compulsive ambition that drives the artist. By namby-pamby standards, it may seem that you are being cruel to your children, but really you are doing them a favor. "They fuck you up, your Mum and Dad" is not therapeutical babbling, but the poet's grateful acknowledgement of his two-headed Muse. As Proust said, "everything we think of as great comes from neurotics. They alone have founded religions and composed masterpieces." He knew this first hand: when he didn't get his customary goodnight kiss from his mother one night at the age of seven, he concluded that love was doomed and was plunged into the lifelong despondency that produced his magnum opus. As his example shows, nothing heavy-handed is required; a forgotten kiss, a strange look, or a rash word are all it takes to spice up a life.

MY NAME IS ADOLF. AT LEAST THATS WHAT MY DADDY CALLS ME. MY REAL NAME IS BILLY. BUT DADDY SAYS ADOLF IS BETER FOR ~~THE~~ ME. HE SAYS I WILL UNDERSTAND ~~WITH~~ WHEN I GROW UP. IT MAKES THE OTHER KIDS AT SKOOL LAUGH. I DONT KNOW WHY. MOMMY IS A PAINTER. SHE PAINTS WITH ME. ~~I~~ I LIKE PAINTING BUT I DONT LIKE BLAK. BLAK IS THE ONLY COLOR MOMMY SAYS I CAN USE UNTIL I AM 9. THEN I CAN USE PINK. I DONT LIKE PINK. ON SUNDAYS DADDY AND MOMMY TAKE ME TO THE MUSE UM. I SIT IN FRONT OF THE PAINTINGS. THEN THEY GO TO THEY GO TO THE BAR. CANT GO BECAUS I AM 8. DADDY SAYS THE PAINTINGS WILBE MY MOMMY AND DADDY FOR 2 HOURS. BUT SOMETIMES ITS 3. I KNOW BECAUS I COUNT THE SEKUNDS IN MY HEAD. I CAN COUNT UP TO 14858. THAT WAS THE MOST THEY WERE IN THE BAR AND I WERE LOOKING AT THE PAINTING. SOMETIMES I DREAM THEY ARE DEAD. DADDY SAID GOOD BOY ADOLF AND GAVE ME RED PAINT FOR MY BIRTH— DAY.

ME AND MY MOMMY AND MY DADDY

Day 133

Today plant marijuana outside a government building and report them to the local newspaper.

Where to plant? Picking a good location to plant your seed is crucial. Ideally you are looking for grass interspersed with trees and small bushes, and available water (bear in mind official lawns are often automatically watered). If the soil is very poor, consider adding a layer of organic topsoil with lime to make it more fertile. Sunlight is a definite plus; four hours a day is a minimum, preferably in the morning. Mid-May is a good time to plant. Plant your seeds about one half-inch deep, with two inches between seeds. To guarantee a decent harvest that will photograph well, allow for 200+ seeds. Planting at night is advisable to ensure an element of surprise.

MORNING HERALD

Hippie mayor high on power

By MOJO

BEST WEED: IT'S OFFICIAL!

By BENDS

...NSTER IN GANJA SCANDAL

Lawyer denies everything

EXCLUSIVE INTERVIEW
PAGE 4, 5, 6

SOME GOOD OUTDOOR SEEDS	EARLY GIRL: EASY TO GROW, NOT TOO POTENT	MASTER KUSH: STRONG EARTHY SMELL
AFGHAN: STRONG AROMA, HEAVY SMOKE	SNOW WHITE: NICE SMOOTH TASTE	CHRYSTAL: GOOD YIELDS, QUICK HIGH

Day 134

Hunter-gatherer day

Hunting-gathering is in our genes, but we could all do with a refresher course. Today practice your prehistorical skills with the help of our chart. When civilization collapses overnight, you'll kick yourself if you didn't prepare.

HUNTINGS							
EDIBLE	NON-EDIBLE	EDIBLE	NON-EDIBLE	EDIBLE	EDIBLE	EDIBLE	EDIBLE
NON-EDIBLE	NON-EDIBLE	EDIBLE	EDIBLE	NON-EDIBLE	EDIBLE	EDIBLE	NON-EDIBLE	NON-EDIBLE
NON-EDIBLE	NON-EDIBLE	EDIBLE	EDIBLE	EDIBLE	EDIBLE	EDIBLE	NON-EDIBLE	EDIBLE
EDIBLE	EDIBLE	EDIBLE	NON-EDIBLE	NON-EDIBLE	NON-EDIBLE	EDIBLE	NON-EDIBLE	NON-EDIBLE
NON-EDIBLE	NON-EDIBLE	NON-EDIBLE	NON-EDIBLE	NON-EDIBLE	EDIBLE	NON-EDIBLE	EDIBLE	NON-EDIBLE
GATHERINGS							
EDIBLE	POISONOUS	DEADLY	POISONOUS	EDIBLE	DEADLY	EDIBLE	DEADLY

Day 135

Benrik are keen to revive communism, a much-maligned ideology that was never correctly applied. What could be simpler and more inspiring than "From each according to his ability, to each according to his need"? To help Benrik implement communism properly, would everyone please e-mail a) their abilities and b) their needs to: commies@benrik.co.uk. Thank you comrades. Watch this space.

Day 136

WEEK OF REVOLUTION!

UNDERGROUND

DOWN WITH THE POST CAPITALIST ORDER!

COMRADES UNITE IN OVERTHROWING THE GOVERNMENT! USE ANY MEANS NECESSARY!

WHY FIGHT FAIR WHEN THE STATE APPARATUS DOES NOT?

REPRESSION BEGETS REACTION! ANARCHY IS TOO TIMID!

RISE AGAINST THE RULING CLASS AND ITS LAPDOG THE MIDDLE CLASS

THEY MAY SPEND MONEY BUT WE WILL SPEND BLOOD! AND LOTS OF IT!!!!!!

WHO IS THE ENEMY? THEY KNOW WHO THEY ARE! AND SO DO WE!

IF YOU ARE A BOURGEOIS JUST SHOOT YOURSELF AND SAVE US TIME

Print your own samizdat

Revolution is made in the mind. Plant its seeds with your very own samizdat pamphlet. Samizdat rules: no pictures or colors are allowed, it's not meant to be enjoyed. Avoid margins, a waste of scarce paper. Simple words are best, in capitals for emphasis. Logic may be shaky, as long as the main thrust is clear.

Day 137

WEEK OF REVOLUTION!

Foment
unrest away
from home

Dear Benrikians

Following yesterday's outburst, you will have been banished. Use this time wisely to make contacts in the revolutionary diaspora. Distribute pamphlets outside offices, speak at covert meetings, rouse the rabble! If you do not come to the attention of the local authorities, you are not fomenting hard enough.

Day 138

WEEK OF REVOLUTION!

Develop your own revolutionary brand today

With so many things to oppose, it's important to give your revolution some individuality. It could be out-of-control facial hair, an unusual scapegoat (the weather?) or a rhetorical device, like starting all your sentences with "But!"

REMINDER: THE STATUS QUO If your revolution is simply a generic one against the status quo, here is a reminder of its basics: our world is dominated by a global elite based on interlocking military economic social and cultural networks, organized to exploit the rest of us as workers and consumers, and configured to exclude even the possibility of serious dissent.

Day 139

WEEK OF REVOLUTION!

REVOLUTION

Hijack a train to the scene of your coup

No revolution is complete without the spectacular arrival from the hills of the bearded revolutionaries. Today board a train and demand that it divert to the government HQ, or better still, the TV station, where you will take over the country, using force of some description.

Day 140

WEEK OF REVOLUTION!
NEW DAWN

Impose your new society

The hardest part is done. Now we must change society. Form neighborhood committees, headed by the local Book reader. Pool all your salaries (including bonuses and benefits in kind) and divide them equally. Put all the houses in a hat and just reallocate them at random. Enforce equality of opportunity. Then take the rest of the day off as a national holiday.

I CAN'T SEE

Day 141

WEEK OF REVOLUTION!

PURGE

Now liquidate absolutely everyone you've met this week

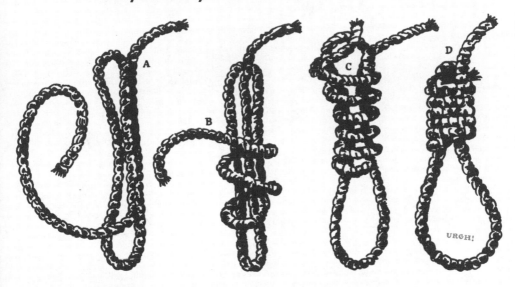

"DON'T THINK. IF YOU THINK, DON'T SPEAK. IF YOU SPEAK, DON'T WRITE. IF YOU WRITE, DON'T SIGN. IF YOU THINK, SPEAK, WRITE AND SIGN – DON'T BE SURPRISED!!!"

Day 142

TODAY CONFUSE FUTURE ARCHAEOLOGISTS BY DATING THINGS WRONGLY

The historian of tomorrow has it too easy. Complicate matters slightly by picking an item of consumer electronics, dating it 23/05/1778 in marker pen, and burying it in your back garden. Thousands of years from now, you could be the cause of a major re-evaluation of Late Second Millennium history.

Slapstick Day

SLIP ON A BANANA PEEL

THROW A CUSTARD PIE

WALK INTO A LAMP POST

HIT SOMEONE WITH A FRYING PAN

DROP YOUR ICE CREAM BALL

LEAVE A WATER BUCKET ABOVE THE DOOR

FALL INTO AN OPEN MANHOLE

STEP ON SOMEONE'S TOE

GET STUCK IN REVOLVING DOORS

Day 144

DROP THIS BOOK ON SOMEONE'S FOOT!

TODAY BE A MODEL CONSUMER

Help the economy by spending exactly $37. Economists have determined that $37 is the optimal figure for everyone to spend at this point in the business cycle. Do your duty for the world economy by purchasing $37 of goods and services during business hours today.

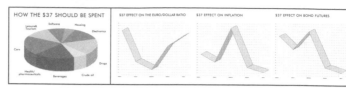

HOW THE $37 SHOULD BE SPENT

Day 145

Muzak!

Carry your own desired musical ambience around with you today. Make a tape of songs appropriate to the mood you wish to convey to those around you, and play it on a beatbox all day long. For instance:

ANGRY

Fight The Power Public Enemy
The Prisoner Iron Maiden
White America Eminem
Fifth Symphony Beethoven
Fuck The Pain Away Peaches
Mutter Ramstein
Injustice For All Metallica
Smells Like Teen Spirit Nirvana
Won't Get Fooled Again The Who
Two Tribes Frankie Goes To Hollywood

Good for: asking for a pay raise, complaining in shops.

SAD

Everybody Hurts REM
Yesterday The Beatles
So Far Away Carole King
Last Christmas Wham!
Moonlight Sonata Beethoven
Crying Roy Orbison
Crying Primal Scream
Tears In Heaven Eric Clapton
Send In The Clowns Frank Sinatra
Do They Know It's Xmas? Band Aid

Good for: dumping partner, telling someone they have a parking ticket.

HUNGRY

Strawberry Fields Forever The Beatles
Candy And A Currant Bun Pink Floyd
Sugar And Spice The Searchers
Starfish And Coffee Prince
Rock Lobster B-52's
Hungry Like The Wolf Duran Duran
Soup Is Good Food Dead Kennedys
Mashed Potatoes The Smashing Pumpkins
Cinnamon Girl Neil Young
Crème Brulee Sonic Youth

Good for: restaurant settings, supermarkets.

Lustful

Horny Mousse T
You Sexy Thing Hot Chocolate
Sex Machine James Brown
Erotica Madonna
Push It Salt'n'Pepa
I Touch Myself The Divinyls
Touch Me Samantha Fox
Suck My Dick Lil' Kim
Can't Get Enough... Barry White
I Want Your Sex George Michael

Good for: first date, public masturbation.

HAPPY

Dancing Queen Abba
Shiny Happy People REM
Beautiful Day U2
Freedom Aretha Franklin
Holiday Madonna
It's Raining Men Weather Girls
Celebration Kool And The Gang
Club Tropicana Wham!
Don't Worry, Be Happy Bobby McFerrin
La Bamba Los Lobos

Good for: winning the lottery, delivering babies.

MAD

Freak Radiohead
Rambling On Procol Harum
Livin' La Vida Loca Ricky Martin
I Talk To The Trees Tony Bavaar
Party Out Of Bounds B-52s
Rock Me Amadeus Falco
Who Let The Dogs Out? Baha Men
O Superman Laurie Anderson
Bat Out Of Hell Meatloaf
Ring Cycle Wagner

Good for: scaring away muggers, scaring away loved ones.

Day 147

Adult Material Day

Go on! You know you want it!

Imagine you, naked, on the internet. Doesn't it give you a great feeling?

Today all readers are to take filthy pics of their exploits and post them on www.thiswebsitewillchangeyourlife.com

Caught at it!

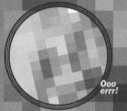

Ooo errr!

Great feeling! Being naked on the internet is perfect!

Naughty!

Being naked on the internet is a great feeling!

Sex! Sex! Sex!

Lots of sex here!

Saucy
Readers behaving BADLY!

Day 148

You scratch mine!
I really needed to itch my back, right
where the shoulder blade is (which is
ungettable, unless you have dislocating
arms) and I thought I should ask a
stranger to scratch it, and then offer to
scratch theirs in return. Wadda ya think?

(no pix: needs photos of objects "I did think
that the page could be made up of various
implements of different kinds that could be
used to scratch ones back. A bamboo stick,
a piece of spaghetti, a fork a CD etc.")

Optional: Then kill them, chop them up and stuff them under the floorboards

Today, make a shrine about someone you don't know but see on a regular basis such as on the bus or train to work, then show it to them.

<u>"John"</u>

John on subway

John at lunch

My painting of John (not finished)

<u>Where John lives:</u> No 12 Hickory Lane

<u>About his home:</u> John lives in a <u>nice house</u> with a garden. The garden <u>has a gate</u> with an old padlock. The house has <u>nice</u> curtains. The living room has a TV <u>wich is often on</u> in the evening, sometimes even past <u>midnight.</u> John lives in the same house as a <u>woman.</u> She looks like a WITCH. She <u>wants to hurt</u> John, but I <u>won't</u> let her haha. ~~When~~ John gets a <u>lot of mail.</u> Here is a <u>postcard</u> from his <u>mum</u> in New Zeeland (Susan):

Welcome To New Zealand

<u>Where John works:</u> John works for an <u>insuranse compa-ny.</u> They have a <u>big</u> office. One day I will visit him. That will be a <u>nice surprise.</u> It's time I met his <u>colleagues.</u>

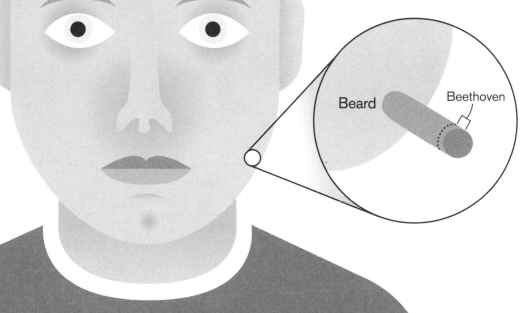

We are all part of Beethoven!

Beard

Beethoven

One billion of your atoms used to belong to Beethoven. Today sue for your share of his royalties. In his *A Short History Of Nearly Everything*, Bill Bryson explains the science behind the age-old belief in reincarnation: "When we die our atoms disassemble and move on to find new uses elsewhere – as part of a leaf or other human being or drop of dew… We are each so atomically numerous and so vigorously recycled at death that a significant number of our atoms – up to a billion for each of us, probably belonged once to Shakespeare. A billion more each came from Genghis Khan and Beethoven." Call up classical record labels and ask for a retroactive share of the profits.

Day 152

Return all unwanted gifts

Don't be a wimp! Go through all your possessions and root out the stuff you never wanted in the first place. Return them to giver with a curt note, and you'll ensure your door is never darkened with space-wasting presents again.

Tonight go to sleep with a bedtime story: No matter how old you are, a bedtime story will help you get to sleep. Ask a friend or a family member to pick a favorite story and sit by your pillow. Stories with a sexual theme are not recommended. Aim to fall asleep as they whisper the words "and everyone lives happily ever after"...

Day 154

CLOUDS

THERE ARE PROBLEMS AHEAD AT WORK, GO ON VACATION.

CATS

YOU NEED MORE INDEPENDENCE, QUIT YOUR JOB AND DUMP YOUR PARTNER.

FIRE

SOMEONE HATES YOU: HATE THEM BACK.

ANGELS

YOUR END IS NEAR, GET LIFE INSURANCE.

DESERT

YOU ARE LONELY. WAKE UP AND TALK TO SOMEONE.

WEB

YOU ARE TRAPPED! RUN AWAY NOW.

SEX

YOU WANT SEX. HAVE SEX.

MIRRORS

YOUR SELF IS DIVIDED, PULL YOURSELF TOGETHER.

CASTRATION

YOU ARE HAVING A CLICHÉD DREAM. WAKE UP IMMEDIATELY!

MOUNTAINS

SYMBOLS OF SPIRITUAL AWARENESS. GO SKIING IMMEDIATELY.

LADDERS

YOU ARE CLIMBING TOWARDS YOUR GOAL. HURRY UP BEFORE SOMEONE BEATS YOU TO IT.

FALLING

YOU FEAR FAILURE. DON'T DO ANYTHING AT ALL TODAY.

Dream analysis

Work out what your dreams are telling you to do and do it!

TREES

YOU NEED EMOTIONAL SUPPORT. HUG A TREE.

ROPES

YOU FEEL ALL TIED UP. NOT MUCH YOU CAN DO HERE.

SERPENTS

YOU ARE BEING DECEIVED BY A PERSON WHO LOOKS A BIT LIKE A SERPENT. KILL THEM.

DEATH

YOU ARE AFRAID OF DYING, GO TO YOUR DR. FOR A CHECK-UP

KEYS

THE SOLUTION TO YOUR PROBLEM IS IN THE CUPBOARD THAT OPENS WITH THOSE KEYS.

Day 155

Send a drink over to someone today

Do not send it to someone if they are with their partner.

It is traditional to send over drinks with alcoholic content only.

Wait until they raise their glass at you, then nod at them knowingly.

Do not send a drink over to someone already visibly drunk.

If they raise their glass at someone else, have the waiter fired.

If they send it back, they probably wouldn't have slept with you anyway.

Day 156

Spend today listening to a loved one's inner workings

Reach new levels of intimacy. Put your ear to their chest, their belly, their groin, and monitor their plumbing noises. Record them carefully below and see if you can discern a pattern.

GURGLE!

BURP!

PITTER! PATTER!

Belch!

FART!

Day 157

JUDGEMENT DAY

Judgement Day is looming! Prepare for it ahead of time with our "Judgement Day Self-Assessment" form below. On the day itself simply hand it in to God, who will appreciate your time-saving efforts and award you a bonus point!

MY GOOD DEEDS	MY SINS	OTHER
Helped blind person across street	Fornicated with strangers	Drank semi-skimmed milk
Comforted crying child	Lied to my own mother	Knitted green pullover
Returned lost wallet	Murdered my father	Tried to repair toaster to no avail
Gave to worthwhile charity	Stole ice cream from a child	Kept CDs in alphabetical order
Loved my neighbor	Engaged in sodomy (repeatedly)	Always sat in front row at movies
Cured the sick	Padded out my expense claims	Preferred pepper to salt
Fed the hungry	Envied everyone I ever met	Holidayed in the Bahamas twice
Did a good turn	Lied about my age to lover	Enjoyed chess as a hobby
Helped the aged	Was gluttonous as a baby	Had a friend named Toby
Saved a cat from up a tree	Chronically undertipped hookers	Kept a goldfish for 4 years
Rewound videos before returning them	Made greed my true religion	Worked in a bar whilst traveling
Planted a tree	Sacrificed goats to Satan	Visited long-lost cousin in Scotland
Forgave an enemy	Talked behind backs	Read mostly non-fiction
Went to church	Secretly despised my children	Broke a leg skiing
Have been a good listener	"Borrowed" library book forever	Went to Jon Bon Jovi concert
Was faithful to my spouse	Shoplifted pornography	Played the lottery regularly
Dried the dishes without being asked	Masturbated uncontrollably	Never really had favorite film
Rescued family from house on fire	Listened to Alice Cooper backwards	Redecorated spare bedroom in fuchsia
Adopted a stray dog	Stole from the cookie jar	Sent total of 658 postcards
Prayed in earnest	Skipped Sunday school	Rose to senior manager position
Found a family for ugly orphan	Told orphan they were ugly	Saw documentary about orphanage once
Total	Total	Total ....

If your sins exceed your good deeds, you're going to hell buddy! Unless you make up the deficit between now and midnight. If your other deeds preponderate, God will decide your fate on a passing whim, or maybe even by tossing a coin, who knows.

Day 158

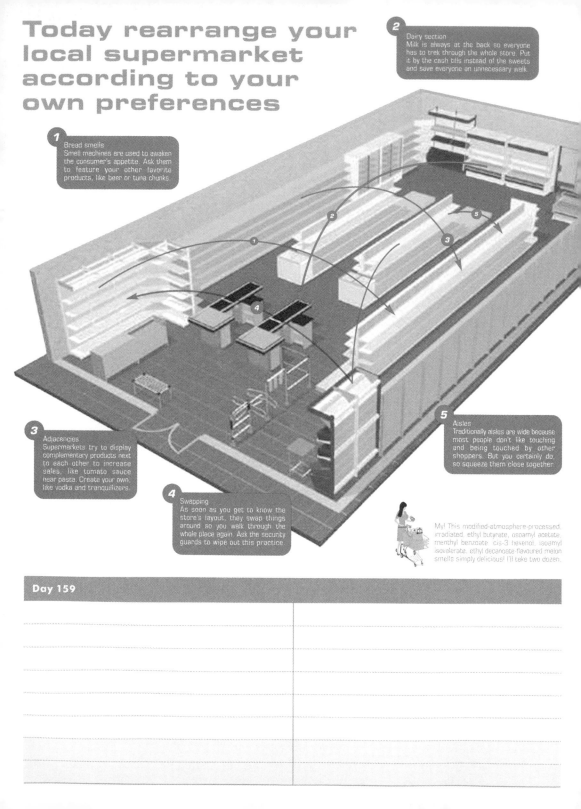

Today rearrange your local supermarket according to your own preferences

2 Dairy section
Milk is always at the back so everyone has to trek through the whole store. Put it by the cash tills instead of the sweets and save everyone an unnecessary walk.

1 Bread smells
Smell machines are used to awaken the consumer's appetite. Ask them to feature your other favorite products, like beer or tuna chunks.

3 Adjacencies
Supermarkets try to display complementary products next to each other to increase sales, like tomato sauce near pasta. Create your own, like vodka and tranquillizers.

4 Swapping
As soon as you get to know the store's layout, they swap things around so you walk through the whole place again. Ask the security guards to wipe out this practice.

5 Aisles
Traditionally aisles are wide because most people don't like touching and being touched by other shoppers. But you certainly do, so squeeze them close together.

My! This modified-atmosphere-processed, irradiated, ethyl butyrate, osoamyl acetate, menthyl benzoate, cis-3 hexenol, isoamyl isovalerate, ethyl decanoate-flavoured melon smells simply delicious! I'll take two dozen.

Day 159

Today imagine you have the lifespan of a beetle

The tiger beetle lives for six weeks on average. What would you do differently over the next six weeks if they were all you had?

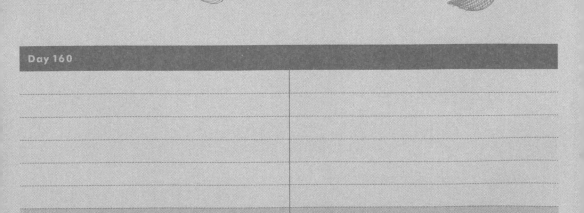

Day 160

NB This does not dispense you from following the Book's next 42 instructions.

Today make people believe you're a billion-dollar cyborg

People believe what they've seen on TV, so stick to this storyline, maybe changing a small detail like your name, and you won't be challenged: you were test piloting a NASA experimental craft when it spun out of control and crashed. In the crash you lost your left arm, your right eye and both legs. You would have died had the government not fitted you with cybernetic body parts that are much more effective than the originals, at a cost of billions. They were going to make you do all sorts of fancy missions on their behalf, but you got a good lawyer and now you're suing them.

BIONIC NEURO LEG
REFERENCE ++XD45678
BIONIC NEURO HAND
REFERENCE ++XD78654-5643A
POWER SUPPLY: PLUTONIUM 0-678 RE:
12KW >SURGE> 50KW
CONFIDENTIAL
CLASS 56/US/UK/AW
BIONIC NEURO LEG
REFERENCE ++XD45678
BIONIC NEURO HAND
REFERENCE ++XD78654-5643A
POWER SUPPLY: PLUTONIUM 0-678 RE:

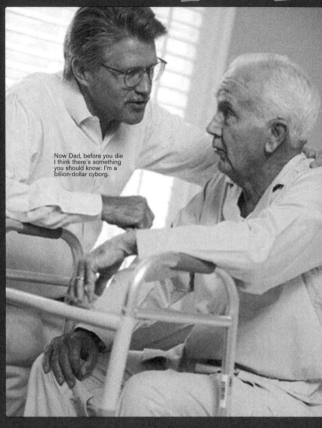

Now Dad, before you die I think there's something you should know: I'm a billion-dollar cyborg.

Day 161

Day 162

Day 163

Today, mouth something obscene to a stranger

Me and you, yes?

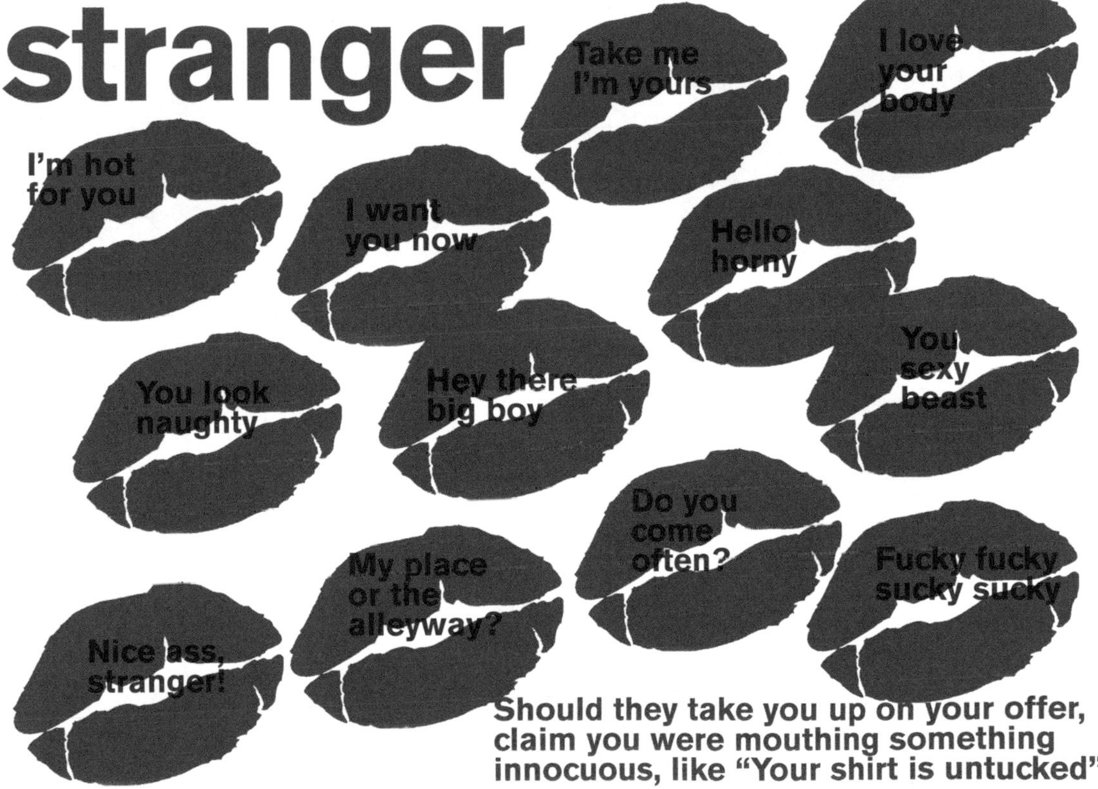

Take me I'm yours

I love your body

I'm hot for you

I want you now

Hello horny

You look naughty

Hey there big boy

You sexy beast

Do you come often?

My place or the alleyway?

Fucky fucky sucky sucky

Nice ass, stranger!

Should they take you up on your offer, claim you were mouthing something innocuous, like "Your shirt is untucked"

Day 164

Today leave a trail behind you, Hansel & Gretel style...

■ GOOD THINGS TO USE
■ BAD THINGS TO USE

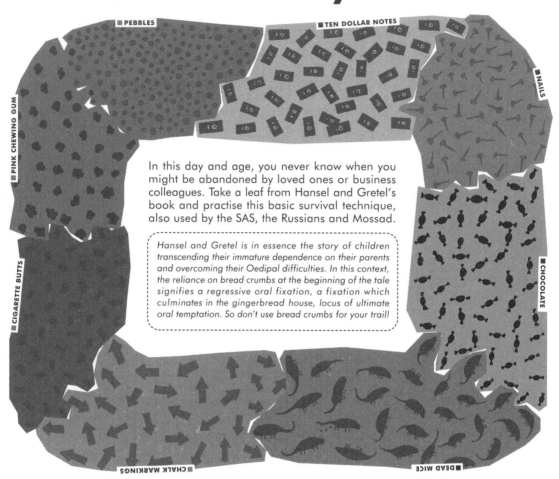

■ PEBBLES

■ TEN DOLLAR NOTES

■ NAILS

■ PINK CHEWING GUM

■ CHOCOLATE

■ CIGARETTE BUTTS

■ CHALK MARKINGS

■ DEAD MICE

In this day and age, you never know when you might be abandoned by loved ones or business colleagues. Take a leaf from Hansel and Gretel's book and practise this basic survival technique, also used by the SAS, the Russians and Mossad.

Hansel and Gretel is in essence the story of children transcending their immature dependence on their parents and overcoming their Oedipal difficulties. In this context, the reliance on bread crumbs at the beginning of the tale signifies a regressive oral fixation, a fixation which culminates in the gingerbread house, locus of ultimate oral temptation. So don't use bread crumbs for your trail!

Day 165

MASS CHEATING DAY

The students of today need all the support they can get. Today help them by reading the tricky bits they can't remember from textbooks out loud with a megaphone outside local college exam buildings.

"On the day of the accession of James the First, England descended from the rank which she had hitherto held, and began to be regarded as a power hardly of the second order. During many years the great British monarchy, under four successive princes of the House of Stuart, was scarcely a more important member of the European system than the little kingdom of Scotland had previously been. This, however, is little to be regretted. Of James the First, as of John, it may be said that, if his administration had been able and splendid, it would probably have been fatal to our country, and that we owe more to his weakness and meanness than to the wisdom and courage of much better sovereigns. He came to the throne at a critical moment. The time was fast approaching when either the King must become absolute, or the parliament must control the whole executive administration. Had James been, like Henry the Fourth, like Maurice of Nassau, or like Gustavus Adolphus, a valiant, active, and politic ruler, had he put himself at the head of the Protestants of Europe, had he gained great victories over Tilly and Spinola, had he adorned Westminster with the spoils of Bavarian monasteries and Flemish cathedrals, had he hung Austrian and Castilian banners in Saint Paul's, and had he found himself after great achievements, at the head of fifty thousand troops, brave, well disciplined, and devotedly attached to his person, the English Parliament would soon have been nothing more than a name. Happily he was not a man to play such a part. He began his administration by putting an end to the war which had raged during many years between England and Spain; and from that time he shunned hostilities with a caution which was proof against the insults of his neighbours and the clamours of his subjects. Not till the last year of his life could the influence of his son, his favourite, his Parliament, and his people combined, induce him to strike one feeble blow in defence of his family and of his religion. It was well for those whom he governed that he in this matter disregarded their wishes. The effect of his pacific policy was that, in his time, no regular troops were needed, and that, while France, Spain, Italy, Belgium, and Germany swarmed with mercenary soldiers, the defence of our island was still confided to the militia. As the King had no standing army, and did not even attempt to form one, it would have been wise in him to avoid any conflict with his people. But such was his indiscretion that, while he altogether neglected the means which alone could make him really absolute, he constantly put forward, in the most offensive form, claims of which none of his predecessors had ever dreamed. It was at this time that those strange theories which Filmer afterwards formed into a system and which became the badge of the most violent class of Tories and high churchmen first emerged into notice. It was gravely maintained that the Supreme Being regarded hereditary monarchy, as opposed to other forms of government, with peculiar favour; that the rule of succession in order of primogeniture was a divine institution, anterior to the Christian, and even to the Mosaic dispensation; that no human power, not even that of the whole legislature, no length of adverse possession, though it extended to ten centuries, could deprive a legitimate prince of his rights, that the authority of such a prince was necessarily always despotic; that the laws, by which, in England and in other countries, the prerogative was limited, were to be regarded merely as concessions which the sovereign had freely made and might at his pleasure resume; and that any treaty which a king might conclude with his people was merely a declaration of his present intentions, and not a contract of which the performance could be demanded. It is evident that this theory, though intended to strengthen the foundations of government, altogether unsettles them. Does the divine and immutable law of primogeniture admit females, or exclude them? On either supposition half the sovereigns of Europe must be usurpers, reigning in defiance of the law of God, and liable to be dispossessed by the rightful heirs. The doctrine that kingly government is peculiarly favoured by Heaven receives no countenance from the Old Testament; for in the Old Testament we read that the chosen people were blamed and punished for desiring a king, and that they were afterwards commanded to withdraw their allegiance from him. Their whole history, far from countenancing the notion that succession in order of primogeniture is of divine institution, would rather seem to indicate that younger brothers are under the especial protection of heaven. Isaac was not the eldest son of Abraham, nor Jacob of Isaac, nor Judah of Jacob, nor David of Jesse nor Solomon of David. Nor does the system of Filmer receive any countenance from those passages of the New Testament which describe government as an ordinance of God: for the government under which the writers of the New Testament lived was not a hereditary monarchy. The Roman Emperors were republican magistrates, named by the senate. None of them pretended to rule by right of birth; and, in fact, both Tiberius, to whom Christ commanded that tribute should be given, and Nero, whom Paul directed the Romans to obey, were, according to the patriarchal theory of government, usurpers. In the middle ages the doctrine of indefeasible hereditary right would have been regarded as heretical: for it was altogether incompatible with the high pretensions of the Church of Rome. It was a doctrine unknown to the founders of the Church of England. The Homily on Wilful Rebellion had strongly, and indeed too strongly, inculcated submission to constituted authority, but had made no distinction between hereditary and elective monarchies, or between monarchies and republics. Indeed most of the predecessors of James would, from personal motives, have regarded the patriarchal theory of government with aversion. William Rufus, Henry the First, Stephen, John, Henry the Fourth, Henry the Fifth, Henry the Sixth, Richard the Third, and Henry the Seventh, had all reigned in defiance of the strict rule of descent. A grave doubt hung over the legitimacy both of Mary and of Elizabeth. It was impossible that both Catharine of Aragon and Anne Boleyn could have been lawfully married to Henry the Eighth; and the highest authority in the realm had pronounced that neither was so. The Tudors, far from considering the law of succession as a divine and unchangeable institution, were constantly tampering with it. Henry the Eighth obtained an act of parliament, giving him power to leave the crown by will, and actually made a will to the prejudice of the royal family of Scotland. Edward the Sixth, unauthorised by Parliament, assumed a similar power, with the full approbation of the most eminent Reformers. Elizabeth, conscious that her own title was open to grave objection, and unwilling to admit even a reversionary right in her rival and enemy the Queen of Scots, induced the Parliament to pass a law, enacting that whoever should deny the competency of the reigning sovereign, with the assent of the Estates of the realm, to alter the succession, should suffer death as a traitor. But the situation of James was widely different from that of Elizabeth. Far inferior to her in abilities and in popularity, regarded by the English as an alien, and excluded from the throne by the testament of Henry the Eighth, the King of Scots was yet the undoubted heir of William the Conqueror and of Egbert. He had, therefore, an obvious interest in inculcating the superstitious notion that birth confers rights anterior to law, and unalterable by law. It was a notion, moreover, well suited to his intellect and temper. It soon found many advocates among those who aspired to his favour, and made rapid progress among the clergy of the Established Church. Thus, at the very moment at which a republican spirit began to manifest itself strongly in the Parliament and in the country, the claims of the monarch took a monstrous form which would have disgusted the proudest and most arbitrary of those who had preceded him on the throne."

BECOME A SUPERHERO TODAY

Don't remain Clark Kent all your life. It only takes a little effort to acquire potentially useful superhero powers. Here's how.

Get a job in a corporate genetic modification lab. Late one night, "accidentally" fall into the experimental seeds centrifuge.
Powers: can clone himself at the drop of a hat.

SUPER GM

In the course of a stroll outside Three Mile Island, get stung by a nestful of unusually large wasps...
Powers: each of her fingertips contains a radioactive sting!

WASPGIRL

Steal an Amazonian tribe's prized medicinal plant for the pharmaceutical industry and be cursed for 1,000 years as a result.

Snakeboy

Powers: with his forked tongue, can lie his way out of any situation.

Fall into the vat of "unfit for human consumption" meat during a guided tour of an abattoir.
Powers: can antagonize vegetarian villains.

MEATMAN

Listen to Sex Pistols album repeatedly until timewarp projects you back to the late seventies.

Powers: her anger can cause any society to implode.

PUNK WOMAN

This one was just born this way, you can't become one.
Powers: turns into a scary monster.

MONSTER MAN

Day 167

BENRIK
SUPERHERO
NECKLACES
ON THE WEB FROM TODAY

Today, write and thank your most influential teacher

You've been very naughty by not doing this much earlier though, so you have to write it 100 times!

Benrik Father's Day!

Assess your Dad's performance so far

Father's name..

Father's age..

Father's age when he met my mother...

Father's age when he had me..

Degree of certainty that he is my father.../10

What I call my father

Dad ☐   Daddy ☐   Father ☐   Papa ☐   Pop ☐   Bastard ☐

Other..

....

....

GENERAL

	YES	NO	DON'T KNOW
My father has provided me with a sense of stability	☐	☐	☐
My father has provided me with a sense of security	☐	☐	☐
My father has provided me with a sense of purpose	☐	☐	☐
My father's relationship with my mother has made me feel that loving relationships are:........the norm	☐	☐	☐
....hard work	☐	☐	☐
....a bitter illusion	☐	☐	☐

In your own words, write your assessment of your father so far, along with suggestions as to how he might improve. *Cut it out and hand it to him on his birthday.*

....
....
....
....
....
....
....
....
....
....
....
....
....
....
....
....

MEN *My father's relationship with me:*

...has been that of a positive role model which has enabled me to identify with him and develop into a well-balanced male ☐

...has been that of an overpowering tyrant, nipping my confidence in the bud and leading to repressed violence and depression ☐

...has been absent, leaving me with an unresolved Oedipal conflict and a confused sexual identity ☐

WOMEN *My father's relationship with me:*

...has allowed me to deal with the Electra complex to the point where I can enjoy fulfilling relationships with men ☐

...has fostered a dependency on overtly callous men whom I normally expect to leave me after a few months at best ☐

...has turned me into a distrustful shrew who avoids men and indeed close relationships in general ☐

Bite animals back today

Here's where to bite those animals that dare to bite humans!

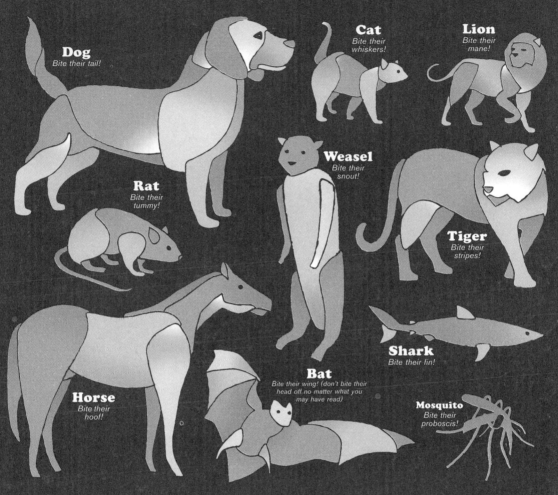

Dog
Bite their tail!

Cat
Bite their whiskers!

Lion
Bite their mane!

Rat
Bite their tummy!

Weasel
Bite their snout!

Tiger
Bite their stripes!

Shark
Bite their fin!

Horse
Bite their hoof!

Bat
Bite their wing! (don't bite their head off no matter what you may have read)

Mosquito
Bite their proboscis!

Day 170	

My Tattoo

This is Frankie Easton. He's tattooed in all kinds of places, but for years he's left his back free for "the big one." Problem is, getting it is such a big step in life that he doesn't know good from bad anymore... Therefore he's asking the Book readers for help.

Help him! He's only getting it done to look cool to you anyway. Out of the following fifteen motifs, which one should he choose? The final design will be printed on his back for all to see. Voting starts now! Feel free to suggest your own design!

Vote at www.thiswebsitewillchangeyourlife.com

Day 171

Downshifting Day

Make your way down the corporate pyramid

Chairman
Chief Executive
Vice President
Senior Executive
Standard Executive
Junior Executive
Personal Assistant
Clerk
Dogsbody
Cleaner

People usually complain of how difficult it is to climb the corporate ladder. But it is even harder to climb back down. How many CEOs are allowed to return to more menial duties? Today demand to be demoted, and cut down on the stress of the high-flying executive lifestyle.

Day 172

Today use your remote control for evil purposes

Don't just point it at the TV! Instead try these functions:

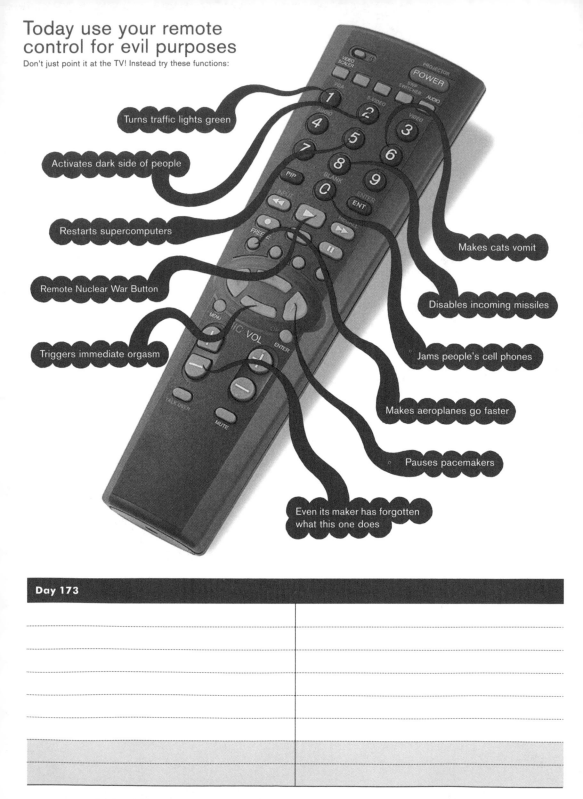

Turns traffic lights green

Activates dark side of people

Restarts supercomputers

Remote Nuclear War Button

Triggers immediate orgasm

Makes cats vomit

Disables incoming missiles

Jams people's cell phones

Makes aeroplanes go faster

Pauses pacemakers

Even its maker has forgotten what this one does

Day 173

Do not attempt this with taxi drivers. In this instance, go straight for sexual favors, no messing about. They like it.

<u>STROKE A BUS OR TRAIN CONDUCTOR AS PAYMENT FOR THE FARE</u> When a bus conductor or other custodian of public transport asks for a fare, admit that you have no money, but offer to stroke him/her in an affectionate but non-sexual manner. It might be interesting to find out exactly how many strokes are equivalent to the appropriate fare.

Day 174

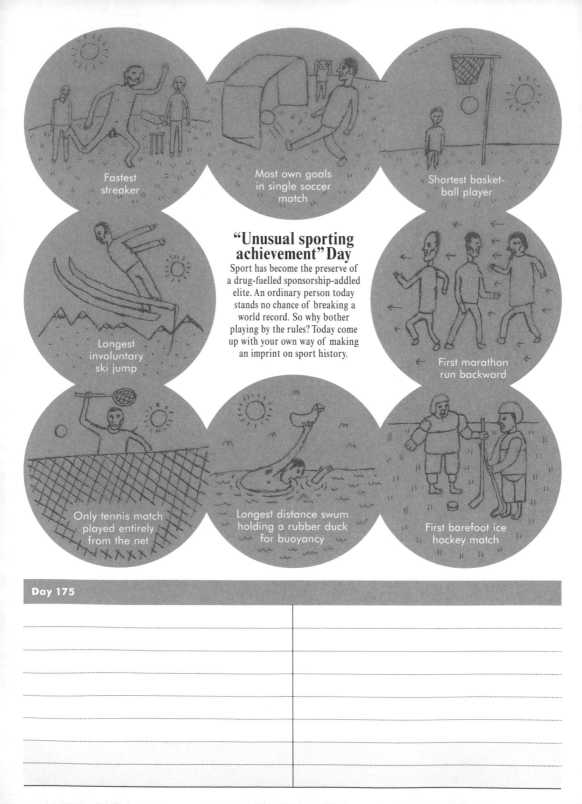

Fastest streaker

Most own goals in single soccer match

Shortest basket-ball player

Longest involuntary ski jump

"Unusual sporting achievement" Day

Sport has become the preserve of a drug-fuelled sponsorship-addled elite. An ordinary person today stands no chance of breaking a world record. So why bother playing by the rules? Today come up with your own way of making an imprint on sport history.

First marathon run backward

Only tennis match played entirely from the net

Longest distance swum holding a rubber duck for buoyancy

First barefoot ice hockey match

Day 175

Benrik Stamp Day

Benrik are exasperated by the tacky selection of stamps available from the postal authorities, and so are launching their very own range. Today circulate these vibrant new design masterpieces and brighten up your correspondence.

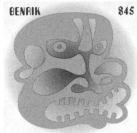

Included in the price of the Book!!!

Day 176

HELP COBBLER
PIOTR SAVE HIS BUSINESS TODAY.

Piotr is putting on a brave face and is known to his (few) clients as a good-humored worker, but as you can see he is deeply troubled by the business cycle.

in Remington, and helped him find a home, premises, and, last but not least, a catchy name. Until the late nineties, business was pretty good, if not exactly booming. But then sneakers became all the rage, and turnover took a hit. Piotr has never liked sneakers ("shoes fit for a lazy peasant") but he has to face the new reality. Benrik are looking for suggestions of how Piotr might reengineer his cobblering skills to the sneakers market. Here are some of the services he might offer to the more discerning customer. Go to his shop and ask for them, and prevent him from sliding into bankruptcy.

Fit your sneakers with crampons for muddy roads

Sew on a personalized logo to stand out from the crowd

Ladies! Get heels fitted for that ladylike look

NEW! The retro clog

Piotr Jareski has been running his business "A Load of Cobblers" in the Mt. Washington suburb of Baltimore since 1991. He learned his trade in his native Poland, where he was apprentice to the famous Konrad Grudzinski of Krakow. He moved over with his family after Grudzinski's death in 1989. His brother was already established as a painter-decorator

Piotr's 17-year-old son Wojtek keeps him in touch with the word on the street. "Retro" is all the rage, which gave Piotr an idea. He called up his old buddy Janusz who took over the Grudzinski business, and ordered a shipment of Janusz's lifelong speciality, the "Krakow clog." Never has anyone seen such a fine clog, from the Baltic to the Ukraine. But Piotr's idea was to adapt it to the Western market. How? By customizing it with the names of all the churches in Pomerania with a simple marker pen. Can you do better?

Day 177

Today hijack a public performance
In the time-honored tradition of the avant-garde, add your twist to a public event. Contemporary composers and playwrights almost expect the audience to erupt at some point, and the dead ones won't mind anyway. If anyone queries your right to shout out FIRE! as a postmodern performative construct, ridicule their philistine literalism and accuse them of disrupting your narrative. BUT! Avoid these clichés, unless you possess superhuman powers of irony:

Day 178

Today presell your memoirs based on your spectacular future achievements

12a Wyman Park Drive
Somerset, NJ 08872
USA

Dear Mister/Madam Publisher,

This is a once-in-a-lifetime opportunity for you to buy my memoirs.

I am Bert Brown, and if you haven't heard of me yet, you sure will! At the present moment I am 29 years of age. In the next ten years, it is my intention to: climb Mt. Everest naked, marry a Hollywood actress (identity to be confirmed), interview the head of the Chinese secret police, and become a chess champion.

After that, in my forties, my plan is to regroup Van Halen with me as drummer, cure cancer of the pancreas (I know someone who had it) and enter the political arena.

My plans for my fifties are a little hazy as it's still a while to go, but I reckon something to do with the Moon (we will live in space by then, don't forget), divorce the famous actress (identity to be confirmed), and become a champion of the oppressed, possibly within the UN if that august international body still exists.

So you see my life will make a GREAT book of memoirs, which I am offering to YOU now. I want $100,000 for it, not a penny less. You have 24 hours or I'm off to your rivals.

Yours,
Bert Brown
(Author)

Day 179

From the Borgias to JFK, poisoning has claimed thousands of victims. Yet few take the necessary precautions against it. Today ask a family member or a waiter to taste your food before you ingest it. Then observe them for 20 minutes for the slightest sign of illness, like vomiting, convulsions or massive internal hemorrhaging. Only then may you relax and enjoy your meal.

Telltale signs that your food is poisoned

Roast chicken
Wings look slightly shrunken

Cod and chips
Chips break in two very easily

Cheeseburger
Cheese has greenish tinge

Steak
Veins bulging (with the poison)

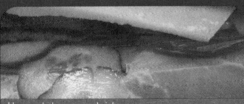

Ham and cheese sandwich
Ham and cheese stuck together

Apple crumble
No visible signs, avoid

Rasputin's top tip: the "mad monk" was the target of many assassination attempts, including one to poison him with huge doses of cyanide. Amazingly, he survived, having deliberately exposed himself to increasing amounts of poison over the years to build up some immunity. Of course he was eventually shot and dumped in a frozen river. Not much you can do about that.

Day 180

TODAY CAUSE AN INTERNATIONAL SECURITY ALERT. FOR YEARS, CONSPIRACY THEORISTS HAVE POSITED THE EXISTENCE OF ECHELON, A SUPERSECRET TRANSNATIONAL EFFORT BY THE WEST TO SPY ON ALL ELECTRONIC COMMUNICATIONS, FROM PHONES TO E-MAILS. THE SYSTEM ALLEGEDLY "RED FLAGS" CERTAIN KEYWORDS IN AN ATTEMPT TO INTERCEPT TERRORIST OR OTHERWISE SUBVERSIVE MESSAGES. TODAY, TEST THIS THEORY BY INCORPORATING AS MANY OF THE FOLLOWING KEYWORDS AS POSSIBLE INTO YOUR E-MAILS. YOU WILL KNOW THE THEORY IS CORRECT IF YOU ARE ARRESTED AND QUESTIONED AT GREAT LENGTH. GOODBYE. ATF OSAMA BIN LADEN FBI DOD WACO TWIN TOWERS RUBY RIDGE PENTAGON OKC OKLAHOMA CITY GUANTANAMO MILITIA WORLD TRADE CENTRE CIA GUN NSA HANDGUN SEMTEX AL QAEDA HOSTAGE MILGOV 9/11 MARTYR RUMSFELD ASSAULT RIFLE TERRORISM BOMB DRUG KORESH ZARQAWI SHARON MOSSAD NASA MI5 CID FALLUJA AK47 M16 C4 REVOLUTION SADDAM HUSSEIN GEORGE BUSH TERROR

Day 181

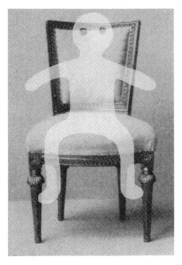

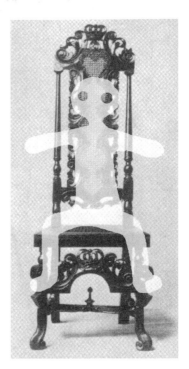
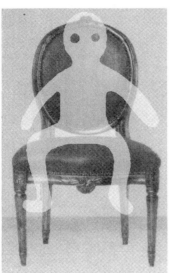

Make people believe in ghosts today

A belief in the paranormal makes life more interesting all round. Today revive your housemates' ancestral fear of ghosts with one or several of the following methods.

- Slam a door and tell everyone it wasn't you.
- Steal someone's keys and replace them the next morning.
- Spray old cologne around while no one's looking.
- Discreetly stamp on the family pet's tail so it snarls inexplicably.
- Paint DEATH! BLOOD! REVENGE!... in blood red on the kitchen ceiling.*

*Try this one last

Audition for Broadway today

Many a star's career started out on Broadway.
If you can sing, why not attend an open call audition?
Check for their location on www.backstage.com, and roll
up with a smile on your face and a song in your heart!

Day 183

PREPARE YOUR OWN DEATH TODAY

Don't leave your posterity in others' hands. Arrange your funeral ahead of time, or spin in your grave as your relatives muck it up.

WRITE YOUR OWN OBITUARY

Who else will do you justice?

BURIAL OR CREMATION?

Just as long as you're definitely deceased.

CHOOSE YOUR OWN COFFIN

Grief-stricken relatives invariably have poor taste.

PICK THE MUSIC

Comedy tunes are only suitable for actual comedians.

SELECT A HEADSTONE

You may crumble, but it shouldn't.

AND FINALLY, WRITE THE EPITAPH

It'll be with you for the rest of your death.

NOW YOU MAY REST IN PEACE

Day 184

SPEND TODAY UP A TREE

How to build a treehouse (optional): Order eight sheets of 3/4" plywood (2m x2m), four 4" lag screws and bolts, and two 2x8 support beams. Prop the support beams up against the branches so that they are level and extend 3" past the branch either side. Screw the lag bolts into the tree and secure the beams using the lag screws. Then nail the platform together using plywood from one of the sheets. Set the platform floor onto the support beams and secure it with 8" nails and nylon rope at each corner. With the remaining 5 sheets of plywood, construct the frame and roof. Screw the plywood walls to the platform using galvanized 2" screws (secure them with rope during construction). Check that the screws hit the plywood centre. Lower the remaining sheet of plywood onto the 4 walls and attach with rope, securing with 3" nails. Create a window and floor entrance using a jigsaw and attach a retractable rope ladder using leftover lumber as a batten. If your treehouse is situated in a public park, don't forget to put a "private" notice up.

Day 185	

Today follow the crowd

As French social psychologist Gustave Le Bon wrote: "Man, as part of a multitude, is a very different being from the same man as an isolated individual. His conscious individuality vanishes in the unconscious personality of the crowd." Today, lose yourself in a crowd...

Day 186

HIDDEN PROMISE DAY

You never know who around you might shoot to fame overnight these days, so collect their autographs now before they're too important to talk to you.

FATHER	NEWSAGENT	LOVER
MOTHER	DRYCLEANER	MISTRESS
BROTHER 1	SUPERMARKET CHECKOUT GIRL	FIRST LOVE
BROTHER 2	GAS STATION ATTENDANT	FRIEND 1
SISTER 1	BUILDER	FRIEND 2
SISTER 2	CAB DRIVER	FRIEND 3
SON	BANK TELLER	FRIEND 4
DAUGHTER	FISHMONGER	ACQUAINTANCE 1
GRANDFATHER 1	GARDENER	ACQUAINTANCE 2
GRANDFATHER 2	CLEANER	ACQUAINTANCE 3
GRANDMOTHER 1	HOOKER	ACQUAINTANCE 4
GRANDMOTHER 2	PSYCHOTHERAPIST	COLLEAGUE 1
AUNT	PERSONAL TRAINER	COLLEAGUE 2
UNCLE	TAX INSPECTOR	COLLEAGUE 3
COUSIN 1	LOCAL VICAR	COLLEAGUE 4
COUSIN 2	LOCAL POLICEMAN	COLLEAGUE 5
NEIGHBOR 1	LOCAL TRAMP	BOSS
NEIGHBOR 2	LOCAL PEDOPHILE	EMPLOYEE 1
TEACHER	LOCAL BUSDRIVER	EMPLOYEE 2
BUTCHER	VILLAGE IDIOT	EMPLOYEE 3
GREENGROCER	SPOUSE	GIRL NEXT DOOR*

*MOST LIKELY TO SHOOT TO FAME: MAKE SURE YOU GET HER AUTOGRAPH!

Day 187

LANDGRAB DAY

There's plenty of public land still to be claimed. Today make a grab for it. Start by ring fencing a small patch (say 1m²) somewhere spacious like Central Park, and expand it gradually until you have enough to build on. After 12 years of unchallenged occupation, it will be yours forever!

Day 188

Today write a letter to your future self

Hello future me.
I'm glad we're still around to read this in the year 2035. What's happened to us in the last 30 years? Obviously I can't speculate too much, but from where I'm standing now, we'll have done well to avoid personal and global annihilation! So if im reading this, things have gone pretty good already. What are my hopes for the future me? I hoped we've lived up to my promise and become a race car driver. I imagine we've married and have kids (2 or 3) though I'll understand if we've become gay. It's because of that Martha bitch isn't it? We never liked her. Anyway, have we gone around the world as planned? I'd have to say I'd be really pissed off if we hadn't as I've just started saving. Also it's my life dream, so if we haven't got a good excuse that makes us a big fat loser in my book. Did we ever get caught for that tax scam?! I'm pretty nervous about it now. I don't imagine we can get away with that in 2035, when computers probably monitor your every move. Maybe we're a famous astronaut? In which case schoolchildren will be reading this and learning about our life! But probably not. Anyway gotta go and live our life, so that's all from 2005. *Your 2005 self*

To: Year 2035 self

Sender: Year 2005 self

Day 189

TODAY SPEAK THE UNSPEAKABLE

In our verbally incontinent society, recover the power of words by finding something you cannot actually bring yourself to say out loud in public.

Day 190

Today, go halfway around the world

For the first time in the history of humanity, we can circumnavigate the Earth in a couple of days! To previous generations, this would have been as unthinkable as going to the moon. And yet anyone can do it. Book a round-the-world flight leaving today first thing, and within 24 hours you'll be on the other side of the planet.

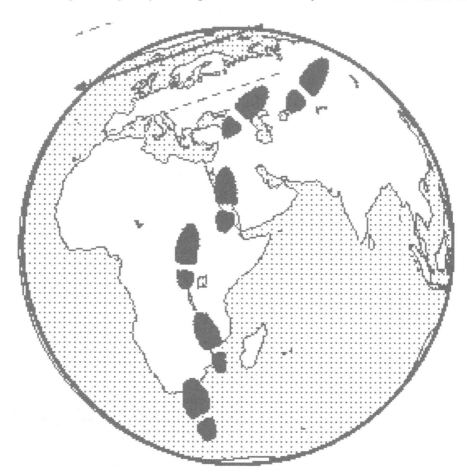

Day 191

Day 192

Today: impulse-buy!

Today use our ouija board to invoke an evil spirit

Instructions: leave the Book open on your knees at this page and gather two or three friends round to begin the seance. It is crucial that you only invite people who treat the board with the appropriate respect, otherwise it will not work. Hold the oracle in your hand, get your friends to put their hands on top of yours and let it drift over the board. Ask a pertinent question to rouse the spirits, like "is anyone there" or "can you hear me Beelzebub." You will sense the board's pull when you reach the appropriate letter. It is perfectly permissible to write down the board's replies, particularly if you are a beginner. Once you have established communication with the other realm, start to conjure up a malevolent spirit with teasers such as "Archatapias, hear my call" or "Lucifer, it is time!" When you are bored of toying with the evil spirit, simply place the oracle on GOOD BYE.

HANDS FREE DAY

We are constantly burdened with accessories, from handbags to cell phones. Today leave them all at home and see how you much freer you feel without all these supposedly essential items.

Day 195

TODAY STARE INTO OTHER PEOPLE'S HOMES

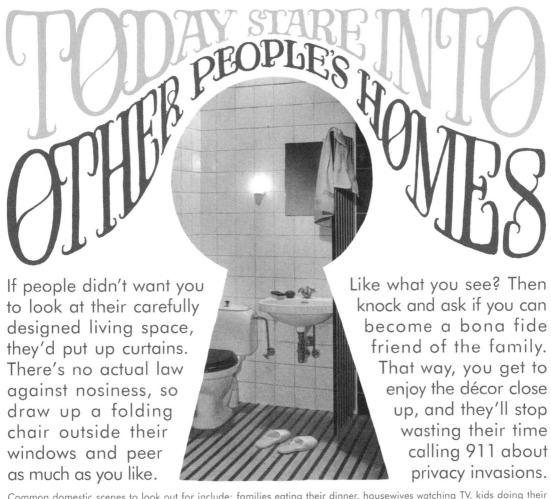

If people didn't want you to look at their carefully designed living space, they'd put up curtains. There's no actual law against nosiness, so draw up a folding chair outside their windows and peer as much as you like.

Like what you see? Then knock and ask if you can become a bona fide friend of the family. That way, you get to enjoy the décor close up, and they'll stop wasting their time calling 911 about privacy invasions.

Common domestic scenes to look out for include: families eating their dinner, housewives watching TV, kids doing their homework, clocks ticking, babies crying, neighbors borrowing cups of sugar, teenagers picking up the phone, salesmen doing their spiel, dogs fouling the carpet, wives cheating on their husbands, husbands cheating on their wives, lovers hiding in closets, bailiffs repossessing the fridge, grannies beating their cats, sadomasochistic suburban orgies, cockroaches jumping in the soup, instances of spontaneous combustion, plots being hatched against civilization itself. Don't get caught peeking!

Day 196

Today, speedread a masterpiece

Everyone means to read *War and Peace*, but few actually do. Don't be daunted by its length;
it's a quick read if you put your mind to it and follow a few basic time-saving guidelines.

Time yourself
Let's say you have 20 hours of reading time today. At 1,200 pages, that means you can devote 60 seconds to each page. Remind yourself of this deadline every time you turn the page.

60

Read only the right-hand pages
This was Marshall McLuhan's method. You'll still pick up most of the plot, but you'll halve your reading time. If the book ends on a left-hand page though, you may break the rule.

Skip the descriptions
Yadda yadda yadda. Sometimes even the greatest novelist can go on a bit. Dialogue is more important, plus it's fun to imagine what the characters are wearing yourself.

Pick out key words
No one knows how this works, but if you squint at the page, your subconscious self somehow spots the key words that really matter to comprehension.

Rename the characters
Work out who the characters remind you of amongst your friends and rename them all accordingly. This provides a useful psychological shortcut.

Already read *War and Peace*? Then just pick another masterpiece from the following list: *Remembrance of Things Past*, *Ulysses*, the Bible, *David Copperfield*, *Anna Karenina*, *Don Quixote*, *Moby Dick*.

CHAPTER I

"Well, Prince, so Genoa and Lucca are now just family estates of the Buonapartes. But I warn you, if you don't tell me that this means war, if you still try to defend the infamies and horrors perpetrated by that Antichrist- I really believe he is Antichrist- I will have nothing more to do with you and you are no longer my friend, no longer my 'faithful slave,' as you call yourself! But how do you do? I see I have frightened you- sit down and tell me all the news."

It was in July, 1805, and the speaker was the well-known Anna Pavlovna Scherer, maid of honour and favourite of the Empress Marya Fedorovna. With these words she greeted Prince Vasili Kuragin, a man of high rank and importance, who was the first to arrive at her reception. Anna Pavlovna had had a cough for some days. She was, as she said, suffering from la grippe; grippe being then a new word in St. Petersburg, used only by the elite.

All her invitations without exception, written in French, and delivered by a scarlet-liveried footman that morning, ran as follows:

"If you have nothing better to do, Count (or Prince), and if the prospect of spending an evening with a poor invalid is not

too terrible, I shall be very charmed to see you tonight between 7 and 10 – Annette Scherer."
"Heavens! what a virulent attack!" replied the prince, not in the least disconcerted by this reception. He had just entered, wearing an embroidered court uniform, knee breeches, and shoes, and had stars on his breast and a serene expression on his flat face. He spoke in that refined French in which our grandfathers not only spoke but thought, and with the gentle, patronizing intonation natural to a man of importance who had grown old in society and at court. He went up to Anna Pavlovna, kissed her hand, presenting to her his bald, scented, and shining head, and complacently seated himself on the sofa.

"First of all, dear friend, tell me how you are. Set your friend's mind at rest," said he without altering his tone, beneath the politeness and affected sympathy of which indifference and even irony could be discerned.

"Can one be well while suffering morally? Can one be calm in times like these if one has any feeling?" said Anna Pavlovna. "You are staying the whole evening, I hope?"

"And the fete at the English ambassador's? Today is Wednesday. I must put in an appearance there," said the prince. "My daughter is coming for me to take me there."

"I thought today's fete had been cancelled. I confess all these festivities and fireworks are becoming wearisome."

Anna Pavlovna = Tracy Baker

Day 197

TODAY DO EVERYTHING IN SLOW MOTION

The reason movies show dramatic events in slow motion isn't just to let us see the details. Accidents and other high-stress situations are actually experienced in slow motion. Scientists speculate that the rush of adrenalin alters our brain's perception of time — what the Greeks called tachypsychia or distortion of the "speed of the mind." Those Greeks!

6.23 PM:

Day 198

AMATEUR PAGE 7

From: Fiona Carey
County Wicklow,
Ireland

You will need:

An audio copy of Pink Floyd's 'Dark Side of the Moon', a copy of 'The Wizard Of Oz on DVD or video.
Now, begin DSotM just as the MGM lion (at the very beginning of WoO) roars for the third time. You know you're right if the title 'Produced by **MERVIN LE ROY'** appears just as 'Speak to Me' fades into 'Breathe'.

You may have heard that pink floyd's 'dark side of the moon' album acts as a sort of soundtrack to 'the wizard of oz'. I tried this the other day and the results are quite exciting if you get it in sync properly. http://members.cox.net/stegokitty/dsotr_pages/dsotr.htm will tell you everything you need to know and includes a list of things to look out for.

Day 199

Attempt to be noticed from space today

There are hundreds of spy satellites orbiting the earth with cameras that can pick out objects a few inches wide. Do something unusual enough to spark their attention. Arrange 100 of your friends into the shape of a giant caterpillar. Dig a nuclear-style crater on the beach. Send a message like "EMPEROR XORG WE ARE READY FOR YOUR ARRIVAL" in Morse with a giant arc-lamp. CIA analysts too need something to lighten up their day.

Day 200

Dumbing Down Day

Today see if you can reduce your IQ by at least 30 points

IQ at 8a.m.

Watch TV for 6 hours, though nothing that contains evidence of thinking

Listen to heavy metal through your headphones at maximum volume

Read the *National Enquirer* from A to Z, paying particular attention to the astrology section

Drink a bottle of Scotch and chase it with some vodka shots

Smoke a couple of joints, take a couple of pills, snort a quick line

Tailor your diet to exclude brain-friendly substances such as fish, avocados, spinach or water

Avoid using human language: instead grunt when people speak to you

Bang your head against a hard surface for a minute

I'M TAKING TODAY OFF; I AM ALREADY STUPID.

IQ at 8p.m.

Day 201

Today mislead a tourist

The world would be a brighter place if tourists got lost more regularly. When an inquisitive foreigner asks his way today, send him off in an unexpected direction. He's read about all the obvious landmarks in his guidebook anyway.

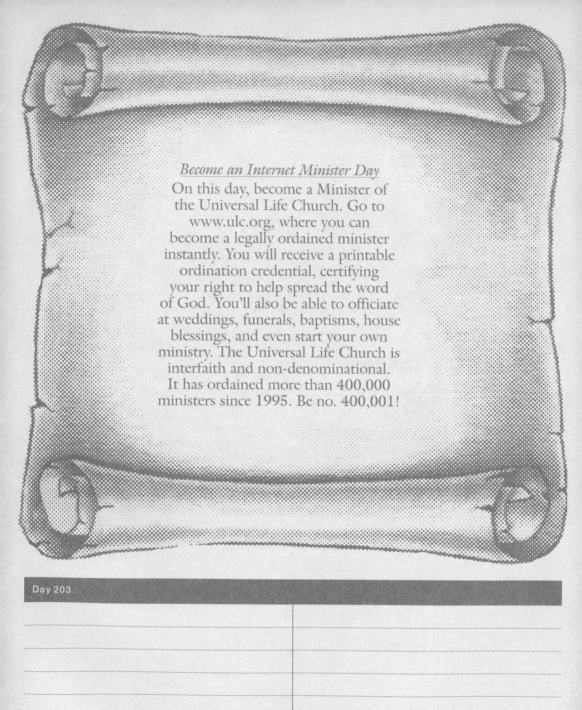

Become an Internet Minister Day
On this day, become a Minister of
the Universal Life Church. Go to
www.ulc.org, where you can
become a legally ordained minister
instantly. You will receive a printable
ordination credential, certifying
your right to help spread the word
of God. You'll also be able to officiate
at weddings, funerals, baptisms, house
blessings, and even start your own
ministry. The Universal Life Church is
interfaith and non-denominational.
It has ordained more than 400,000
ministers since 1995. Be no. 400,001!

Day 203

TODAY TAKE PART IN THE GREAT CYCLE OF LIFE

We humans stand too aloof from the basic processes of our planet. And yet we are as crucial a part of the Earth's ecosystem as fruitflies or plankton. Today make a conscious effort to play your part in the cycle of life.

Let a mosquito bite you
Shit in the vegetable patch
Feed your hair to the dust mites
Carry pollen from one flower to another
Discard fruit seeds in a park
Help worms find the cemetery
Let yourself be eaten by a lion

Day 204

Today keep an eye out for subtle body language

Students of psychology know that hands on hips signifies confrontation, or that touching your nose means lying. But the truly significant emotions are more deeply repressed, and thus are revealed in extremely subtle ways. Today learn to look out for these and many others.

LITTLE FINGER BENT 45°
Betrays lying, deception on a colossal scale

BLINKING 5% MORE THAN USUAL
Person is questioning your sexual orientation

NIPPLES ERECT
Indicates love at first sight

STOMACH MUSCLES TWITCHING
Signifies deep discomfort with your clothing

EYES FOCUSING 4M AWAY
Person is plotting against your country

LEFT EAR FULLY OPEN
Signifies desire for urgent sexual congress

NOSTRILS FLARED
Person will physically attack you within 20 seconds

BUTTOCKS CLENCHED
Shows desire to evacuate bowels

LEG HAIR RAISED
Appreciates your sense of humor

FOOT TILTED TOWARDS MECCA
Indicates person will agree with you just so as to go home

Day 205

TODAY FIGHT FOR YOUR COUNTRY!

Today find out from the government which wars your country is fighting, and volunteer to do your duty, even if you don't agree. It's your country, right or wrong dammit!

MAY THE BEST MAN WIN!

WWW.THISWEBSITEWILL
CHANGEYOURLIFE.COM

Day 206

Today, appear on TV!

These days anyone can appear on one of the thousands of shows that welcome the public, from *Jerry Springer* to *Stupidest Criminals*. Today apply to feature on one and enjoy the media spotlight.

Criteria for disqualification:

Stark nakedness

Tourette's syndrome

Possession of a weapon

Family link with Benrik

Aged over 39

Previous appearance on Big Brother

Wearing of visible sponsorship

Wearing of motorcycle helmet

Hidden agenda

Day 207	

Today, ask everyone you meet to jump

Life photographer Philippe Halsman invented "jumpology," a simple technique to reveal people's true personality to the camera: he'd ask them to jump. "In a jump the subject, in a sudden burst of energy, overcomes gravity. He cannot simultaneously control his expressions, his facial and his limb muscles. The mask falls. The real self becomes visible." Today ask everyone you meet to jump and reveal their true selves.

Day 208

The Village!

The Headmaster...

SWAZILAND DAY

Benrik have a small but loyal fanbase in Swaziland. The children of Kaphunga are all doing their best to follow them, though it is sometimes difficult as they have limited resources. But they appreciate encouragement and visits from other Benrik fans worldwide. Write to them c/o Myxo, Box 2455, Manzini, Swaziland, and donate $18 to help them purchase the latest edition.

TOP TIP! *When in Swaziland, stay at Myxo's!* Myxo's Place is set in a beautiful location in central Swaziland and is run by Swazis. Learn siSwati, enjoy traditional food, chat with laid back owner Myxo, and visit all the children at school! DIRECTIONS: 6km outside Manzini on the Big Bend Road, Pass the Imphilo clinic. Turn left at the Big Surprise Bottle Store and follow the signs. Call 268 505 8363 for reservations.

Day 209

Learning math!

SWAZILAND

Swaziland is the jewel at the heart of South Africa. Its 1.1 million people are known for their hospitality. It is ruled by King Msawti III, member of the Dlamini dynasty. Its inhabitants depend mostly on agriculture, although tourism is booming. Foreigners come for the unspoilt nature reserve of Malolotja and the whitewater rafting on the wild Usutu river, as well as to meet the people! Business hours are 08h00 - 13h00 and 14h00 - 17h00 Mondays to Fridays. Bank hours are 18h30 - 14h30 Mondays to Fridays and some banks, 08h30 - 11h00 on Saturdays. Post offices are open 08h00 - 16h00 Mondays to Fridays and 08h00 - 11h00 on Saturdays.

Today grimace as the wind changes and sue the weather bureau if your face freezes forever

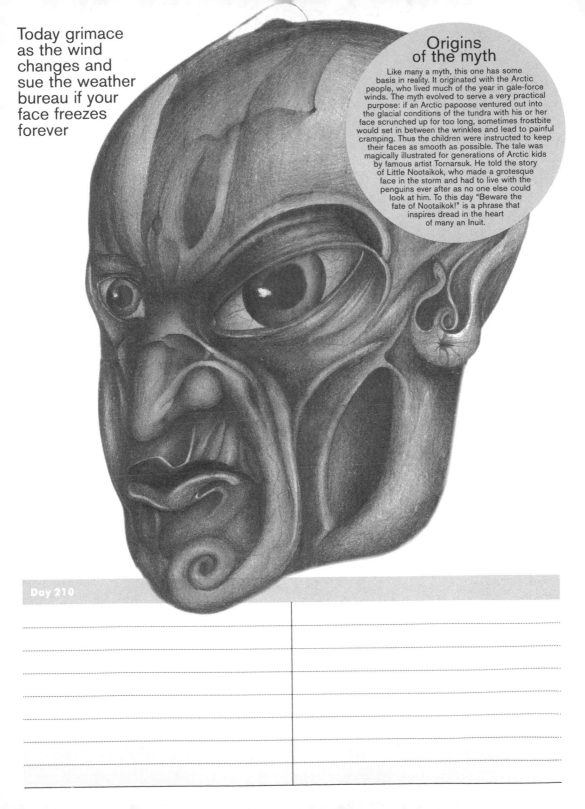

Origins of the myth

Like many a myth, this one has some basis in reality. It originated with the Arctic people, who lived much of the year in gale-force winds. The myth evolved to serve a very practical purpose: if an Arctic papoose ventured out into the glacial conditions of the tundra with his or her face scrunched up for too long, sometimes frostbite would set in between the wrinkles and lead to painful cramping. Thus the children were instructed to keep their faces as smooth as possible. The tale was magically illustrated for generations of Arctic kids by famous artist Tornarsuk. He told the story of Little Nootaikok, who made a grotesque face in the storm and had to live with the penguins ever after as no one else could look at him. To this day "Beware the fate of Nootaikok!" is a phrase that inspires dread in the heart of many an Inuit.

Day 210

Shush
Corner

Shush
Bird

Shush
Leaves

Shush
Sky 1

Shush
Sky 2

Shut the
fuck up
roof-fuck

Shush
Branch

Minute Of
Silence Day

Shush
Tree

There is no reason minutes of silence should be
reserved for public calamities. Personal tragedies are
just as deserving. Today, hold a minute of silence for
the end of a romance, the failure of a business deal,
or the death of your goldfish. Encourage others to
observe it out of respect for your grief.

Shush
Door

Shush
Benrik

Shush
Ants

Day 211

Shush Day-box

Call a sex line and ask to speak to the manager. Claim you are unsatisfied with the service and try to get them to give you your money back. Possible grounds for complaint include:

Operator was faking pleasure

Operator used foul language

Operator sounded bored

Operator was overly familiar

Sex talk was unchristian

Sex talk was clichéd

Scenario was implausible

Scenario was demeaning towards women

Sex talk was grammatically flawed

Scenario was tasteless

Today, assess people's potential for evil, and act in consequence

MCCCL

CMX

MCMXLVI

MDCCIX

MMV

MCMXIV

Adolf Hitler outlined his plans for the Jewish people in *Mein Kampf*, published in 1923. If someone then had taken them seriously enough and killed him to prevent them, millions of deaths would have been averted. Today, probe those around you for murderous designs, and, should you find any, take history into your own hands.

Day 213

Today put yourself up for sale on eBay!

Tips to help you sell yourself

Include a photo: No one will be interested in buying you unless they can see what you look like. Make sure the photo is a recent one. No naked photos, unless you are looking to be sold as a sex slave.

Give a description: As eBay themselves advise, "give some thought to describing your item. What are its most appealing characteristics?" Be specific: "proficient at computer software installation including Windows XP and Mac OSX" beats "quite friendly."

Choose the right category: The right category is: Everything Else > Weird Stuff > Slightly Unusual.

Pick a realistic starting price: Research shows that $100 is all that most people are prepared to bid initially for an average human being. Unless you are beautiful or famous, start at $100 and work your way up through the auction process.

Let us know the result: Benrik are interested in your well-being, wish to follow your progress, and will claim their 10% off your eventual price.

Day 214

Internet Vigilante Day. Today police the internet yourself.

<cutie69er> asl
<cutie69er> im 13
<LuvinBoy> 16,m,malaysia
<Ready> hello cutie
<cutie69er> hi
<LuvinBoy> 3 years older]
<LuvinBoy> hehe
<Vigilante> Hey you two are underage!
<LuvinBoy> hi
<hottiewithabody> no freedom im am too! haha
cassandra sets mode: +b *!*@26E1AC.EBA119B.7903A39D.IP
<MasterYoda> bored bored bored bored
aziz is now known as SwEeT_BoY_MsN
<cutie69er> hi
<Vigilante> cutie69er isn't it past your bed-time?
<LuvinBoy> wazzup...
*some^boy thinks freedom2fight4 is wrong
<handsomeboy_932> 18,mmalaysia
<cutie69er> nm
<sexypip> any m wnt chat, 15 f uk
<Freedom2Fight4> sure u are hottie
<LuvinBoy> nm?
<Freedom2Fight4> whys that some boy
<CKY_17> hi

<hottiewithabody> i am if you knew me you would agree too
<Vigilante> enough of this lechery let's talk about something else guys and girls
*some^boy isnt too coward to state facts that are insulting... freedom2fight4 u suck.... (an insulting fact)
<cutie69er> hi any hot guys?
gangsta_18 is now known as Wolf_King
<some^boy> :)
<some^boy> lol
<DrPel_6931> Any girl who wants to have a real talk pvt me
(Spanish,German.Italian,French, language iis not a problem-)
<Vigilante> Dr? You don't sound like a teen, get out of our chatroom
<Freedom2Fight4> well i dont and thats why im neutral at the moment
<DrPel_6931> Any girl who wants to have a real talk pvt me
(Spanish,German.Italian,French, language iis not a problem-)
<hottiewithabody> im in this HUGE fight right now with a few ppl just b/c i stated the facts
<Freedom2Fight4> sure u are someboy
<some^boy> lol

l_6931> and u r a moron who's only a man behind a computer 8-)
<Vigilante> cutie69er pvt me and I'll help you fight these degenerates
*SEXYIRISHGIRL sits on the arms chair
*SHAZ hey some^boyyyyyyyyyyyyyyyyyyyyyyyyyyyyyyyyyyyy
<DrPel_6931> and u r a moron who's only a man behind a computer 8-)
<nurse> hiya everyone
<Vigilante> a nurse? Whatever next?
cassandra sets mode: +b *!*sweet_gi*@*
nurse is now known as nurse_538
*Web_Cam_BoY please Àù want WEB CAM girls
<Baby_Bunny> ANY1 FOUND ANY PERVES 2NI
<Vigilante> it's full of perverts raaaaaghh hhhh
DrPel_6931> :S damn it
<DrPel_6931> someone dropped me :S
<hobby> where are hot girls ?
<Vigilante> where are they those dripping hot ones?????????!!!!!!
*SHAZ hb some^boy
<scrpion1> hiiiiiiiiiiiiiiiiiiiiiiiiiiiiiiiiiiii
<nurse_538> he wants a three some y u not up 4 that
cassandra sets mode: +b *!*araCroft@*
<hobby> any girl wanna chat
<LuvinBoy> anybody want to tok dirty pvt me
<Vigilante> DIRTY LITTLE WHORES OF BABYLON!!!!!!!
<beachgirl> hi room
<samiekins_3469> here!
*SEXYIRISHGIRL sneezes
<hobby> hi beach girl
<samiekins_3469> yeah n e fit guys wntin sommat gooooood pvt me
<Vigilante> that's better. Bye for now.
*some^boy is back... again
<samiekins_3469> :P

Day 215

Day 216

NO:

YES:

KIDNAP A WORM DAY

There's no law against it!

SCIENCE DAY!

Worms lead surprisingly busy—albeit short—lives. During the course of its two-week lifespan, a worm will travel 5 miles, and ingest 100kg of earth! Worms are also noted for their unique self-regenerating ability. Today, kidnap a worm, chop it in two and dump one half into the posher bit of the park. Return every day to see if the two halves lead different lives.

THE WORM'S MOTHER CRYING:

THE WORM'S COUSIN CRYING:

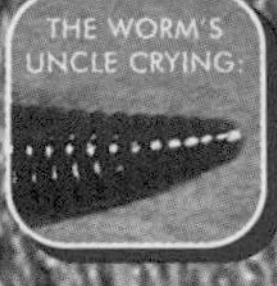

THE WORM'S UNCLE CRYING:

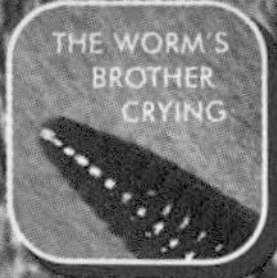

THE WORM'S BROTHER CRYING

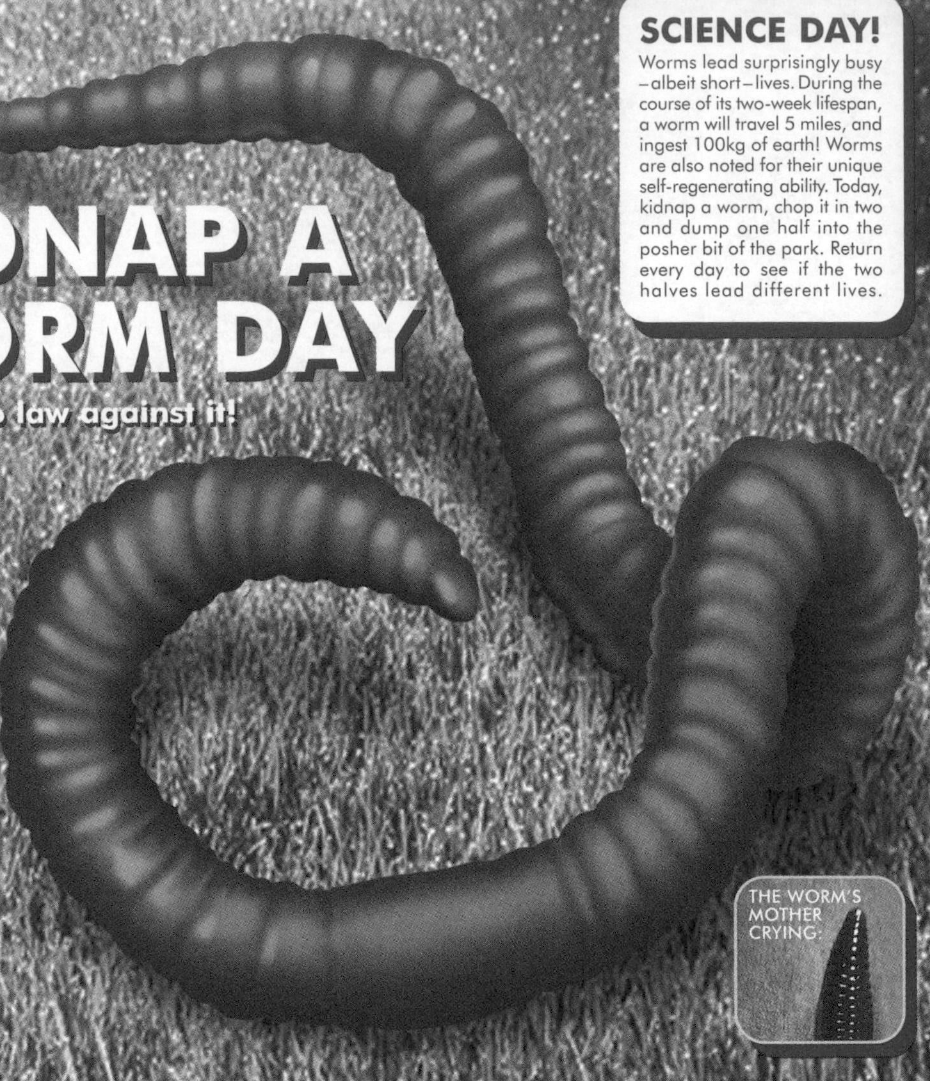

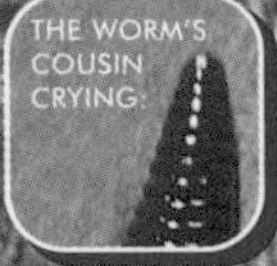

Day 217

On the face of it, this well-known work by Algerian-born painter Khaled Reghine presents us with a straightforward narrative. Entitled *Number 12*, it weaves the tale of two boys who have (just?) competed in a wheelchair race. One has won and is holding the trophy. The other (the eponymous "Number 12") has lost, one of his wheels lying on the ground. Also he seems to be a werewolf. The locus is a simple one: we as spectators are enjoined to feel sympathy for No12, who holds us in his tearful gaze.

Yet this deceptively simple scene conceals a web of conflicting narratives which a closer textual/ pictorial interpretation will reveal.

Consider the winning boy more closely. Even though he has won, he is still angry with the werewolf. Indeed, he is not only holding the trophy, but also threatening or preparing to throw it. Next to him, his mother or lover congratulates and kisses him (she is dichotomous). They stand as one pictorial mass, conjoined also to the forest, symbol of motherhood and refuge. No12, by contrast, sits alone. He is triply isolated: from the forest, from the other two, and last but not least, from us the viewers – he is stranded in the foreground of the canvas, floating in the perspectival abyss between the field of our gaze and the "grounded" plane of conifers behind him.

This is a quintessentially Freudian mise-en-scene. The second boy has crossed the Oedipal bridge to the point where he is at one both with his mother (he has conquered her affection and respect) and with his lover. It is no coincidence that the pine trees in the background stretch to the sky, erect. He brandishes his trophy/penis, keen to hurt his rival with it in a display of brute testosterone-filled caveman machismo.

Yet this is only one strand in this many-faceted masterpiece. For the wheelchairs provide a second key (clef) to the text. Both competitors are it seems disabled. They are formally similar too in

Number 12, by Khaled Reghine (1921-1984) (Musee De L'Art Populaire Algerien, Wahran)

that their wheels are perfectly aligned – save of course for the werewolf boy's left wheel which has come off. Many critics have sought to explain this in strictly narrative terms. Was it an accident? Did the winner push him right off the road, or even sabotage the wheelchair? Post-Marxist aficionados of Reghine in particular have found this a rich vein of analysis, positing the broken wheel as a symbol of the internal contradictions of our technocapitalist society literally coming off their axis, leaving us bereft of escape routes. All that is left to us is self-defeating faceless (numbered) struggle in a dog-eat-dog world.

But this is simplistic. The true import of the wheels is to be divined at a more formal level. For the broken wheel disrupts the picture's visual field, shattering the perspective both in its positioning and through its (abnormally small) size.

And this is where we intuit the force of "Number 12." The werewolf boy is doubly other: he is disabled, indeed, but beyond that he is in radical rupture with the dimensions (three) of the rest of his world, the world of the canvas. Two corresponding circles signify this, both lying flat against the viewer's eye: his lost wheel, and his moony face, grotesquely malformed by the transformation *unter* werewolf, that archetypal Other of our culture. He is alienated from his world, from his condition. He can no longer condone the dread illusion. He faces us directly, not merely as representation, but as mirror to our lost selves ("mon semblable, mon frère" indeed). We, like him, are pure form. He cries not at the other boy but at us and for us, for we are he, and he is us...

Day 218

Today: Living History Day
Today, enjoy the lifestyle of a 13th-century peasant.

Wake at dawn as the pig you share your straw bed with relieves himself on your foot. Shake off the fleas, flies and lice, and prepare to meet the day! Skip your bath as usual, you had one last year. Wake your spouse and your eight (or is it nine?) children, and enjoy a breakfast of tasty dry bread, washed down with ale (you don't drink the water from the river - it tastes foul as a result of being used as a sewer). You notice your ox in its wisdom has decided to bash in part of the house's wall. Make a mental note to patch it up with mud when you have two seconds, or maybe with some of the copious manure the ox produced overnight. But for now, off to the fields you go, not to your own strip, but to work on your lord's. It's harvesting time, so grab your sickle, a rusty bit of metal as likely to land you with a tetanus cut as to help you harvest. The crop this year is pretty weak, because it rained for two weeks continuously in June. So you don't want to tire yourself out completely, since there might be little food to help you recuperate. On the other hand if you don't work hard, there'll be no food at all and you'll starve to death. In any case the lord's reeve will be keeping an eye on you and you'll get fined or beaten if you don't pull your weight. Time for lunch, not a moment too soon as you're hungry. You're hungry most of the time anyway though, so it's nothing to complain about. Lunch is more dark bread, with a bit of rat-nibbled cheese if you're lucky. And ale. More work, maybe on the church's land this time. There are other peasants working nearby, but there's not much time for gossip with

Don't forget the shoes.

Hans, Will or Sal (they have no surnames and neither do you. You don't need a surname as there's only a few dozen of you in the village you were born in and which you'll probably never leave in your 13th century life in any case. Not that you know what century you're living in.) Anyway as the sun sets you down tools and head home. Tonight's supper is pottage, a stew of oats with the odd turnip. You're exhausted but you might attempt some rather clumsy intercourse with your spouse, never mind the kids and animals. They've seen and heard it all before. Repeat tomorrow. And every day for the rest of your life, which will probably end around age 45 if you're lucky.

You will need: ❶ Mud ❷ Rats ❸ A straw bed ❹ A pig ❺ Cloth ❻ An ox ❼ A field ❽ Leprosy ❾ Ale ❿ Turnips ⓫ Manure

---

Day 219

Acupuncture is now widely recognized as an effective cure for a wide variety of ills. However it is still beyond the reach of many, while others still may feel slight embarrassment at exposing themselves for treatment. That is why Benrik are providing this self-acupuncture chart. Simply buy some needles and stick them in at the relevant acupuncture points, taking care not to push them in too far (half an inch is about right). Soon your Qi will flow unimpeded again, and your troubles will abate.

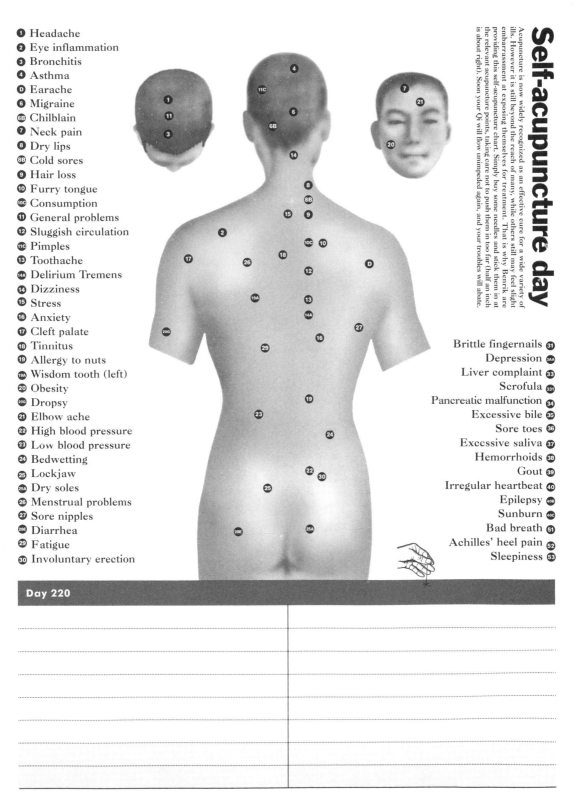

1 Headache
2 Eye inflammation
3 Bronchitis
4 Asthma
D Earache
6 Migraine
6B Chilblain
7 Neck pain
8 Dry lips
8B Cold sores
9 Hair loss
10 Furry tongue
10C Consumption
11 General problems
12 Sluggish circulation
11C Pimples
13 Toothache
14A Delirium Tremens
14 Dizziness
15 Stress
16 Anxiety
17 Cleft palate
18 Tinnitus
19 Allergy to nuts
19A Wisdom tooth (left)
20 Obesity
20G Dropsy
21 Elbow ache
22 High blood pressure
23 Low blood pressure
24 Bedwetting
25 Lockjaw
25A Dry soles
26 Menstrual problems
27 Sore nipples
28E Diarrhea
29 Fatigue
30 Involuntary erection

Brittle fingernails 31
Depression 3AA
Liver complaint 33
Scrofula 33I
Pancreatic malfunction 34
Excessive bile 35
Sore toes 36
Excessive saliva 37
Hemorrhoids 38
Gout 39
Irregular heartbeat 40
Epilepsy 40B
Sunburn 40C
Bad breath 51
Achilles' heel pain 52
Sleepiness 53

Day 220

TODAY CARRY A HIDDEN WEAPON

With street crime allegedly rife, perhaps you should go armed. Today conceal some means of defending yourself, like scissors or a hammer. Do you feel safer? Or does it merely ramp up your insecurity?

NOTE TO THE POLICE
This fine gentleman/lady/child is carrying a dangerous weapon as part of a Benrik mind experiment into the psychosociology of crime. Please do not arrest them. Benrik vouches for their peaceful nature.

Day 221

Today,

YOU MUST STOP HORSING AROUND.

YOUR LIFE UP UNTIL TODAY HAS

BEEN NOTHING BUT HORSE PLAY

AND NOW IT'S TIME TO STOP IT,

YOU IDIOT.

Signed

DAVID SHRIGLEY

Day 222

Our guest David Shrigley does great drawings for a living. www.davidshrigley.com

Day 223

Today have a sleep somewhere random

AMATEUR PAGE

8

From:
William Tiernan
Whyteleafe,
UK

1) Beginner (somewhere else in your own bedroom e.g. under your bed)

2) Novice (another room in the house e.g. kitchen)

3) Intermediate (somewhere within your own (or parents') property e.g. garden, garage or car)

4) Expert (anywhere else e.g. on top of a bus shelter or up a tree in the park)

Day 224

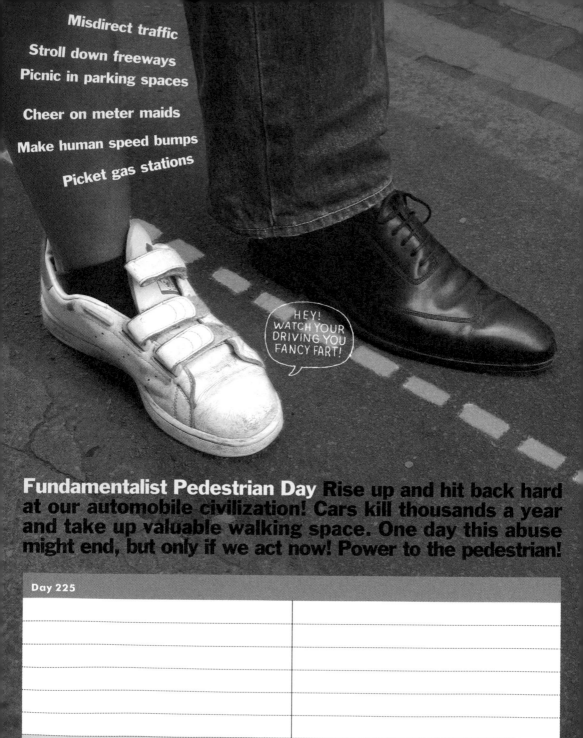

Misdirect traffic
Stroll down freeways
Picnic in parking spaces

Cheer on meter maids

Make human speed bumps

Picket gas stations

HEY! WATCH YOUR DRIVING YOU FANCY FART!

Fundamentalist Pedestrian Day Rise up and hit back hard at our automobile civilization! Cars kill thousands a year and take up valuable walking space. One day this abuse might end, but only if we act now! Power to the pedestrian!

Day 225

TODAY DRAW GOD

IT DOESN'T NEED TO BE A MAN. IT DOESN'T HAVE TO BE A WOMAN. IT DOESN'T EVEN HAVE TO BE A PERSON. BUT: IF YOU DRAW HIM/HER/IT BADLY YOU GO TO HELL!!

Day 226

Nanonap Day

Scientists have discovered that the age-old tradition of sleeping for hours on end may not be the most efficient way to rest. Instead, "nanonaps" are being mooted as the future of sleep. Astronauts first alerted the scientific community to the phenomenon, when they found they felt more energetic after many small naps than after one long one. A nanonap only lasts for 20 to 30 seconds, and may take place anywhere – at the office, on the train, at school. Napoleon is said to have prefigured them by sleeping upright on his horse during brief lulls in the battle. Test the theory today by taking up to 100 thirty-second nanonaps at regular intervals. Rest your head on this page with your mouth over our waterproof "dribble zone." Dribbling only occurs during deep sleep, so you will have a reliable measure of how well you have slept. If your dribble spreads out beyond the box, nanonaps are for you!

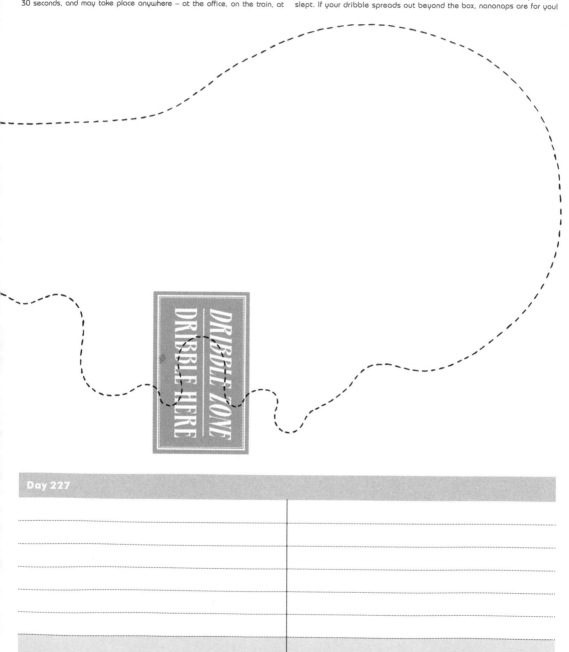

DRIBBLE ZONE
DRIBBLE HERE

Day 227

Day 228

Today, price tag all your possessions

Everything has its price. Work it out and stick it on your possessions today with the understanding that anyone who meets that price can buy them. Factor in sentimental value; if an old teddy bear was your first friend, then it's perfectly legitimate to value it in the thousands. Restrictions: human beings are legally impossible to buy or sell, but pets are fair game.

SALE PRICE

The coat in which I lost my virginity 1988.
$6.99

Day 229

Make someone hate you today

Hatred is as mysterious and volatile an emotion as love. It is relatively easy to pinpoint why we dislike someone. Dislike is socially acceptable, one of the inevitable lubricants of our close-quarters living. Hatred is socially disruptive. Its intensity is pathological. It overrules rational argument and shreds the social fabric. What drives anyone to hate? Find out today by trying to make someone hate you. It can be someone who already dislikes you, or you can start from scratch with a stranger or a friend. Good luck, and don't forget to tell them it was a joke tomorrow!

Illustration taken from Hell's Angels rule-book under the headline "Tattoos that we accept you to have on your face in our club."

Ignore them

When your receptionist smiles and says hello as usual, pretend she's invisible, pause for a moment as if trying to locate the source of a particularly nasty smell, and stride on into the elevator.

Attack their family

Ask your neighbor over the garden fence if she minds that her husband sees the dominatrix in Pond St. every other Monday evening on his way home. Say you assumed she knew as everyone else seems to.

Insult their beliefs

Your great aunt has been praying fervently all her life to get to heaven. Get her a free subscription to *Science* magazine with instructions to look out for articles on what actually happens after death.

Day 230

ZAPPING DAY

Today, we've picked the best programs for you, so follow our TV-watching schedule to the minute and relax.

	CH1	CH2	CH3	CH4	CH5	CH6	CH7	CH8	CH9	CH10	CH11	CH12	CH13	CH14	CH15	CH16	CH17	CH18	CH20
8:00a.m.													■						
8:12a.m.						■													
8:50a.m.										■									
9:10a.m.															■				
9:12a.m.			■																
10:01a.m.													■						
10:18a.m.								■											
10:59a.m.																			■
11:30a.m.																			
11:50a.m.	■																		
12:05p.m.							■												
12:32p.m.												■							
1:13p.m.				■															
1:48p.m.																	■		
2:10p.m.																			
2:51p.m.			■																
3:35p.m.													■						
3:39p.m.																			■
4:05p.m.						■													
5:15p.m.											■								
5:41p.m.		■																	
5:52p.m.																		■	
6:00p.m.				■															
6:15p.m.												■							
6:40p.m.																	■		
6:50p.m.	■																		
7:00p.m.						■													
7:30p.m.												■							
7:45p.m.										■									
8:48p.m.																			
8:49p.m.															■				
8:50p.m.			■																
9:20$^{1/2}$p.m.		■																	
9:30p.m.													■						
9:50p.m.								■											
10:00p.m.																	■		
10:40p.m.					■														
10:52p.m.												■							
11:10p.m.																			
11:50p.m.			■																■

Day 231

Today, stick a message on a banknote

Banknotes are the ultimate media, circulating between millions every day free of charge. Benrik believe that their use for communication purposes would reinforce the social tissue and make the spending experience a lot more "fun."

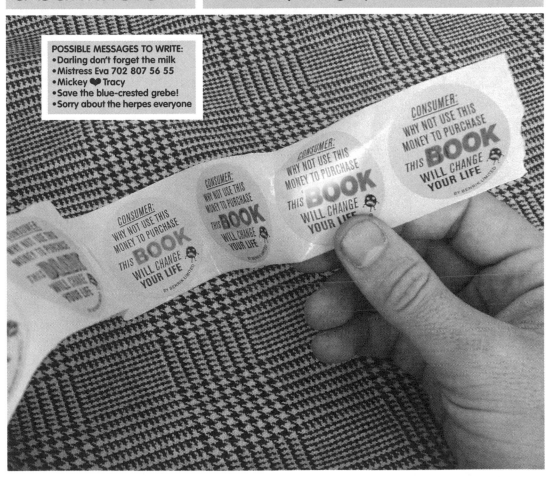

POSSIBLE MESSAGES TO WRITE:
- Darling don't forget the milk
- Mistress Eva 702 807 56 55
- Mickey ♥ Tracy
- Save the blue-crested grebe!
- Sorry about the herpes everyone

Day 232

TODAY LET A DOG WALK YOU

WATCH OUT!
Dogs must clean up after their humans. Humans with a history of dangerous behavior are prohibited. Humans must be licensed and vaccinated. Humans must be wearing a collar with identification at all times. Leaving humans unattended is prohibited. SCOOP THE POOP!

THE PEOPLE
(FOULING OF LAND) ACT 1996.

CLEAN IT UP!
MAXIMUM FINE $1000

Day 233

Discover who you were in a past life

Our past lives are stored in our subconscious. It is said that Buddha remembered all 500 of his when he fully Awakened! You can't compete with that, but try and remember your last one, using this simple technique: close your eyes and move your finger around this page at random whilst chanting "Nam-myohorenge-kyo" 10 times. Your finger will stop on your previous life, and the memories should start flooding back.

Which one of these were you?

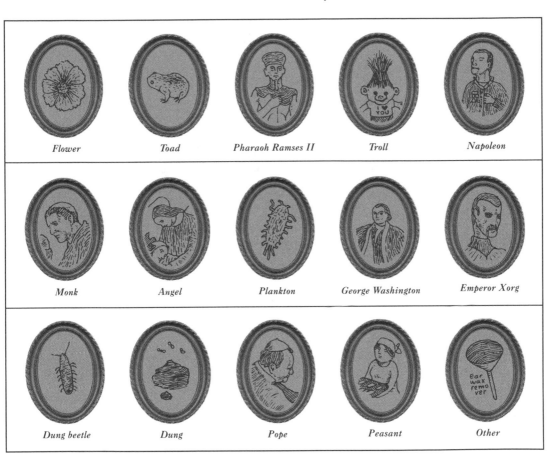

Flower	*Toad*	*Pharaoh Ramses II*	*Troll*	*Napoleon*
Monk	*Angel*	*Plankton*	*George Washington*	*Emperor Xorg*
Dung beetle	*Dung*	*Pope*	*Peasant*	*Other*

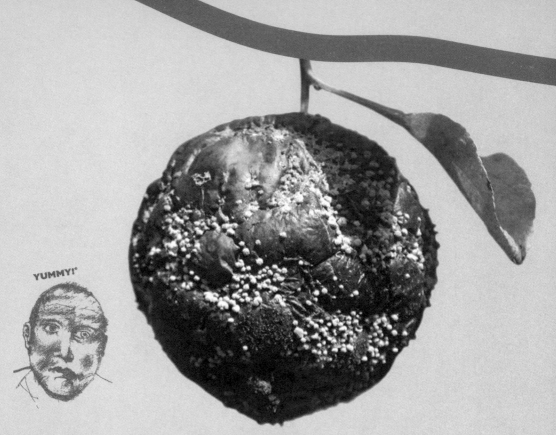

YUMMY![*]

Extreme Fruitarianism Day

Vegetarianism is murder! If you eat something that is alive, you kill it, whether meat, vegetable or fruit. Even the so-called enlightened diets are genocide on a grand scale. There are only two acceptable alternatives. 1) Breatharianism, which means surviving on love and fresh air, but which still needs some practical fine-tuning. 2) Extreme Fruitarianism, where you may only eat fruit that has fallen off the tree of its own accord. There are over 3,000 extreme fruitarians worldwide, mostly living near orchards. The rules are strict: you may not shake the branch or even touch the tree in order to make the fruit fall. Eating fruit with worms is forbidden, of course. However, you may eat fruit that the wind has shaken off the tree. The benefits are manifold: clearer conscience, clearer skin, light-headedness and medically significant weight loss.

Day 235	

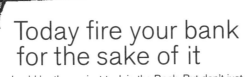

Today fire your bank for the sake of it

This should be the easiest task in the Book. But don't just send them a one-liner ending it. Explain in great detail why you are booting them out of your life, in small print.

YOU'RE FIRED!

Thank you for being my bank over the last few years. Now it's time for us to part and I'd like to explain why clearly and succinctly. When you raised "first-time" buyer interest rates from 5.6%* to 6.1%** on 12/08/05 (7.56% APR), my overall ratio of debt to overdraft rose to 345%, adjusted for inflation (231% in real terms, based on 2004 Treasury figures). My salary dropped to 78% of my expenditure as a result, from a mid-2004 low of 94%. Over the last few years you have caused an increase in my blood pressure of 2.3% (1999), 2.7% (2000), 2.8% (2001), 4.6% (2002), 7.8% (2003), 9.9% (2004 estimated). This represents a cumulative rise of 23.5%, adjusted for natural ageing of the arteries. Typical example: $78,987 mortgage (87%): Purchase price $110,500, mortgage over 25 years, charged at a discounted 3.1% variable rate for 36 months, then 7.55% variable rate (standard plus account with Breakthru discount + 0.5%, exclusive of fees). 36 payments of $566.78 gross then 294 payments of $897.04 gross. Total amount payable over the term $234,879.56 excluding fees. Fees include: solicitor's fee $235, valuation fee $270 (standard valuation***), lawyers transfer fee $34. APR (VARIABLE) 6.9% calculated over the term of the mortgage. If mortgage is redeemed within 16 months, a charge of $5,876 will apply, along with redemption charges of 1.4% of total value of the mortgage over the term. Redemption administrative fee $545. Redemption administrative fee if remortgaging with your current lender $445. Rates correct as of 13/04/03, subject to variation. Interest will be payable on the mortgage from the date on which the check (or telegraphic transfer) is issued until the following December 31. In each succeeding year, interest will be charged on the balance of the whole debt outstanding at the end of the preceding year. In addition, if any further sums become owing during any year, interest will be charged from the date such sums become owing until the end of that year. In the year of repayment of the whole debt, interest will be charged on the whole debt outstanding at the end of the preceding year (and on any further sums becoming owing during that year) up to and including the date on which cleared funds are received by the society to repay the whole debt in full. Interest will accrue from day to day but will be payable partly in advance (if appropriate having a regard to the payment date) and partly in arrears by monthly instalments during the year (each month being treated for this purpose as a twelfth of the year). Your home is at risk if you do not keep up repayments on a mortgage or other loan secured on it. Payment holidays, overpayments and equity transfer are subject to status, terms and conditions. For interest only mortgages, you should arrange an appropriate repayment vehicle. It is strongly advised for any mortgage that you take out suitable life insurance cover. Written quotation available on request. Security required. Only available to US residents aged between 21 and 68, subject to status and to terms and conditions. In this section, "me," "my" and "I" refer to my person as a legal entity. "You," "my bank" and "you evil bastards" refer to your plc, your holdings plc and any subsidiaries, associated and affiliated companies. If I have not delivered the standard of explanation you require, or if you think I have made a mistake, please let me know. I will then investigate the situation and, if appropriate, attempt to remedy the situation with steps to prevent you contacting me ever again. If you remain dissatisfied, there is precious little you can do about it. Me and you submit to the non-exclusive jurisdiction of the courts of the United States of America.

Day 236

*5.6% before deduction of tax **APR: gross rate compounded ***advanced valuation recommended $345 fee includes test for rising damp, dry rot, condensation, woodworm, electrical wiring, masonry and structural problems.

Censored page

After consultation with our editors, lawyers and the District Attorney for the State of New York, we have no choice but to remove the task for today from the print edition of *This Book Will Change Your Life, Again!* Readers are invited to view it online on www.thiswebsitewillchangeyourlife.com. We have been asked to remind our readers that "pranks" may well be in violation of the law, and that humor does not constitute a valid defense. In other words, have fun, yes, but responsible fun.

Thank you, Benrik Limited

Day 237

Let children rule the world today

Children are pure and innocent. If we all do their bidding, the world can only become a better place. Do nothing today without first asking for instructions from the nearest available child.

Armies to be composed of pets. Grrr. Grrr.

Beat up the fat kids.

Only cartoons on TV.

Detention for all teachers. Naughty Boy

lolly-mountain
Spend all money on candy.

Parents in bed by 8. stories

Breakfast: Lunch: Dinner:
Burger and chips every meal.

Today make sure your body survives you

Upon death your soul and body will part ways, but that's no reason to abandon your corpse entirely. Your body is an integral part of you and deserves to survive to preserve your memory. Pick one of the three options below and make the necessary arrangements today.

- Boy, the scavenger termites did a really great job stuffing that human.
- Yeah it's scary how real it looks.

1) PLASTINATION Invented by celebrity professor Gunther Von Hagens, plastination impregnates the body with reactive polymers such as resin and silicone rubber. This is a marvellous way of preserving your body, although do note they remove the skin. You may volunteer your body for plastination by contacting the Bundesverband der Korperspender (Federal Association of Body Donors). Write c/o Institut fur Plastination, Rathausstrasse 11, D-69126, Heidelberg, Germany, or call the Body Donation Office direct on +49 6221 33 11 50.

2) TAXIDERMY Taxidermy has been around since the hunter-gatherers in one shape or another. Yet only in recent history has it reached a state of refinement where it is now possible to "mount" human beings with any degree of artistic success. The main advantage over plastination is that your body retains its outer form. The disadvantage is that your innards go. Still, if you are less interested in what's under the skin, try calling a taxidermist in your area. To find one, look in the yellow pages, or write to: the International Guild of Taxidermy (President: Joe Boggs), 411 George Street, Aurora, IN 47001. Phone: (812) 926-4868.

3) STATUARY This is very much the old-fashioned option. Get a local sculptor to cast you in plaster. You will be covered in hot sticky goo for the best part of the day, and lose any body hair, probably for good. However, it's cheaper than the above two options, and will look decorative in your descendants' garden. Note: if you want the authentic "lost an arm at Troy" look, get it chopped off from the final statue, and not prior to modelling.

Day 239

TODAY, TOPPLE A DICTATOR USING ONLY THE INTERNET

The information revolution is a direct challenge to authoritarian states. With its many points of access and its decentralized, disembodied nature, the internet is the perfect rallying point for change. Yet it has still to claim its first direct dictator scalp. Book readers can change that today by e-mailing them and convincing them to step down from power with a few well-chosen arguments.

Kim Jong Il (North Korea)
www.korea-dpr.com

Hu Uintao (China)
www.govonline.cn

Fidel Castro (Cuba)
www.cuba.gov.cu

Robert Mugabe (Zimbabwe)
www.gta.gov.zw

Than Shwe (Burma)
www.myanmar.net

Omar Al-Bashir (Sudan)
www.sudan.gov.sd

Saparmurat Niyazov (Turkmenistan)
www.mct.gov.tm

Alexander Lukashenko
(Belarus)
www.president.gov.by

Crown Prince Abdullah (Saudi Arabia)
www.shura.gov.sa

Day 240

$$$

Today ask Bill Gates for money

Bill Gates is happy to give money to worthy causes, like AIDS or malaria. Why shouldn't he give to you? Write to him asking if he could spare you just 0.001% of his fortune. Address: Bill Gates c/o Microsoft, Redmond, WA 98052, USA. (Don't forget to include your bank account details.)

Bill Gates, Microsoft,
Redmond, WA 98052, USA

Dear Bill,
We are Benrik and we write books. It's a tough life and we could use some more dough.
Here's our offer: if you give us, say, a couple of million out of your $26 billion fortune,
we'll mention you in our next book. For another $500,000 (nothing to a man such as you),
we include a full-color photo. It's a pretty sweet deal we think you'll agree.
Our bank details are:
Xxxxxxxxxxxxxxxx
Xxxxxxxxx-xxxxx-xxxxxxx

Yours gratefully,
Benrik

PS By the way, we just love your software products. Keep up the good work!

Sample Sample Sample

Day 241

Today fight for your right to party

Mothers can be unreasonable, insisting that you attend school against your express wishes. Teachers may attempt to demean in front of your peer group, particularly if you have failed to attend or complete your assignments. Fathers may deny you the right to smoke, even if they themselves use tobacco products on a regular basis. Such are the downsides of residing with your parents. Others may include the confiscation of adult material, censorship of your attire and hairstyle, and lack of empathy for your taste in music (and particularly the self-styled "Beastie Boys" combo). In the face of this, you must make a concerted effort to retain your right to enjoy yourself, develop your own hobbies, and choose recreational activities that suit you as an individual. (Translated from the original.)

Day 242

MORAL MAJORITY DAY:
ENFORCE MORALITY TODAY!

Morality is the shared set of values that holds our tolerant Judaeo-Christian civilization together. Some people just can't seem to get that through their thick skulls however. Today, look out for the following immoral types and prevent them from ruining civilization for everyone else.

UNMARRIED COUPLES
Stop them from fucking

HIPPIES
Stop them from smoking

LIBERALS
Stop them from voting

DRUGGIES
Stop them from injecting

PUSHERS
Stop them from pushing

ABORTERS
Stop them from killing

HOMO-SEXUALS
Stop them from touching

VILLAGE VOICE READERS
Stop them from reading

HOOKERS
Stop them from whoring

YOU ARE ALL GOING STRAIGHT TO HELL!

Moral majority 49% Immoral minority 48% Don't know 3% (ABC Research poll 05/06, 2,000 adults)

Day 243

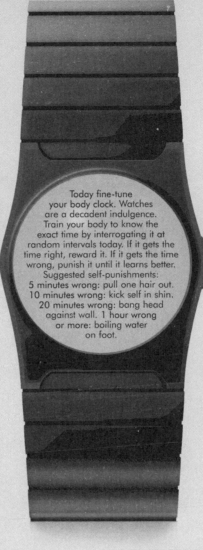

Today fine-tune
your body clock. Watches
are a decadent indulgence.
Train your body to know the
exact time by interrogating it at
random intervals today. If it gets the
time right, reward it. If it gets the time
wrong, punish it until it learns better.
Suggested self-punishments:
5 minutes wrong: pull one hair out.
10 minutes wrong: kick self in shin.
20 minutes wrong: bang head
against wall. 1 hour wrong
or more: boiling water
on foot.

Day 244

GO BACK TO SCHOOL TODAY

Maybe you weren't well. Maybe you skipped it without realizing its importance. But through no real fault of your own, you missed a crucial lesson, undermining your life since then. Today, go back to your local school and insist on attending a class you missed.

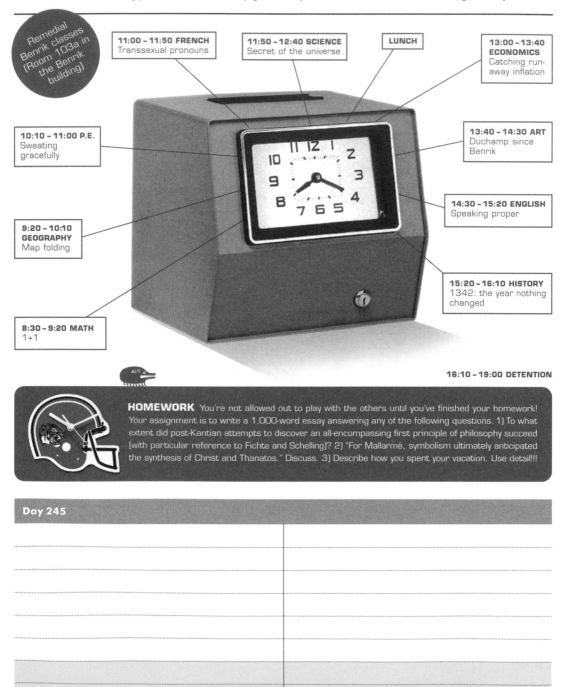

Remedial Benrik classes (Room 103a in the Benrik building)

11:00 – 11:50 FRENCH
Transsexual pronouns

11:50 – 12:40 SCIENCE
Secret of the universe

LUNCH

13:00 – 13:40 ECONOMICS
Catching run-away inflation

10:10 – 11:00 P.E.
Sweating gracefully

13:40 – 14:30 ART
Duchamp since Benrik

9:20 – 10:10 GEOGRAPHY
Map folding

14:30 – 15:20 ENGLISH
Speaking proper

8:30 – 9:20 MATH
1+1

15:20 – 16:10 HISTORY
1342: the year nothing changed

16:10 – 19:00 DETENTION

HOMEWORK You're not allowed out to play with the others until you've finished your homework! Your assignment is to write a 1,000-word essay answering any of the following questions. 1) To what extent did post-Kantian attempts to discover an all-encompassing first principle of philosophy succeed (with particular reference to Fichte and Schelling)? 2) "For Mallarmé, symbolism ultimately anticipated the synthesis of Christ and Thanatos." Discuss. 3) Describe how you spent your vacation. Use detail!!!

Day 245

MAKE AN INSECT'S DAY

YOU ARE NUMBER ONE

THE LIFE OF AN INSECT IS GENERALLY NASTY, BRUTISH AND SHORT. BRING A LITTLE WARMTH TO BEAR ON THIS MISERABLE EXISTENCE TODAY BY GIVING ONE OF THEM THE EXPERIENCE OF AN INSECT LIFETIME.

- POUR A PUDDLE OF HONEY IN THE PATH OF AN UNSUSPECTING ANT
- CAPTURE A BEE AND LET IT LOOSE IN A FLOWER SHOP
- CHASE A MOSQUITO INTO A PACKED SAUNA
- PLACE A GRASSHOPPER ON A TRAMPOLINE
- FURNISH A TERMITE COLONY WITH A LOUIS XIV COMMODE
- SMUGGLE A FLY INTO A MORTUARY

YOU ARE TO INSECTS WHAT GANDHI WAS TO HUMANS

Day 246

Today, change the weather

Try the Sioux Rain Dance, dancing in a circle four times around a jug of water

Try the Hopi Rain Dance, holding a live venomous snake in your mouth

Try the Zuni Rain Dance, whirling yourself around acting like the wind

Try those old aerosols with CFCs that cause global warming

"Everybody talks about the weather, but nobody does anything about it"
Mark Twain

Day 247	

Could you be the face of...

Today think of the brand you could be a great spokesperson for, and contact them to become rich.

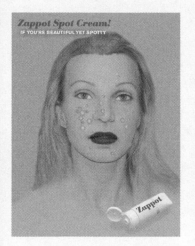

Zappot Spot Cream!
IF YOU'RE BEAUTIFUL YET SPOTTY
Zappot

Whitex Toothpaste!
If you have great teeth

Aunt Edna's Thick Soap
If you have a thick mustache

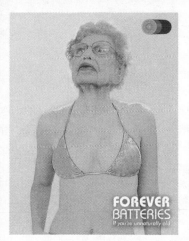

FOREVER BATTERIES
If you're unnaturally old

YUMYUM CHOCOLATE
IF YOU'RE FAT BUT HAPPY

SMOOTH CIGARETTES
IF YOU'RE DEAD

Day 248

Save someone's life today

They will be eternally grateful. They will be your friend for life. They will talk about you to everyone they know. They will hug you often. They will dedicate their autobiography to you. They will name their children after you. They will include you in their will. Nothing but good can come of this day.

Day 249

Keep an eye out for genuine opportunities to save a life. Should one not arise, however, force your luck. Leave a flower pot teetering over a window ledge and push someone out of the way as it falls. Elbow someone discreetly on a crowded train platform and pull them back as they wobble. Jump on top of someone and claim a sniper had his laser sights trained on them. Don't worry how implausible your story is, no one wants to be ungrateful to their savior.

EIGHT MILLION WAYS TO DIE

We all have to die of something. Today make your preference known by ranking this selection of ways to die from 1 to 100.

Hit by truck.................................../100
Hit by car....................................../100
Hit by bus..................................../100
Volcanic eruption........................../100
Earthquake.................................../100
Meteorite on head........................./100
Cancer../100
Burnt alive.................................../100
Flower pot falls on head................./100
Fall under train............................/100
Pushed under train......................./100
Plane crash................................./100
Parachute jammed......................../100
Cocaine overdose........................./100
Heroin overdose.........................../100
Painkiller overdose......................../100
Trampled at rock concert................/100
Struck by lightning........................./100
Ebola virus.................................../100
Snake bite..................................../100
Snake constriction........................./100
Tarantula...................................../100
Scorpion....................................../100
Swallowed wasp.........................../100
Broken heart................................/100
Nuclear bomb.............................../100
Anthrax in mail............................./100
Friendly fire................................./100
Spontaneous combustion................/100
Eaten by sharks............................/100
Eaten by cannibals......................../100
Eaten by piranhas........................./100
Eaten by dinosaurs ..../100
Eaten by zombies........................../100
Eaten by flesh-eating bug.............../100
Drowned....................................../100
Hanged......................................./100
Lynched....................................../100
Strangled...................................../100
Decapitated................................./100
Crucified...................................../100
Sliced up..................................../100

Disembowelled............................./100
Eviscerated.................................../100
Microwaved................................./100
Vaporized..................................../100
Shot in head................................/100
Shot in heart................................/100
Shot in stomach........................../100
Shot in foot................................./100
Dropped on head........................./100
Gangrene...................................../100
Choking......................................./100
Choking on a bone......................../100
Choking on a nut........................../100
Unexpected nut allergy................./100
Elevator brake failure.................../100
Spacesuit leak............................./100
Stabbed....................................../100
Stabbed in the back....................../100
Bludgeoned with baseball bat....../100
Abducted by aliens for tests........./100
Gas../100
Paper cut..................................../100
Lethal injection............................/100
Electric chair................................/100
Guillotine...................................../100
Duel../100
Suicide../100
Suicide-bombed.........................../100
Suicide-bomber........................../100

Food-poisoned............................/100
Alcohol-poisoned........................./100
Poison-poisoned........................../100
Poisoned umbrella tip.................../100
In my sleep (N/A)........................../100
Machine-gunned........................../100
Hypothermia................................/100
Heart attack................................/100
Malaria......................................./100
Measles....................................../100
Mumps../100
Smallpox...................................../100
Cholera......................................./100
Whooping cough........................../100
Black death.................................../100
Car accident................................/100
Mafia../100
Buried alive................................./100
Prematurely cremated.................../100
Routine surgery gone wrong........./100
Bondage session gone wrong....../100
Superman impression gone wrong./100
Russian roulette........................../100
Murdered by serial killer.............../100
Assassinated............................../100
Ransom unpaid by family.............../100
Caught in crossfire......................./100
Fall into vat of acid....................../100
Hara Kiri....................................../100

Supplementary information

If you have to be tortured
first, which would you prefer?
A Beatings
B Cigarette burns
C Psychological
D Water torture

Please hand
this to any
kidnappers.

Day 250

Today learn a sex trick from an animal

Human sex lives are fairly boring compared to what goes on in other species. Observe what goes on in the animal and insect kingdoms today, and expand your copulatory range.

DO IT IN FLIGHT Many birds, such as the chimney swift, mate in mid-air. Don't forget your parachutes.

DO IT IN PUBLIC Humans are the only creatures to have sex in private. Break the taboo!

EAT THE MALE IMMEDIATELY AFTER COPULATION The praying mantis is famous for getting the munchies after sex. But girls, who doesn't?

DO IT HANGING FROM A TREE The orangutan's favorite position: you'll need strong arms, and a strong branch.

Advanced: caress an animal lasciviously. Beware: bestiality is illegal! Do not engage in actual sexual relations. The purpose of this experiment is solely to discover if the animal freaks out in horror at your perversion.

ANIMAL BESTIALITY
JUST SAY NO!!!

Day 251

Today insult an alien

All radio waves are beamed up into space at the speed of light, and can travel millions of miles towards faraway galaxies. So, even an amateur CB radio can be used to communicate with other worlds. Today, check it's working ok by radioing up an appropriate insult, such as "your mother is a venusian whore" or "you stupid alien, come and get some." (When the alien arrives, tell him you weren't serious.)

R U TALKIN' TO ME?

day 252

TIME LAPSE DAY

Shoot your typical day on video, and speed it up from 24 hours to one hour. Then watch it and find out if you've accomplished anything useful.

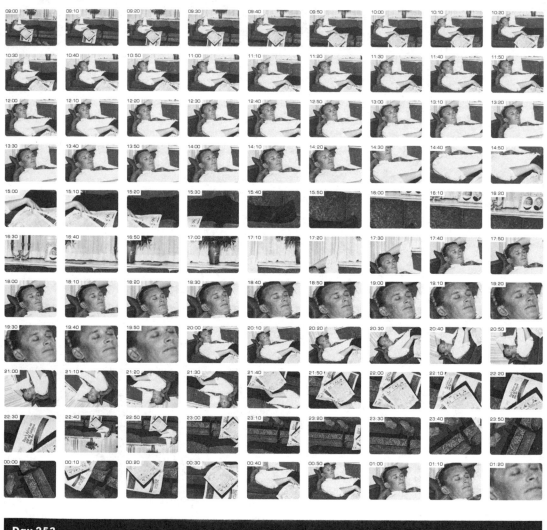

Day 253

TRY TO SELL YOUR USED KNICKERS TODAY

In Japan, schoolgirls make decent pocket money by selling their underwear. Why shouldn't you? Just make sure you've worn it for a full eight-hour day, otherwise it's not legally "used."

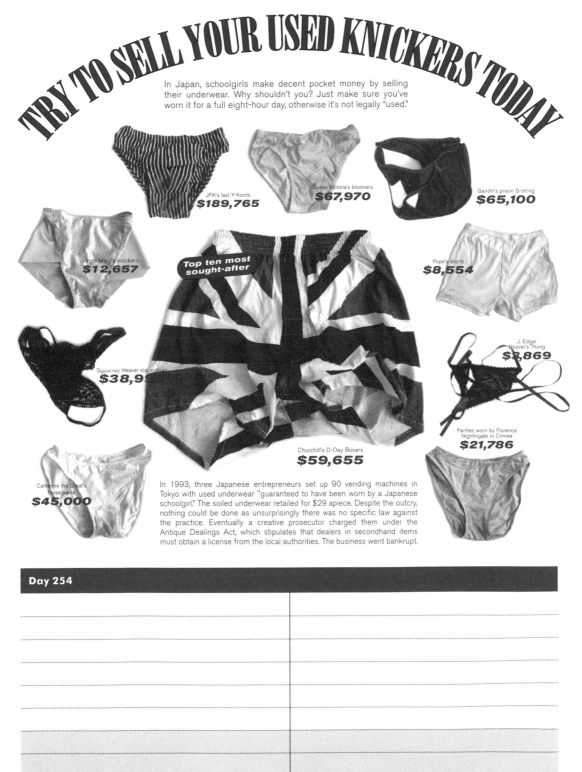

JFK's last Y-fronts
$189,765

Queen Victoria's bloomers
$67,970

Gandhi's prison G-string
$65,100

Virgin Mary's knickers
$12,657

Top ten most sought-after

Pope's shorts
$8,554

Gigourney Weaver slip in Alien
$38,99

J. Edgar Hoover's Thong
$3,869

Panties worn by Florence Nightingale in Crimea
$21,786

Catherine the Great's horse pants
$45,000

Churchill's D-Day Boxers
$59,655

In 1993, three Japanese entrepreneurs set up 90 vending machines in Tokyo with used underwear "guaranteed to have been worn by a Japanese schoolgirl." The soiled underwear retailed for $29 apiece. Despite the outcry, nothing could be done as unsurprisingly there was no specific law against the practice. Eventually a creative prosecutor charged them under the Antique Dealings Act, which stipulates that dealers in secondhand items must obtain a license from the local authorities. The business went bankrupt.

Day 254

Change your name to Benrik by court order

YES! You can change your boring old name to a more exciting one for free with our legally valid court order! The only restrictions on name changes are that it mustn't be impossible to pronounce and it can't include numbers, symbols or punctuation marks (except apostrophes). So you are perfectly entitled to change your name to Clark Kent, Booty Licious or Jack Kennedy. "Benrik," however, is much more suitable.

Order Granting Change Of Name

THIS CHANGE OF NAME DEED *made this* .... *day of* .... *by me the undersigned* BENRIK *of* ....*now or lately known as* ....*(former name) a citizen of* ....*by birth.*

WITNESSES AND IT IS HEREBY DECLARED *as follows:*

1. I absolutely and entirely renounce relinquish and abandon the use of my said former name of............................ ....*(former name) and assume adopt and determine to take and use from the date hereof the name of* benrik *in substitution for my former name,*.................................... ....*(former name).*

2. I shall at all times hereafter in all records deeds documents and other writings and in all actions and proceedings as well as in all dealings and transactions and on all occasions whatsoever use and subscribe the said name of BENRIK *as my name in substitution for my former name of*.................................... ....*(former name) so relinquished as aforesaid to the intent that I may hereafter be called known or distinguished not by the former name but by the name of* BENRIK *only.*

3. I authorize and require all persons at all times to designate describe and address me by the adopted name of BENRIK.

IN WITNESS *hereof I have hereunto subscribed my adopted and substituted name of* BENRIK *and also my said former name of*.. ....*(former name) and have affixed my seal the day and year first above written. Signed sealed and delivered by the above-named* Benrik *in the presence of*

Witness 1..

Witness 2..

Seal (from stationer's shop)

Send it for safe keeping to your Attorney and any relevant State Authorities (Immigration and Naturalization, Criminal Justice System if applicable). Alternatively just show this Court Order to government departments and other organizations and ask them to change your records.

Egg&Spoon Day

Carry an egg in a spoon all day long without dropping it. You are not allowed to put it down. If you are going to be indoors, use a boiled egg for safety. If you drop it, start again tomorrow, and again until you complete a whole day. Don't rush! This isn't a race.

Day 256

Discreetly give the finger to people all day today

FIG. A: What's
in my eye?!

FIG. B: Just
chilling out...

FIG. C: Hmmm...
I wonder...

FIG. H: I like to
stay informed

FIG. D: Everything's
in order, officer

FIG. F: Rich
pickings...

FIG. G: Is there
something in my teeth?

FIG. E: Sure, take
the last seat!

Day 257

GO TO PRISON TODAY!

Prison has proved a life-changing experience for many illustrious personalities, from Winston Churchill to Mahatma Gandhi. Nelson Mandela, the most famous prisoner of the 20th century, learnt to overcome his anger at the apartheid regime and forge a new path for South Africa as a result of his 27 years in prison. If it worked for Mandela, it could work for you! Experience prison for yourself today by committing a very minor offense and refusing to pay the fine (one-day sentences have been passed for the peaceful blockade of an arms fair, for instance, or assaulting highway traffic cones).

Day 258

Day 259

Today, Dance with Death

We are only ever one minute away from the end. Today, experience death's insane proximity so as to savor life all the more. Stand next to a running chainsaw. Stumble on the train platform. Stare over the edge of the cliff. Run a red light. Insult a skinhead. Just don't take anyone with you though.

In 1976, installation artist Bruce Mercer created "Untitled 22," which involved setting up a loaded gun in a gallery, pointed at the audience and primed to fire once at a random moment over the following 20 years. The exhibition attracted record numbers. The gun fired just after dawn on October 6, 1993, nearly injuring a cleaner.

Work out your alcohol tolerance level scientifically today

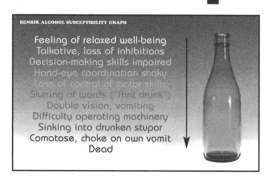

BENRIK ALCOHOL SUSCEPTIBILITY GRAPH

Feeling of relaxed well-being
Talkative, loss of inhibitions
Decision-making skills impaired
Hand-eye coordination shaky
Loss of control of motor skills
Slurring of words ("Aint drunk")
Double vision, vomiting
Difficulty operating machinery
Sinking into drunken stupor
Comatose, choke on own vomit
Dead

Everyone's reaction to alcohol is different. Today work out the exact levels at which you become drunk. Start on an empty stomach for accuracy. Procure a 700ml bottle of vodka. Drink it one measure every 5 minutes, and use our graph to work out how many minutes it takes you to become drunk (V). Now open a bottle of red wine and repeat. The red wine result is R. Repeat again with a gallon of beer (B). Your average number of drinks to get drunk is $(V+R+B) - age/1.15 + weight (kgs)/34.5$.

Day 260

Today, praise an unsung achievement

Dear Sir,

I would like to say how much I enjoyed your review of *Driving Miss Daisy* in today's *TV Weekly*. "Funny in parts but disappointing ending, watch if you're in" is as succinct and perspicuous a critique as one could wish to read. Thank you.

Dear Madam,

I was very taken by your weather update this morning on television. The way you explained the anticyclone's movements across Florida was pure poetry in motion and brought meteorology to life for me.

Dear Sir/Madam,

I purchased a pack of your toothpicks yesterday and I must confess I have never come across such marvellously crafted specimens! My mouth has not felt this clean for 65 years! Keep up the good work.

Gentlemen!

Please pass on my congratulations to the receptionist who transferred my call to your sales department this afternoon at 3:43p.m.; she did it so smoothly and in such a friendly manner that I hardly noticed the wait!

Dear neighbor,

Sorry for bothering you with this note, but I can no longer keep quiet. The way you deal with your trash never fails to inspire me. Your bags are beautifully tied yet quite hermetic and resistant to squirrels. You have all my respect.

Officer,

I live at 34B and watch you patrolling the street every day. Your posture is magnificent. You strike the perfect balance between scaring off the criminal mind, and reassuring the householder. Bravo! (I have sent a copy of this letter to your superiors.)

Day 261

AMATEUR PAGE
9

From:
Audrey Hantla
Sioux City,
Iowa, USA

DARLING ERNEST, IN THIS TEMPERATE WEATHER

YOUR EYES ARE LIKE TWO PINK FLAMINGOS, BEATING THEIR

Write a love letter to the mailman.

Wear your red heels. Hold back no reserve. Confess your undying passion. "Darling, Neither rain nor hail nor sleet nor snow will keep me from your arms, 9-5, Monday through Saturday,"or, "I think of you when I lick stamps." Hand it to him personally.

MY THOUGHTS TURN TO YOU AND OUR LONG STROLLS TO THE SUPER-MARKET.

Day 262

Dear Audrey, this was a good attempt. May we point out however, that your drawing skills are moderate. To highlight the topic of love in your concept you could have used a photograph, like this one for example (a postman in his sexual prime):

Benrik Check-up

By accepting this Book as a gift or purchasing it, you have legally committed yourself to following it. Today Benrik need to check on your progress. If you have been diligent, you have nothing to fear from this test. If you fail, however, we will know you have not been doing your daily tasks, and will have to ask you to return the Book to the bookshop.

Answer this multiple choice test and send it to us. You will be notified of the results within 3 weeks.

NO PEEKING!

1. For how long were you asked to think about Ada Peach?
a)30 seconds b)15 minutes c)5 hours

2. What word terrifies the Arctic papoose?
a)Nootaikok b)Amaguq c)Nanootik

3. Who do Benrik suggest you draw on Day 226?
a)Donald Duck b)God c)Benrik

4. Jonas Jansson's sexuality is best described as?
a)Mainstream b)Gay c)Confused

5. Which Benrik amateur wrote "Everybody scream today"?
a)Joel Moss Levinson b)Alex Nicholson c)Tracy Shiraishi

6. How many dollars did the model consumer need to spend?
a)36 b)37 c)38

7. What kind of bird should you release for peace?
a)A pigeon b)An eagle c)A dove

8. How much money do Benrik suggest you transfer on Day 34?
a)$17.99 b)$1000 c)All your money

9. Who wrote "Spazzing: the art of inarticulacy"?
a)D. Heisenger b)G. Klage c)S. Weissmarker

10. How does the winning genetic code on Day 130 end?
a)ATTAGTA b)AAAGGTA c)GGGATTGG

11. Which small African country counts the most Benrik fans?
a)Lesotho b)Angola c)Swaziland

12. Which phone area code people are dark and mysterious?
a)323 b)212 c)716

13. What is the Esperanto word for dominatrix?
a)Domino b)Dominati c)Seksmastrinon

14. How deep can the Drillmaster II dig?
a)10m b)50m c)200m

15. What is the going rate for Japanese schoolgirl soiled underwear?
a)$29 b)$56 c)$99

16. What is the name of Celine's baby?
a)Henri-Martin Dupre b) Rene-Charles Angelil c)Louis-Celine Dion

17. How much do Benrik's lawyers charge per hour?
a)$150 b)$350 c)$700

Send to: Benrik Limited
You should know the address by now!

Day 263

PLEASE WEAR THIS STICKER ON YOUR BACK TODAY

If this sticker's message is not appropriate to your location, circumstances or personality, here are some others you may enlarge with a color photocopier.

Day 264

CALL A CALL CENTER IN INDIA AND GET THE STAFF TO TEACH YOU ABOUT THEIR CULTURE FOR A CHANGE

More and more companies are outsourcing their call centers to India, where the workforce is cheap and all speak perfect English. Staff are even made to watch TV programs like *Friends* or *Dharma and Greg* in order to understand American culture. But why should the cultural interchange be one-way only? Take this golden opportunity to ask questions and learn about everyday life in India. Don't worry how long the telephone call lasts, it's courtesy of some multinational corporation!

Day 265

TRY ANY TOLL-FREE NUMBER AND GET THROUGH TO BANGALORE!

HELP THE HOMELESS!

**Thousands on our streets!
Please give generously!
Winter is coming!**

AFRICA ACTION
**MILLIONS ARE AT RISK.
MILLIONS FACE DROUGHT.
MILLIONS LOOK TO YOU...**

TODAY, DO SOME GOOD FOR A CHANGE: WALK THE STREETS RAISING MONEY FOR CHARITY. THERE'S NO NEED TO REGISTER, JUST FIND A TIN AND A RATTLE, AND GLUE ONE OF THESE FINE HANDY CUT-OUTS AROUND IT.

EVERY YEAR 100's OF ELDERLY DIE. PLEASE HELP US SAVE THEM

BENRiK

THESE AUTHORS BADLY
NEED YOUR CASH TO
FUND THEIR UNHEALTHY
LIFESTYLE CHOICES

Day 266

Get struck by lightning today

Getting struck by lightning has many beneficial side-effects, such as curing major illness and bestowing psychic powers. It's also an interesting conversational tidbit, provided you survive. Here's how you make it happen, weather permitting.

1. WAIT FOR A STORM

2. FIND AN OPEN FIELD

3. STAND ON THE HIGHEST GROUND

4. HOLD UP AN UMBRELLA

5. GET STRUCK – OUCHHHHH!

Day 267

TODAY LIST ALL YOUR FRIENDS AND ACQUAINTANCES AND PRUNE THEM.

According to anthropologist Robin Dunbar, the part of the human brain that deals with social interaction is only wired to cope with 150 people. Beyond that, alienation and aggression rear their ugly heads. List everyone you know below, and cut the dead weight.

FRIENDS

1.....................
2.....................
3.....................
4.....................
5.....................
6.....................
7.....................
8.....................
9.....................
10....................
11....................
12....................
13....................
14....................
15....................
16....................
17....................
18....................
19....................
20....................
21....................
22....................
23....................
24....................
25....................
26....................
27....................
28....................
29....................
30....................
31....................
32....................
33....................
34....................
35....................
36....................
37....................
38....................
39....................
40....................
41....................
42....................
43....................
44....................
45....................
46....................
47....................
48....................
49....................
50....................

ACQUAINTANCES

51....................
52....................
53....................
54....................
55....................
56....................
57....................
58....................
59....................
60....................
61....................
62....................
63....................
64....................
65....................
66....................
67....................
68....................
69....................
70....................
71....................
72....................
73....................
74....................
75....................
76....................
77....................
78....................
79....................
80....................
81....................
82....................
83....................
84....................
85....................
86....................
87....................
88....................
89....................
90....................
91....................
92....................
93....................
94....................
95....................
96....................
97....................
98....................
99....................
100...................

101...................
102...................
103...................
104...................
105...................
106...................
107...................
108...................
109...................
110...................
111...................
112...................
113...................
114...................
115...................
116...................
117...................
118...................
119...................
120...................
121...................
122...................
123...................
124...................
125...................
126...................
127...................
128...................
129...................
130...................
131...................
132...................
133...................
134...................
135...................
136...................
137...................
138...................
139...................
140...................
141...................
142...................
143...................
144...................
145...................
146...................
147...................
148...................
149...................
150...................

GET RID OF THESE GUYS

151...................
152...................
153...................
154...................
155...................
156...................
157...................
158...................
159...................
160...................
161...................
162...................
163...................
164...................
165...................
166...................
167...................
168...................
169...................
170...................
171...................
172...................
173...................
174...................
175...................
176...................
177...................
178...................
179...................
180...................
182...................
183...................
184...................
185...................
186...................
187...................
188...................
189...................
190...................

NOW YOU'RE JUST LYING

191...................
192...................
193...................
194...................
195...................
196...................
197...................
198...................
199...................
200...................

Day 268

HELP REMOVE THE METEORITE!

METEORITE ZELDA On April 4th, 2008, meteorite Zelda crashed through the ionosphere and straight into London. Known since then only as "404," this cataclysmic event immediately wiped out 6,500,000 lives, a third of them across the channel as a huge tidal wave engulfed the French, Belgian and Dutch coasts. Since then half of Europe has been reduced to three hours of (faint) sunlight a day, as the dust from the impact still saturates the atmosphere. The Gulf Stream has reversed course, a state of emergency has been declared on both sides of the Atlantic, and food rationing is back. The core of the meteorite is still embedded in the remains of what was once known as "England's garden." Today join the thousands who make it their business to remove it chunk by chunk. Let's do it for our greatgreatgreatgreatgreatgreatgreatgreatgreatgreatgreatgreatgreatgreatgrandchildren!

Day 269

Today make a pact with the devil

Fill in this standard satanic contract with your own blood, which must be drawn from your left arm.

Dear Lucifer

I, ..., wish to make a pact with you.

In exchange for my soul, you will grant me great power/vast wealth (cross out) for the next .... years (to be agreed). I undertake to abide by the rules of the damned, accept the Devil's mark, sacrifice children to you and generally make a satanic nuisance of myself.

Signed and dated in my blood,

....

To register this pact with the devil, stand within a magic circle and recite the following invocation: LUCIFER, Emperor, Master of All Rebellious Spirits, I beseech thee to be favorable to me in calling upon thy GREAT MINISTER which I make, desiring thus to make a pact with him. BEELZEBUB, Prince, I pray thee also, to protect me in my undertaking. ASTAROTH, Count, be propitious to me and cause that this night the GREAT DEMON appear to me in human form and without any evil smell, and that he grant me, by means of the pact which I shall deliver to him, all the treasures of which I shall have need. GREAT DEMON, I beseech thee, leave thy dwelling, in whatever part of the world you may be, to come speak with me; if not, I shall thereto compel thee by the power of the mighty words of the Great Key of Solomon, whereof he made use to force the rebellious spirits to accept his pact. Appear then instantly or I shall continually torment thee with the mighty words of the Key: AGLON, TETRAGRAMMATON, ICION, STIMULAMATHON, EROHARES, RETRASAMATHON, ONERA, VAYCHEON, ESITION, EXISTIEN, ERYONA, CLYORAN, ERASYN, MOYN, MEFFIAS, SOTER, EMMANUEL, SABAOTH, ADONAI. I call you. AMEN. When the demon appears, simply hand him the pact and get a receipt. Congratulations! You have successfully sold your soul. May you rot in hell!

Day 270

TODAY COMMUNICATE BY ULTRASOUND ONLY

Why limit yourself to the conventional sound waves? All manner of animals obey instructions in the language of high frequencies. There is a rich conversation out there which humans don't participate in as much as they could. Today get hold of a dog whistle from your local pet store and enter the fascinating world of ultrasound communication.

How to use your dog whistle ultrasound device (THAT YOU WILL BUY TODAY!)

Set it to audible tone so you can hear a very faint version of what's really going on. Place the whistle between your lips, holding it in place with forefinger and thumb, and press lightly with your tongue, changing the pursing of your lips as you blow. Do not blow too hard or you will end up with a whistle full of dribble. Eventually, after a few years, when you master it, you will no longer need to hold it with your hand as much.

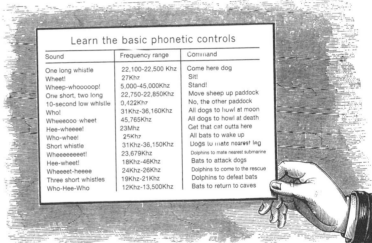

Learn the basic phonetic controls

Sound	Frequency range	Command
One long whistle	22,100-22,500 Khz	Come here dog
Wheet!	27Khz	Sit!
Wheep-whooooop!	5,000-45,000Khz	Stand!
One short, two long	22,750-22,850Khz	Move sheep up paddock
10-second low whistle	9,422Khz	No, the other paddock
Who!	31Khz-36,160Khz	All dogs to howl at moon
Wheeeooo wheet	45,765Khz	All dogs to howl at death
Hee-wheeee!	23Mhz	Get that cat outta here
Who-whee!	25Khz	All bats to wake up
Short whistle	31Khz-36,150Khz	Dogs to mate nearest leg
Wheeeeeeeet!	23,679Khz	Dolphins to mate nearest submarine
Hee-wheet!	18Khz-46Khz	Bats to attack dogs
Wheeeet-heeee	24Khz-26Khz	Dolphins to come to the rescue
Three short whistles	19Khz-21Khz	Dolphins to defeat bats
Who-Hee-Who	12Khz-13,500Khz	Bats to return to caves

Day 271

TODAY, GIVE YOURSELF
A HAIRCUT.

FIG. 1

FIG. 2

I never got your e-mail.

I paid you for that coffee a minute ago.

I gave you that report yesterday!

Of course I'm wearing a condom.

The president just got shot!

Be a pathological liar for a day

He's a well-known child molester, I read it in the paper.

You don't have a daddy.

Don't worry, I'm a doctor.

What do you mean you're my wife? I've never even met you before.

Today lie your ass off about absolutely everything and enjoy a much more stimulating existence.

Day 273

**Today, fake your own kidnapping
and see if anyone pays the ransom**

We HAVE......................
NOthiNG WiLL HarM
HeR/hiM if $50,000
are Left HeRE:
..........................by
SAtuRDay at NOOn.
Do Not coNtact
the pOLiCe or sHe/
he WiLLdiE HoRriBLy.
NO TriCKs!
SignEd: AnOnyMUs

Today, make your childhood complete. Was there ever anything you really wanted as a child but you never actually got? Maybe there was a toy you wanted but never got, maybe there was a film you wanted to see but weren't allowed to, maybe a place you wanted to visit? Spend today plugging that gaping hole in your childhood.

Day 275

ACT LIKE A MAJOR ASSHOLE

Today, call the phone book people saying they've misspelt your name and you'll sue unless they pulp and reprint all current copies

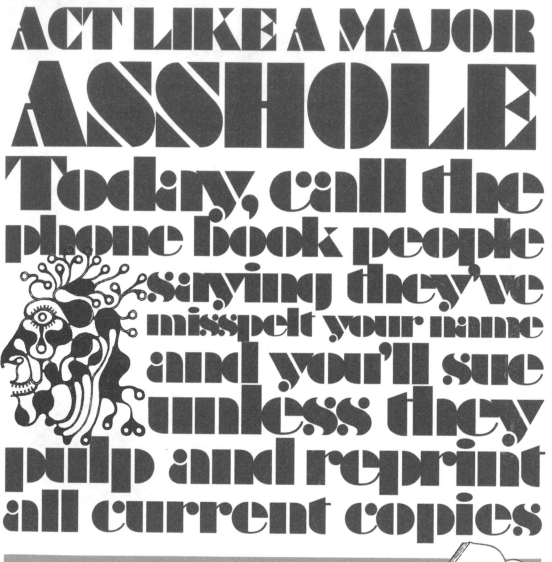

Day 276

Today act like you're invisible

Experience one of mankind's oldest moral quandaries: what would you do if you could get away with anything? Plato tells the tale of Gyges, shepherd to the King of Lydia, who finds a golden ring that confers invisibility on he who wears it. As soon as he realizes his power, Gyges gets sent to the court where he sleeps with the Queen and assassinates the King, taking his place. You may not want to go quite as far, but explore your hold on justice nonetheless. Would you steal, grope, murder? As ever, Benrik's legal disclaimer applies...

"If you could imagine anyone obtaining this power of becoming invisible, and never doing any wrong or touching what was another's, he would be thought by the lookers-on to be a most wretched idiot, although they would praise him to one another's faces, and keep up appearances with one another from a fear that they too might suffer injustice." (Plato, The Republic, Book II)

Day 277

Today

Traffic Russian Roulette is all the rage amongst the restless youth in the vast suburbs of Ukrainian dormitory towns. It's easy to take part, less easy to win. The idea is simply to cross the road without looking. Start with an easy road and progress to the trickier ones.

1 *Path in your local park*
Threats: dogs, joggers, pushchairs.
Risk: low.

2 *Country lane*
Threats: cows, tractors, idiots in sports cars.
Risk: some.

3 *Main road*
Threats: cars, buses, trucks.
Risks: high.

4 *German autobahn*
Threats: Mercedes, BMW, Porsche.
Risks: insane.

Day 278

GIVE ME A HUG **GOD DAMN IT!**

Give away free hugs

Spread a little love today you sexy beast you...
Here are the six officially recognized hugging styles

Standard hug

Grandma hug

Sexpest hug

Pickpocket hug

Self-hug

Porno hug

Freeform hugging Freeform hugging is only to be attempted when you have mastered the above.
Many amateur huggers have developed cramps, injuring both themselves and the huggee.

Day 279

Day 280

CLASS ACTION LAWSUIT DAY

Benrik are filing class action lawsuits on behalf of their readers. If you feel you qualify for damages based on the description of the class action, then mark the relevant lawsuit(s), fill in the detailed form below and send it to our legal team.

■ THE SCHOOL SYSTEM
For wrongful imprisonment between the ages of 4 and 18, in violation of the Declaration Of Rights Of The Child (1959, Part 1 Art.3.1.2 & 3.1.3).

■ MAKERS OF CUDDLY TOYS
For instilling us with feelings of affection for inanimate objects, the memory of which later stunted our emotional and sexual lives.

■ THE MASSACHUSETTS INSTITUTE OF TECHNOLOGY
For allowing Edward Lorenz to discover chaos theory, thereby undermining 20th-century man's already shaky relationship with the universe.

■ SOFT DRINK MANUFACTURERS
For funding the oppressive communist regime in Angola in the 1970s, perpetuating the legacy of oppression of the Portuguese.

DATE OF INJUSTICE:..................................Details of complaint (damages you have suffered, including emotional damages)...
I want at least this much compensation ....$

A class action lawsuit is a lawsuit in which the plaintiff represents a number of people, all engaged in similar claims against the defendant. The plaintiff is known as the class representative. A plaintiff may for instance bring a claim against the manufacturer of a drug with hidden side-effects, on behalf of him or herself and others affected by the side-effects. Class action lawsuits make it economically and logistically possible for hundreds or thousands to sue a large wrongdoer, where pursuing their claims individually would prove difficult and expensive in relation to likely damages. The class members share any eventual damages amongst themselves.

Day 281

Today start your very own religion

Religion doesn't just cater to spiritual needs, it's also very big business. Most of the current faiths have been around for a long while, so it's time for a new kid on the block. Today invent your own set of beliefs and cash in on people's deepest fears.

Name

If you have a catchy surname, like Christ, then you'd be daft not to use it. Examples of good names include Stern, Ryke or Kharg – basically anything that sounds important with -ology or -ianism appended. Less good names might include Smith, Brown or Crawford. It helps if the name sounds vaguely eastern and hints at animal sacrifice.

Gods

You may want to feature several gods for the sake of variety. If so, try to link them to awe-inspiring animals, like the lion, the eagle, the serpent or perhaps the owl. The modern approach, however, is to concentrate on one god. It helps the believers focus, and is so much easier from a branding viewpoint. Again, scary names work best. Think Urgg, Drakkar or Achaemon.

Book

You will need a Holy Book, wherein you codify your religion. This is to guarantee your intellectual property rights over the religion. Sales of the Holy Book will also provide a valuable revenue stream. Be sure to write it in vague language, so that you will need to be consulted as to its precise meaning. Claim that the Book was dictated to you on a hill of some sort, by Urgg, Drakkar, Achaemon or other.

Rituals

Worship is a major part of religion, and gives your believers something to do. Provide for daily prayers, but keep them short and sweet. No one has time for lengthy get-togethers these days. You will want to create one special day a year though, where you will gather with your flock. Again, animal sacrifice does seem to draw the crowds, although communal singing is also a firm favorite.

Afterlife

This is pretty important. People will be more likely to sign up if there's a reward. You'll find it difficult to beat the Christian combination of Heaven for the faithful and Eternal Hell for the rest. Perhaps some form of cloned immortality might do the trick, although science could beat you to it. Certainly unbelievers need an incentive scheme to join.

Prophet

People want to hear it straight from the horse's mouth. If you want to be taken seriously, you will have to take on the mantle of prophet yourself. This is not without its dangers. Would-be prophets have been shot, burned and drowned, not to mention crucified. But the rewards are substantial. Fame, money and women could be yours, provided your religion allows them. Good luck!

Tip: Aliens provide a plausible basis for religion. Try to include them in some shape or form, if only to attract the affluent Californian market.

MEET YOUR MAKER   LET THE KIDS COME TO ME   FATHER, FORGIVE THEM   I AM THE LIGHT   WALK THIS WAY   MY CLOSEST FRIEND IS ALWAYS NEAR ME   A CHILD IS BORN IN BETHLEHEM   WATERWALKER

Day 282

CORPORATE GAMES DAY

Don't let office routine get you down this year. Liven up proceedings by insisting that everyone in your company spend Friday afternoon playing. The following games are team-building, lessen workplace stress, teach modern corporate values, and they're fun!

HIDE & SEEK Everyone hides from the boss, those who don't get found in the first five minutes get fired for absenteeism.

SIMON SAYS Also known as Roger says, Gerry says, Richard says, Hilary says, Peter says, depending on the name of your boss.

TAG One player is labelled "office loser." He/she chases the others and tries to touch them to transfer the "office loser" label.

SPIN THE BOTTLE
Everyone sits around the boardroom table. Players spin the bottle, and have to sexually harass the player the bottle points at.

Day 283

SPEED DAY

TODAY YOU MUST GO ABOVE 100MPH

The rush to the head that speed provokes is the defining sensation of our times. We've even named a drug after it. Today fly, drive or ride a rollercoaster. Only make sure you break your speed limit.

The world's magnificence has been enriched by a new beauty: the beauty of speed. A racing automobile with its bonnet adorned with great tubes like serpents with explosive breath ... a roaring motor car which seems to run on machine-gun fire, is more beautiful than the Victory of Samothrace (Filippo Tommaso Marinetti)

Too bad he was a fascist

ACHTUNG! If you choose to drive, make sure you're on an autobahn!

Day 284

Today, eat or drink something older than yourself

There is something deliciously unnatural about ingesting matter that predates you on this planet. Pick one of the following and consume it.

WINE (0 TO 150 YEARS)

Nothing could be simpler than drinking wine older than yourself; stroll down to the nearest merchant and buy a bottle from the year before your birth. Bordeaux is a safe bet, although the risk-takers might pick a Burgundy. If the wine is very old, it will react extremely quickly to air. Leave it for 10 minutes to dissipate any "bottle-stink," then enjoy it in the next half an hour, before the evanescent aroma of decades vanishes into thin clear air.

WHISKY (10 TO 70 YEARS)

A great bottle of single-malt Scotch should keep for the average human life span. It is only after 12 years in cask that it can truly be considered for drinking. If you can afford it, try the 1937 Glenfiddich, which only became fully drinkable in 2001. It's the oldest whisky in the world. There are only 60 odd bottles left worldwide. One will cost you $80,000 at the very least. But you're guaranteed a taste of history.

DRIED MUSHROOMS (50 TO 70 YEARS)

In the north of Japan, farmers preserve Maitake mushrooms by drying them on the slopes of the Ishikari volcanic mountains. Then they use a unique mix of whale blubber and spices to seal them into man-sized urns, which they bury for a minimum of 50 years. The result? A moreish treat with delicate yet earthy overtones, prized for its cancer-inhibiting properties. Simply brush off the dirt, soak in 23°C water for 5 hours, and fry gently for 10 minutes in extract of soya oil.

HANGAI YAK CHEESE (14 TO 60 YEARS)

This hard cheese is the longest-lived milk-based product in the history of food preservation. This is due in no small measure to the freezing climate of the Mongolian lowlands, where it is produced. The Hangai yak feeds on relatively acidic grasslands that provide the milk with some natural preservatives, which the Mongols then top up with rennet. The cheese itself is an acquired taste. Dense and pungent, with an inch-thick rind, it is normally enjoyed as a meal on its own.

SALTED BEEF (5 TO 50 YEARS)

Salting of meat is an ancient preservation technique, particularly favored by the Romans. Perhaps this is why some of the best salted beef comes from the Italian region of Trentino. By using only the finest cuts and mixing in some salpeter, the locals are able to hang them for up to 50 years, by which time they have developed a layer of scrumptious fine moss. Once you've got your hands on some (no easy task!), just bring it to boil and leave to simmer with some marjoram for three hours per kilo. Serve cold with beetroot and/or radishes.

100-YEAR-OLD TURTLE SOUP

If your palate is jaded or you are already older than most of these delicacies, there is but one treat left for you: Chinese turtle soup made from century-old turtles. You will need to travel to Hunan, as export of food made from this endangered species is prohibited. There, you will need to scour the backstreets for the wily peasants who are still proficient in the art of hunting and deboning these increasingly rare ancestral beasts. The going rate for a bowl of this soup of soups is $3,000. NB: This trip is not recommended for anyone over 95 years old.

Day 285

PASS A NOTE ON PUBLIC TRANSPORT TODAY

PLEASE PASS THIS ON TO:
YOU LOOK TIRED. WOULD YOU LIKE TO COME AND SIT ON MY LAP?

PLEASE PASS THIS ONTO: WERE WE NOT AT SCHOOL TOGETHER? YOUR FACE IS STRANGELY FAMILIAR.

PLEASE PASS THIS ON TO: WHERE IS THIS BUS GOING AGAIN? I'VE COMPLETELY FORGOTTEN

Please pass this on to: STOP STARING AT MY CLEAVAGE OR I'LL CALL U A PERVERT OUT LOUD.

PLEASE PASS THIS ONTO: THE GUY IN FRONT OF ME HAS DANDRUFF! TELL THE OTHERS!

Please pass this on to: YOUR SHOELACE IS UNTIED, YOU IDIOT. FALL OVER DON'T YOU!

Please pass this on to: May I compliment you on your hat? I have the same at home.

Please pass this on to: This train has been hijacked by extremists. Be ready to act when I say.

PLEASE PASS THIS NOTE ON TO: I HAVE RUBBED THIS NOTE ON MY GENITALS! AND NOW YOU'VE TOUCHED IT!

On the bus to work i'm never alone

Day 286

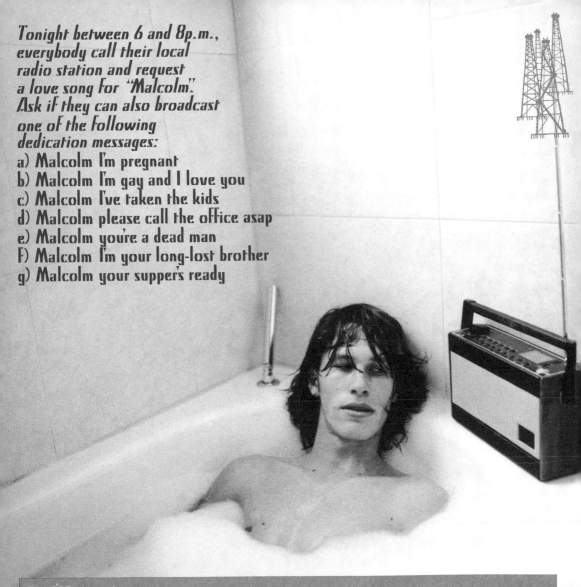

Tonight between 6 and 8p.m., everybody call their local radio station and request a love song for "Malcolm". Ask if they can also broadcast one of the following dedication messages:
a) Malcolm I'm pregnant
b) Malcolm I'm gay and I love you
c) Malcolm I've taken the kids
d) Malcolm please call the office asap
e) Malcolm you're a dead man
f) Malcolm I'm your long-lost brother
g) Malcolm your supper's ready

Day 287

Today
Sabotage Hollywood

Go to movies and shout out the ending to help people realize
how predictable most big studio productions are.

APOLLO 13
They don't make the
moon, but return safely.

BASIC INSTINCT
Sharon Stone did it!

CASABLANCA
Ilsa leaves Casablanca
without Rick.

DEEP IMPACT
The shuttle crew blow
themselves up with the
comet and save us.

E.T.
The other aliens
rescue him.

FORREST GUMP
Forrest's Mum and Jenny
die, but leave Forrest with
a baby.

GLADIATOR
Russell Crowe kills the
emperor but dies.

HALLOWEEN
They think they've killed
him, but they haven't!

INDEPENDENCE DAY
They disable the alien
shield and nuke them all.

JAWS
Schneider blows
the shark up and
swims home.

KARATE KID
Daniel wins.

LOVE ACTUALLY
The Prime Minister
marries the tea lady.

**MISSION:
IMPOSSIBLE**
Everything has been set
up by Jon Voight.

NOTTING HILL
They get
married,
she gets
pregnant.

**OCEAN'S
ELEVEN**
The SWAT team
are the conmen.

PEARL HARBOR
The Japanese lose the war.

QUIZ SHOW
The hoax is exposed.

**RAIDERS OF
THE LOST ARK**
Indy recaptures the Ark
for the US government.

**SAVING PRIVATE
RYAN**
The old man at the
beginning is Ryan.

**THELMA
AND LOUISE**
They commit suicide by
driving off
a cliff.

**USUAL
SUSPECTS**
Kevin Spacey has
made everything up.

VANILLA SKY
Too
complicated
to explain.

**WHEN HARRY
MET SALLY...**
Meg Ryan and Billy Crystal
eventually get together.

XXX
Vin Diesel
triumphs over the bad
guys.

**YOU'VE
GOT MAIL**
Meg Ryan and Tom Hanks
eventually get together.

ZULU
The Zulus
recognize their bravery
and let them survive.

Day 288

Today add "von"
to your surname
to see if people treat
you differently

The German nobility has an undeniable mystique. From medieval knights to temperamental Hollywood directors, the "von" prefix oozes aristocratic reserve. Adopt it and notice the deference.

Before   *After*

Danny Higgins   Danny Von Higgins

How to substantiate your claim to noble German descent: unfortunately, a "von" alone is no guarantee of pedigree. In Northern and Eastern Germany, a large number of families use it purely to indicate their town of origin e.g. Johann von Freiburg. Should some nosy snob demand proof of your lineage, you may resort to the following double-bluff: "My great-great-grandfather killed the King and so was expelled from the family who erased all records and exiled him to America. I know this because my great-great-aunt told me with her last dying breath."

Day 289

AMATEUR PAGE

10

From: Billy Wagar
Crawley,
UK

Today get everyone in the office, classroom, street etc to whistle the same tune as you untill every one you know cannot get it out of their head.

Day 290

Today, divine the will of your ancestors

There is no reason why the ancient Etruscan art of haruspicy, better known as entrail-reading, cannot be practiced in our day and age. Before you roast a chicken tonight, take time to "read" it and learn what fate has in store.

Swollen liver?
You face
military defeat

Enlarged goiter?
Your tumble dryer
will break down

Unusually
protuberant veins?
You will miss
your plane

Purple spots?
Your daughter
will elope with a
Nubian

Dry patches?
The Furies are
after your head

Dark yellow
kidneys?
This chicken is past
its sell-by date

Small oesophagus?
Go into exile now

Fatty tissue?
Prepare to face
a tax audit

Strange little
white bones?
You are entrail-
reading a fish

And remember – it used to have a life – just like you and me!

Day 291

MAKE YOUR BOSS NOTICE YOU TODAY.

Walk back and forth in front of his office in deep thought, yelling out EUREKA. When you're on the phone, shake your fist in triumph. Crack open a bottle of champagne whenever he looks up. Your boss will form the impression that you're the one to watch and you'll be guaranteed a fat pay raise.

Day 292

!!!POISONED PAGE!!!

Today make your mortal enemy touch this page, which is poisoned with a cyanide compound ink. The ink will kill your enemy for good within 3 minutes, just long enough for you to explain your motives and chuckle as they writhe in agony. As you do so their tongue will turn green and attempt to slither out of their mouth. Their innards will gently liquefy, their eyeballs retract into their skull, their saliva boil, and they will feel overall pain.

HOW TO CONVINCE THEM TO TOUCH IT:

YOU'RE TOO CHICKEN TO TOUCH THIS AREN'T YOU?

NO IT'S NOT POISONED THAT'S A TYPO DON'T WORRY.

I PROMISE YOU WON'T WRITHE IN AGONY.

LOOK AT THE PRETTY COLOR, DON'T U WONDER WHAT IT FEELS LIKE TO TOUCH?

Day 293

Benrikchalking Day

American hoboes in the Depression communicated through rough chalk symbols on sidewalks, fences and buildings, to let each other know what to expect in that area. More recently it's been used to advertise wireless access points. But the potential is much greater. Today, chalk the streets near you in Benrik signs, to let your fellow readers know the salient features of your neighborhood.

Hobo sign language

Kind hearted lady	Unsafe place
Talk religion to get food	Work available
Judge lives here	No alcohol town
Bad water	Hoboes arrested on sight
Free telephone	Rich people live here

Bad tempered owner	Crooks!
Owner out	Gentleman
Man with guns	Hold your tongue
Vicious dog here	Good place to catch a train

Benrik sign language

Dog with diarrhea	Woman with evil laugh
Bad haircuts here	Conscientious butcher
Celebrity often has coffee here	Small child pees from balcony
Household with widescreen TV	Watch your change in here
Very loud kettle	Double pram zone

Don't order the prawns in here!	Nudist couple in window above
Farty shopkeeper	Road rage intersection
Housewife with forlorn smile	Cappuccinos extra frothy
Man plays saxophone badly	Pee here if really can't hold it

Day 294

Last year, Benrik asked readers to help create the world's longest poem, starting with the line "Mercy, cried the popinjay to the pope." The results have been impressive, so much so that we only have room to print 5% of the poem below. We still have not seen a suitable final line, though. Today, contribute one on www.thiswebsitewillchangeyourlife.com so we can end the poem!

Today make your heart beat faster

Martial arts masters learn to control the "autonomic" body functions, like the heartbeat or blood pressure, which theoretically are outside our conscious control. Today make an effort to accelerate your subconscious vital functions and find out if you have a knack for it.

Heart rate
Normal: 60–180 bpm
Target today: 300 bpm

Day 296

LIVE BY THE SCOUT CODE OF HONOR TODAY

Some chaps say scouting is just for kids. Well, that idea is plain wrong! The high-minded principles laid down by Robert Baden-Powell in 1907 are just as useful to grown-ups. Today, even if you've never had a scouting experience as a child, endorse those fine values and put them into practice in your daily life.

First up, take the Scout Promise

> On my honor I promise that I will do my best,
> To do my duty to God and to the Queen,
> To help other people at all times,
> And to obey the Scout Law.

Repeat this promise to yourself at least once set each. Now, read on to work out how to apply the Scout promise and the Scout Laws to your lifestyle.

Approach a homeless chap and make inquiries. Why does he lie there in such unscout-like spirit instead of fetching himself a job? Urge him to shape up at the double, or you'll see the law on the fellow!

Volunteer for the Samaritans. When chaps feel down in the mouth, what they need isn't hangdog advice, but some cheery companionship! Tell the funny beggars to stop being bloody milksops and to start wearing a merry smile!

Stop a fight. Sometimes when pals have had one too many beverages (!), they quarrel and think it fun to have a bout. Ask them to desist and exchange the heartiest of handshakes. And don't mind if they scoff at you.

The Ten Scout Laws

> A Scout's honor is to be trusted
> A Scout is loyal to Queen and Country, other scouters, parents, and employers
> A Scout obeys orders of his parents, and scout authorities
> A Scout's duty is to be useful and to help others without reward
> A Scout is a friend to all no matter to what nationality, class, race or creed they belong
> A Scout is courteous
> A Scout is a friend to animals and nature
> A Scout smiles cheerfully even under difficulties
> A Scout is thrifty and self-reliant
> A Scout is clean in word and deed

Day 297

Make a non-obscene phone call today
Call a stranger at random and whisper
nice things about them down the line

Your phone has
a lovely ring

I admire the way you
keep your front garden
so well-tended

Your voice is so strong
I bet you're a baritone

Do I hear
children in
the back-
ground,
they sound
beautiful

I noticed your name
as soon as I opened
the phone book

Every word you say has
the feel of self-confidence

If no one's home, leave a message: Hello this is just to
prepare you mentally for when I come up to you in the
street and hug you tight you don't know me but I feel
like I've known you a very long time now and I just
think you're super, so don't worry, I could tell you what
I look like but that would ruin the surprise anyway I
look forward to meeting you very soon good night
CLICK

I bet if we met
we'd be friends
straightaway

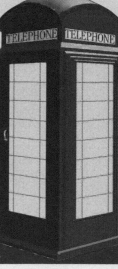

Maybe it's a fancy, but I could swear I can
smell your sweet scent down the phone

Even when you swear it
sounds like pure poetry

Don't hang up, I want this
conversation to last forever

TODAY LOBBY CELINE DION TO SING ABOUT YOU

Celine Dion has enjoyed a meteoric rise to global fame. She has sold over 130 million records worldwide and now stars in one of the most successful live shows in the history of entertainment. But her wide repertoire of songs has not yet featured you. Today write to her and suggest yourself as a fertile song topic, detailing your life story and how you think you would fit thematically into her oeuvre.

WRITE TO: CELINE DION, A NEW DAY, CAESARS PALACE, 3570 LAS VEGAS BOULEVARD, LAS VEGAS, NV89109, USA

Here is Celine's life to inspire you with emotional connections between your journey and hers.
Celine was born in 1968 in a picturesque small town in Quebec named Charlemagne. The youngest of 14 children (!), she learned the art of entertainment early on, performing with her siblings for the benefit of the locals in her parents' pianobar. At the age of 12, she announced to her mother that she wanted to sing. They composed a song together and contacted one of Montreal's pre-eminent managers, Rene Angelil, in January 1981. Rene was so entranced by Celine's voice that he cried. He then remortgaged to finance her first album and set about introducing her talent to the world! She became an overnight sensation in her native Quebec with her French-language single "La voix du bon dieu" ("The voice of God"), written by Eddy Marnay – apparently the words that Marnay exclaimed when he first heard her sing. International success swiftly followed, when she won the gold medal at the Yamaha World Song Festival in Tokyo barely a year after her debut. The next five years saw her become a huge star in the French-speaking world, with classic hit albums such as "Du Soleil Au Coeur" and "Incognito," which went platinum.
Her global breakthrough came in 1988, when she won the Eurovision Song contest, singing "Ne partez pas sans moi" for Switzerland, wowing 600 million viewers throughout the world in the process! In September 1990 she capitalized on this by releasing *Unison*, her first English language album, which scored a huge hit in the US with the Top 5 single "Where Does My Heart Beat Now." But this was just the beginning! In 1991 she sang the title soundtrack for Disney's *The Beauty and the Beast*, which rocketed to No.1 and won an Academy Award as well as a Grammy. Celine by now was unstoppable, with her eponymous album *Celine Dion* spawning no less than FOUR more hit singles.
To top it all off, Celine had found love. Rene Angelil was 26 years her senior, yet love knows no such barriers. Their admiration and respect for each other had grown into something more, and on December 17, 1994, they married in Montreal, to the delight of her fans.
Meanwhile her worldwide success showed no sign of abating. "D'Eux" broke through the French language barrier in 1995 to become the biggest-selling French hit in history, netting Celine the knighthood of the order of arts and letters from the French government for being the "best ambassadress of the French language." Merci beaucoup! In Britain she topped the charts for weeks with the ballad "Think Twice," which sold over a million copies.
This success, however, was all but eclipsed in 1996 and 1997 when successive albums *Falling Into You* and *Let's Talk About Love* sold roughly 30 million worldwide – each! The song "My Heart Will Go On," movie theme song of *Titanic*, won an Oscar and became a favorite wedding song for fans of Celine. The Nineties were fittingly topped by an authorized biography by Georges-Hebert Germain and a collection of greatest hits, *All The Way...A Decade of Song*, which featured such classics as "The Power Of Love," "Because You Loved Me," and "If You Asked Me To," along with some brand new songs.
By the end of 1999, Celine was long overdue for a break! She decided to take some well-deserved time off from her hectic schedule. In spite of this, there was an unexpected release for her fans in 2001: her baby son, Rene-Charles Angelil, born on January 25!
After two years off, Celine returned to showbiz in 2002 with a new blockbusting album, *A New Day Has Come*, an immediate No.1 across the globe, with fans reassuring Celine she had not been forgotten! If anything, her schedule has got busier since her break, with several new albums, a perfume launch, and in March 2003, the opening of her own show at Caesar's Palace Las Vegas! Bravo Celine!!!

Day 299

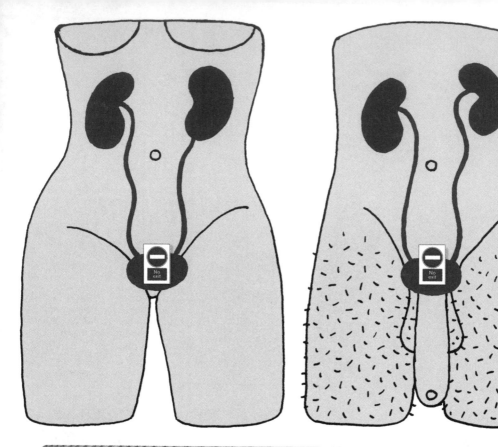

DON'T PEE AT ALL TODAY

When we're all down and out it can be good to know how lucky we are, to be able to pass water for example. Today do not urinate until tomorrow to give you that future satisfaction of knowing that when times are bad, they COULD be worse!

AND KEEP AN EYE ON THIS IMAGE WHILE YOU'RE AT IT WHY DON'T YOU! HAHAHA!

Day 300

TODAY SPEAK LIKE JIM MORRISON
TODAY ONLY SAY THINGS LIKE "5 TO 1, 1 IN 5, NO-ONE HERE
GETS OUT ALIVE NOW," OR "THE MINISTER'S DAUGHTER'S IN
LOVE WITH A SNAKE WHO LIVES IN A WELL BY THE SIDE OF
THE ROAD" OR "HER CUNT GRIPPED HIM LIKE A WARM
FRIENDLY HAND," OR FINALLY, "FATHER, I WANT TO KILL
YOU." RECORD PEOPLE'S REACTIONS.

Day 301

Patronize people all day

Officer, are you quite sure this is illegal?

You've got a real knack for vacuuming darling.

Your novels are very accessible, aren't they?

"In flagrante delicto" - it's latin, your honor.

Oh 'nother, I wish you'd grow up.

Surely you mean 3√454 *(fx-55612165/32.8887)=6, professor?

Aren't you wearing your stethoscope the wrong way round?

That crown is so cute your Majesty, it really suits you.

I admire the way your wife just refuses to follow fashion.

Day 302

Baby Talk Day

Today communicate only as a baby would. You may squeal, giggle, produce wordless noise or cry. If someone breastfeeds you, you've succeeded.

Day 303

Today walk into a police station, announce you're finally giving yourself up, and refuse to say another word.

Shout with joy, then tell the nearest stranger you've just won the lottery. See if they try to become a friend for life.

TODAY JOIN THE FRENCH FOREIGN LEGION

This has always been one of the swiftest ways of changing your life. Leave your sordid past behind and enter a world of French camaraderie and bracing physical standards. The Legion's motto is "March Or Die," which is no longer taken literally, but gives a flavor of their attitude towards slackers.

HOW TO ENLIST:

Simply pop into one of the recruiting centres in France *(like Fort de Nogent, Fontenay sous Bois, 94120, just outside Paris)*. You have to be 18 to 40, unmarried and male. You need to be physically fit, i.e. be able to run a minimum of 3km in less than 12 minutes, do 30 push-ups, and climb a 20ft-long rope without using your feet. If successful (and fewer than 1 in 30 are), you will sign a contract for 5 years and be shipped off to some remote part of Africa to fight anyone who has displeased the French government. If you haven't deserted after your minimum 5 years, you may acquire French citizenship (this is optional). Aux armes!

THE CODE OF HONOR

You will need to memorize this perfectly before receiving your *képi blanc*, the white hat that all legionnaires sport. Learn it and recite it at interview to double your chances.

1. Légionnaire, tu es un volontaire servant la France avec honneur et fidélité.

2. Chaque légionnaire est ton frère d'arme quelle que soit sa nationalité, sa race, sa religion. Tu lui manifestes toujours la solidarité étroite qui doit unir les membres d'une même famille.

3. Respecteux des traditions, attaché à tes chefs, la discipline et la camaraderie sont ta force, le courage et la loyauté tes vertus.

4. Fier de ton état de légionnaire, tu le montres dans ta tenue toujours élégante, ton comportement toujours digne mais modeste, ton casernement toujours net.

5. Soldat d'élite, tu t'entraines avec rigueur, tu entretiens ton arme comme ton bien le plus précieux, tu as le souci constant de ta forme physique.

6. La mission est sacrée, tu l'exécutes jusqu'au bout, à tout prix.

7. Au combat, tu agis sans passion et sans haine, tu respectes les ennemis vaincus, tu n'abandonnes jamais ni tes morts, ni tes blessés, ni tes armes.

FIN

DON'T FORGET TO COMMIT A CRIME FIRST!

Day 306

Fine Dine with Benrik!

The highest bidder will be wined and dined by the authors of *This Book Will Change Your Life, Again!* at a suitably exclusive restaurant. Please send your bid in a sealed envelope c/o Scott Waxman, 85th Avenue, Suite 1101, New York, NY10011. The results will be announced on www.thiswebsitewillchangeyourlife.com.

What's included
If you bid $5-$10: we go dutch
If you bid $10-$20: the apéritifs are on us
If you bid $20-$50: Benrik pay for the drink
If you bid $50-$100: we'll shout you dessert
If you bid $100-$500: the whole meal is on us
If you bid $500-$1000: we tell you the secret of our success
If you bid $10.000 and upwards: one sexual favor of your choice

Day 307

Don't be afraid to draw dinosaurs. According to the latest scientific theories, dinosaurs and men coexisted. God created them both at the same time, and they lived happily together to begin with, at least until foolish Adam and Eve were thrown out of Eden. When the Flood came, the dinosaurs were harder hit because of their size. They drowned in huge numbers, leaving the fossilized remains we've discovered today. The dinosaurs on Noah's Ark survived, however, and went on to breed, in smaller numbers of course. Humans of all cultures have simply known them as dragons. Still today, there is evidence that some may survive deep under the sea. The idea that dinosaurs existed millions of years before Man is mere atheistic propaganda against the Young Earth scientific theory.

Day 308

Attend court today and offer your verdict to the judge

Most trials are open to the public. You've watched enough TV series to know the legal basics. Now put your knowledge into practice. Listen carefully to the evidence, weigh up the pros and cons in your mind, and shout out your verdict as soon as you reach it. The judge will be grateful for your input.

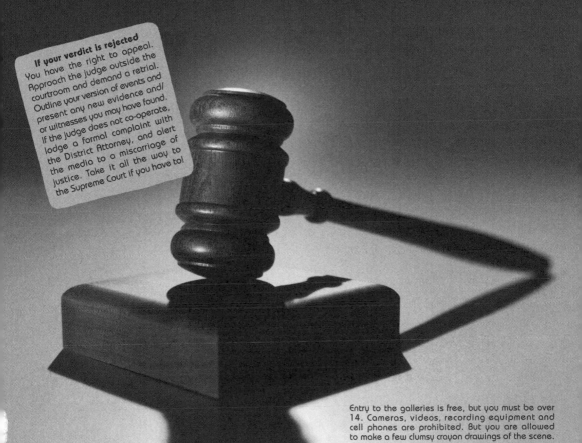

If your verdict is rejected
You have the right to appeal. Approach the judge outside the courtroom and demand a retrial. Outline your version of events and/ or present any new evidence and/ or witnesses you may have found. If the judge does not co-operate, lodge a formal complaint with the District Attorney, and alert the media to a miscarriage of justice. Take it all the way to the Supreme Court if you have to!

Entry to the galleries is free, but you must be over 14. Cameras, videos, recording equipment and cell phones are prohibited. But you are allowed to make a few clumsy crayon drawings of the scene.

Day 309

Found an entirely new city today

Every city once started from scratch, no matter its present size. So will yours. And have patience: Rome wasn't built in a day. This is what you need:

THE FIRST BRICK: this is how cities start, with the founder laying the first brick. Choose a premium handmade brick, that will ensure your city's longevity. You don't need any bricklaying qualifications, as professionals will finish the city for you, but it helps if you try and lay it flat.

A FIELD: find a field with enough room around it for your city to grow (10 miles in every direction should be plenty). If possible the field should be near a major river, as this will help turn your city into a major trading hub. Also, make sure the farmer who owns the field is vaguely aware of your plans.

A NAME: Paris, Milan, Tokyo, Los Angeles...These are glamorous names that have inspired millions of backward peasants to up sticks and move to the bright lights. Tip: try imagining it on a fashion house's letterhead. "Paris Milan Geneva Petaluma," for instance, doesn't work and should have been vetoed.

A STORY: Rome was founded by son of "Mars the war god" Romulus, who was nearly drowned by his evil uncle as a baby, but survived after being suckled by a she-wolf, and returned to kill his uncle, and, soon after, his own brother Remus. Try to come up with something equally catchy.

NEW YORK 1615: BUILT IN 9 DAYS.

LONDON 202 AD: BUILT IN 17 DAYS.

TOKYO 431 BC: BUILT IN 34 DAYS.

PARIS 23 BC: BUILT IN 12 DAYS

Day 310

Today invent a new perversion

The human mind is the ultimate sexual organ, capable of conjuring up erotic pleasure from almost any object. Today test its limits by coming up with a new fetish.

Examples:
These are trademarked. Trying them costs $1 a go, payable to Benrik upon orgasm.

Animalhibitionism
Can only achieve satisfaction if watched by a pet

Opraphilia
Enjoy intercourse in front of live television

Speedophilia
Use of an egg timer in sex play

Masofonism
Aroused by being kept on hold indefinitely

Mediatism
Sex with people who look like a celebrity

Clonophilia
Sex with people who look like you

Day 311

Today make the world a more beautiful place

We're only on Earth for a short while, so we should do our very best to make it pleasant. It doesn't take much: pick up some litter, repaint a fence, or simply stand on a street corner if you're particularly good looking. But do something to prettify our planet today.

Day 312

GET IN TOUCH WITH YOUR HERO TODAY

There is nothing more uplifting than meeting the person you admire most in the world. Take the first step today by approaching your hero and requesting an encounter. Here are some suitable potential heroes if you can't think of any.

Mikhail Gorbachev, Nobel Peace Prize
39 Leningradsky Prospect, bdg. 14,
Moscow 125167, Russia

Jane Fonda, Peace and fitness activist
c/o Fonda, Inc.
PO Box 5840, Atlanta, GA 31107, USA

Nelson Mandela, Nobel Peace Prize
Office of the President
Pretoria 0001, Republic of South Africa

Javier Perez De Cuellar, Fifth UN Secretary
General, c/o UN, United Nations Plaza,
New York, NY 10017, USA

Bjorn Borg, Winner of 5 Wimbledon titles
Stadgarden 10, Box 154 15, 10465
Stockholm, Sweden

Bono, Singer and debt campaigner
Temple Hill, Vico Road
Killiney, Co Dublin, Ireland

Noam Chomsky, Professor/activist
MIT Linguistics and Philosophy Dept.
77 Massachusetts Avenue Bldg. 32-D808
Cambridge, MA 02139, USA

Jimmy Carter, Nobel Peace Prize
Carter Center
One Copenhill, Atlanta, GA 30307, USA

Nana Mouskouri, Singer, UNICEF Goodwill
Ambassador, c/o Mercury – Universal 22, rue
des Fossés St-Jacques, 75005 Paris, France

Day 313

Day 314

Play the stock market today

There's huge money to be made on the stock market, but people are often put off by its seeming complexity, and let's face it, the sheer numbing boredom of trying to fathom those endless figures. And yet it's not rocket science. Benrik have tried to make it more fun, so that anyone can enjoy the experience. Follow our instructions and you too will double your investment and become a trillionaire in no time*.

SELL Any share you can't pronounce immediately (though you can't ask for your money back).

INVEST In high yield bonds (aka "junk" bonds). They go up and down a lot which is more exciting all round.

SELL Shares in companies who do not answer the phone within three rings.

SELL Shares whose price is closest to 666.

GO LONG On Electronics.

GO WIDE On Tobacco.

START By buying a couple of hundred shares at random, while you still enjoy beginners' luck.

BUY Any shares that end in –ex.

SPREAD A rumor that world supplies of salt are about to run out, and buy pepper stocks.

GO SHORT On Mining.

CLOSE by selling everything and pocketing the profits (10% to Benrik).

In 1999, Swedish artist Ola Pehrson hooked up his yucca plant to a computer that bought shares according to the tiny electrical currents the plant generated. If the shares beat the index, the plant was rewarded with sunlight and water. If the shares did badly, the plant was left in the dark... The plant outperformed the Stockholm stock market by 12% over 4 weeks. This is a risky strategy though, which we do not recommend.

THIS COULD BE YOU...

...TALKING TO HER

Benrik Limited shares

Coincidentally, Benrik Limited is floating today on the NASDAQ. Our readers get a 5% negative discount, so make sure you pop into your broker's and pick up your allocation. See our accounts at the end of this Book to decide if you want to invest. Or visit www.thiswebsitewillchangeyourlife.com to start trading today.

Day 315

*If you were a billionaire to start with of course!

Today women are to take charge of the world

Feminist thinkers have long argued that the world would be a better place for all if women had more say in vital matters. Today, any men following this Book should relax, make sure to use their mother's surname, and look to the nearest woman for guidance. Women should take the lead and construct a more caring sharing society, free of war, want and worry. Take charge!

This Book is brought to you by Ben Harden and Henrik Bengtsson. They are both men though, so does that mean following this day is patriarchal? What a headache!!

Day 316

Nostradamus Day

Benrik are asking their readers to predict the future in the year 2015. Simply answer the questions below and complete the tie-breaker. The winning answer will be disclosed on December 31, 2015, and the winner hailed as the Nostradamus of their time!

CLOTHING
In 2015, we will all be wearing space suits
In 2015, we will all be wearing birthday suits
In 2015, we will all be wearing Gap

....

TRANSPORT
In 2015, petrol-fueled cars will be banned
In 2015, cyclists will be a majority
In 2015, the robot-horse will be the norm

....

GEOPOLITICS
In 2015, Israel and Palestine will be at war
In 2015, the USA and China will be at war
In 2015, the Earth and Omega Centauri will be at war

....

BUSINESS
In 2015, genetics will be the No1 industry
In 2015, the Dow Jones will hit 30,000
In 2015, Microsoft will invade a small country

....

DESIGN
In 2015, clutter will be back
In 2015, the zero-gravity bookshelf will be a huge hit
In 2015, whole books will be devoted to this doodle

....

INTERNET
In 2015, the internet will be wired into our brains
In 2015, the most visited site will be "alienhotties.com"
In 2015, search engines will find true love and settle down

....

ART
In 2015, art will run out of taboos to break
In 2015, perspective will make a come-back
In 2015, rebel artists will seize Jupiter

....

SPACE
In 2015, mankind will be exploring Pluto
In 2015, mankind will be exploring
  the Andromeda galaxy
In 2015, mankind will be getting the hell
  out before the second meteorite hits

....

TIE-BREAKER
What would be a good slogan for the breakfast cereal of the year 2015? (200 letters max.)

....
....
....
....
....
....
....
....
....
....
....
....
....
....

Bake it Naked Day

today liberate yourself from clothes. walking around your pad naked is not radical anymore. bring yourself up to a new level of coolness -- bake something naked [and then invite friends over for a bake-tasting]. Possible things to bake: a cake, bread, cookies, casserole, chicken, pudding, fish, potatoes.

WARNINGs:

1. watch out for pubic hair or sharp objects near that area.
2. it's a good idea not to tell your friends how the baking was done until food is eaten and at least few glasses of wine [or any other alcoholic beverages] consumed.
3. the baking method disclosure might result in minor arse kicking [or equivalent, depending on kind of friends you gather].

Day 318

Today record something only you have noticed

Forty missing since last time

Scenes like these are made of glass

I STAMPED ON IT!

Stones are not alive. They don't belong in the wild.

They're always barefoot.

The further away you stand from something, the less you understand it.

He is thinking about what to do next

431 stones, 40 kg dirt

This bird was Esperanto-Speaking. It's true!

End of the fence but only in the picture. It goes around the whole park

The bottom one tries to climb up to the other three

Everything you have two of is never in the middle.

Day 319

THE Cycle of CRIME ←

LITTERING

ZERO TOLERANCE DAY

Small crimes encourage bigger ones. In a community where seemingly minor offences such as littering are tolerated, serious ones like muggings will flourish. Today tell your fellow citizens off for the smallest of deviations and watch those crime figures drop.

MUGGING OF OLD LADIES

ARMED ROBBERY

BURGLARY

SHOPLIFTING

CHEWING GUM WITH MOUTH OPEN

NOT TUCKING IN SHIRT

BULLYING OF NEIGHBORS

GANGLAND BEATINGS

SPITTING ON PROPERTY

DRIVING WITHOUT SEAT BELT

EATING FAST FOOD ON SUBWAY

SWEARING

SWEARING (4-LETTER WORD)

PARKING ON KERB

DRIVE BY SHOOTINGS

Day 320

Order off- menu to-day

Sauteed foie gras with yuzu-sesame-wasabi-soy vinaigrette

Rabbit bisque with truffle-infested wild garlic croutons

Baby octopi with lavender-smoked borlotti topped with caviar

Siberian scallops on a bed of crispy mango-dipped noodles

Smoked-sturgeon pasta with creamed red aubergine sauce

Mille-feuille of squid with coulis of its own fresh ink (in season)

Peasant-style roast poussin with jus d'escargot and tomato concassee

Maitake mushrooms with marjoram vinaigrette and stuffed petits pois (v)

Can't decide?
Go to a Chinese restaurant and order items 24, 45 and 72.

"The menu" is food in a straitjacket. Refuse it point blank and order from your imagination. The waiter will respect you for it, and other customers will think you're a player. Here are a few dishes that any half-decent chef should be able to rustle up in a few minutes. Bon Appétit!

Day 321

REBIRTH!

Today ask your beloved parents to help you stage a realistic reconstruction of your birth.

Strange how little we know about the details of the most important moment of our life: its beginning. And yet there are witnesses to the act! Enlist them to recreate that magical instant where you burst forth. Only by understanding where you came from will you fully understand where you're going.

GET IT RIGHT!

Details to check and replicate:
- When and where did the waters break?
- How did you get to hospital?
- What time was it?
- How long did the delivery take?
- What drugs were administered?
- Were stirrups involved?
- Was the father in the room?
- Did you put up a fight?
- Which bit came out first?
- Did you cry when spanked by the nurse?
- Who cut the umbilical cord?

Warning: Do not attempt to recreate a Caesarian without qualified medical assistance

---

Day 322

Information Overload Day

Are you exposed to more information than you can process? Today read all the papers from A to Z, watch all the news, and listen to all the radio bulletins. At 11:30p.m. write down all you can remember about the day's events (in the bicycle). This will give you an idea of how much you are truly able to absorb.

WRITE HERE:

Day 323

DARWIN DAY

Evolution guarantees the survival of the fittest and the end for everyone else. Today, try mutating to keep ahead of the pack.

APE

DARWINIAN ADVANTAGE: *Abundant body hair*

PERSONALITY TRAITS: *Dumb*

TIMELINE: 7 million years BC HEIGHT: 4ft

HOMO ERECTUS

DARWINIAN ADVANTAGE: *Use of stone tools*

PERSONALITY TRAITS: *Few social graces*

TIMELINE: 2 million to 300,000BC HEIGHT: 5 1/2ft

NEANDERTHAL

DARWINIAN ADVANTAGE: *Upright posture*

PERSONALITY TRAITS: *Still rough around the edges*

TIMELINE: 230,000 to 30,000BC HEIGHT: 5 3/4ft

DARWINIAN ADVANTAGE: *1450cc brainsize*

HOMO SAPIENS

PERSONALITY TRAITS: *Gregarious*

TIMELINE: 130,000BC to now HEIGHT: 6ft

Possible future mutations to try today:

Antennae Darwinian advantage: extra sensory perception

Even bigger brain Darwinian advantage: prodigious intelligence

Gills Darwinian advantage: underwater breathing

Cockroach Darwinian advantage: survive nuclear winter capability

Day 324

DARWIN YOU OLD FART! NEWTON WAS MUCH BETTER THAN YOU.

Get mugged today

Investigate the reality of street crime for yourself: stroll around a dodgy neighborhood with a shiny camera, a new wristwatch and a laptop bag, and see how long it takes for some kid to approach you for your possessions. Hand them over, but only on condition he tells you all about his deprived childhood and his drug problem.

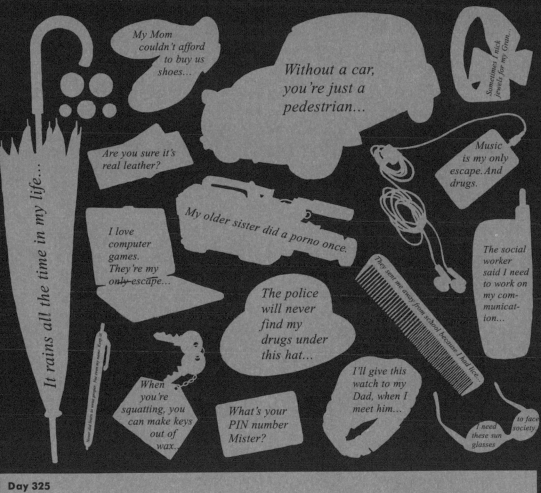

Day 325

Today, let power corrupt you

We all enjoy some form of power: today let it go to your head and abuse it...

Make the check-out girl ring all your purchases through again

Force the pizza delivery guy to go back for extra anchovies

Oblige the shoe store assistant to look for another model

Order the wine waiter to get you a cleaner glass

Demand that your secretary retype the letter in italics

Insist that the receptionist change the flowers' water

Bully your family members to let you hold the remote

Return this book to us for a refund, claiming it's rubbish

Require your visitors to take off their shoes

Day 326

Ask public transport to make a detour for you

Urban planners are busy people and can't always be expected to get it right the first time. Buses, trains and other subway services often stop hundreds of yards away from where you need them to. Remedy this by asking the drivers to divert via your choice of destination. Remember to check the other passengers don't mind; you'll probably find that's where they wanted to go too, only they were too shy to ask! This is only a stopgap measure, until the local authorities commit resources to servicing you properly. To help them, draw up your proposed route and send it to them for implementation. Here is an example.

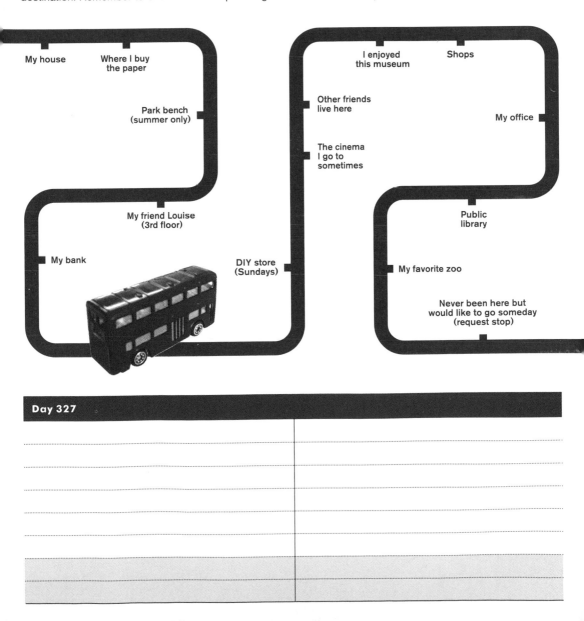

My house   Where I buy the paper

Park bench (summer only)

I enjoyed this museum   Shops

Other friends live here

My office

The cinema I go to sometimes

My friend Louise (3rd floor)

My bank

DIY store (Sundays)

Public library

My favorite zoo

Never been here but would like to go someday (request stop)

Day 327

Today is Neighborhood Watch Day

Today keep an eye on your neighbors. Who is cheating on their spouse? Who is living beyond their means? Who isn't recycling? Log each infraction in your neighborhood watch booklet and hand it in to the police tomorrow morning.

Gosh!!! Sue hasn't watered her plants for like 2 days now! Oh, here comes her cat. Doesn't it look a bit hungry? Maybe I should feed it poison!!! Hahaha. The Sampsons has put up their christmas decoration three days later than last year. I wonder if something is wrong with their family. They are awfully quiet. And the son looks like he is not getting enough food. Oh, that bad housewife! Nothing like what I could have been!! I will give them three days-no more no less, to prove to me that they are shaping up! Otherwise I will call the social service. THAT DAMN KID IS PLAYING THAT MUSIC AGAIN! They are retarded that's what they are-both men and women. Oh, I heard Simons car park outside! Here he is now... WITH SUE! That BITCH! Leave Simon alone, he is not for you! Good, they went seperate ways! Here is old Peter now, haha, in his wheelchair from like -44. Looser, he can't even do his shopping himself. I heard he's never had a wife either, that kinda tell you something about that whole thing don't you think? Blemming old man, he was surely a builder who fell down drunk from whatever he was building or something old fart! What's this? Simon is coming back out again!!! With a bottle of champagne Please come here, please come, come to me!!!! No no no! Nooo! He's knocking on her door. As usual

SPECIAL TEST!

Write your name and address on this label. Stick it on a letter. Put the letter in your next door neighbor's letterbox to make it look like a postman's mistake. See if your neighbor passes it on to you. Check if they haven't opened it!

VALUABLE CONTENT

TOP SECRET

To:

....

....

....

....

FOR YOUR EYES ONLY

Day 328

Today solve a world-famous mathematical problem

The Riemann hypothesis states that the nontrivial Riemann zeta function zeros all lie on the "critical line"

$$s = R[s] = 1/2,$$

where $R[s]$ denotes the real part of s.

Prove it and your fortune is assured.

You may use this space to prove it:

Call someone with your telephone number but a different area code. See how long they're willing to talk about your common bond.

Here is a quick guide to the personality traits associated with some prominent area codes, so you can be better prepared for their reaction when you call.

503
Portland

773
Chicago

716
Buffalo

303
Denver

513
Cincinnati

212
New York

323
Los Angeles

225
Baton Rouge

305
Miami

323 people are dark and mysterious. This can be difficult for loved ones, but means they are often thrilling company!

Those with area code 305 are filled with zest for life. Meeting new people is a pleasure and a treat for them.

The people of area code 716 are wary of strangers. For them, patience and endurance are the uppermost virtues.

Many 225 people function on an intuitive level, and love animals and nature above all. Others are more withdrawn.

773 area code people display huge ambition and charisma. Nothing stops them: beware those who get in the way!

Sensuality and seduction are central themes in the lives of 212ers. They exude a magnetic charm that few can resist…

The people of area code 303 are sometimes capable of malice, but get to know them and you will discover their softer side.

513 people are dominating personalities. They take up leading roles in society and mark the times they live in.

The hedonistic individuals of area code 503 are not interested in anything beyond pleasure: all play and no work!

Day 330

Today stalk someone

Spot someone interesting in the street and follow them around. Who are they? What do they do? Where do they live? What does their lover look like? Are they running late? Where do they shop? What do they order for lunch? What articles do they read in the paper? What makes them special? What moves them? And who are they stalking?

Day 331

Today, take the lift to an unknown floor

(23)	HUMAN RESOURCES
(22)	AL QAEDA
(21)	ACCOUNTS
(20)	OPUS DEI HQ
(19)	C.I.A
(18)	DISTRIBUTION
(17)	BORDELLO
(16)	MARKETING
(15)	SALES

EMPLOYEE OF THE DAY

Today make a note of all the customer service you receive, and make the most deserving serviceperson your "EMPLOYEE OF THE DAY"!

EMPLOYEE OF THE DAY
5 stars ★★★★★
Name:
Employer:
Job:
Motivation:
PHOTO GOES HERE
WELL DONE!

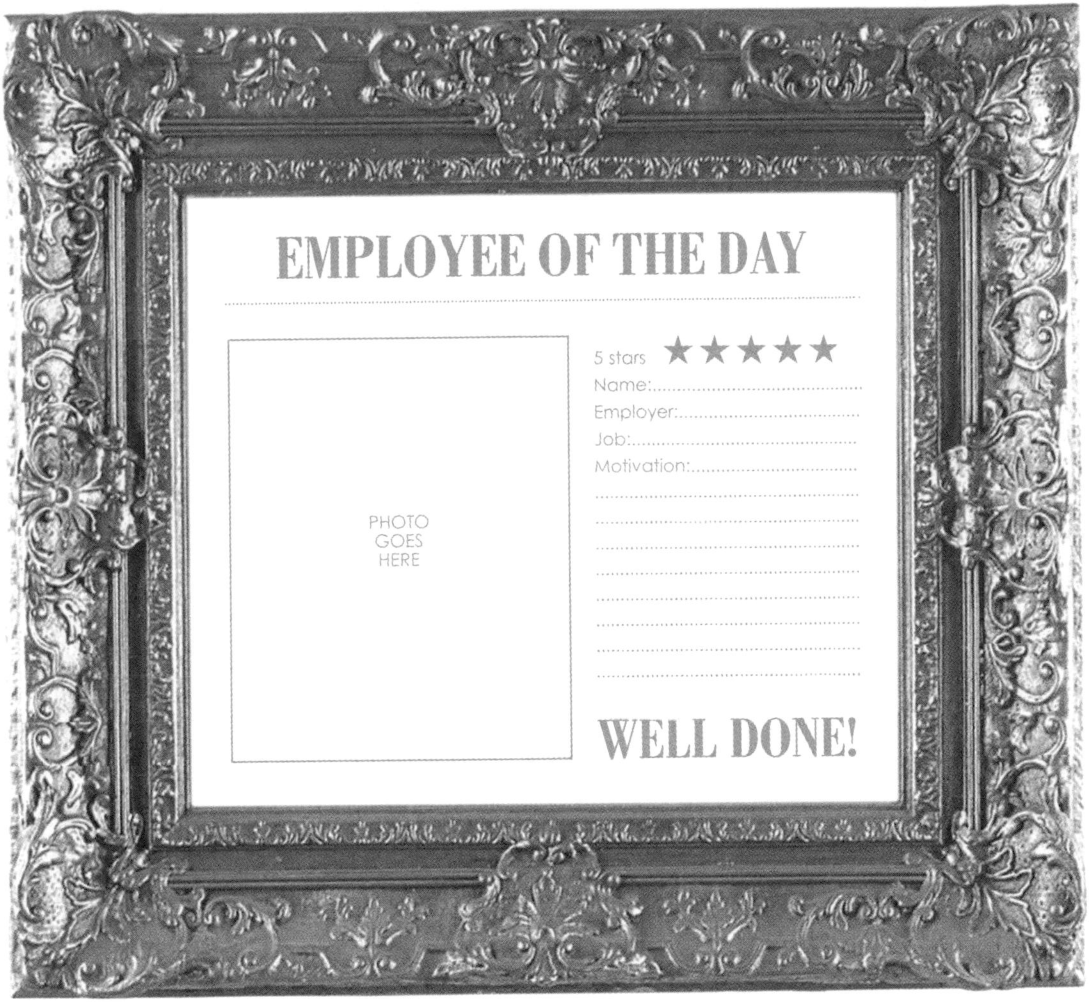

Day 333

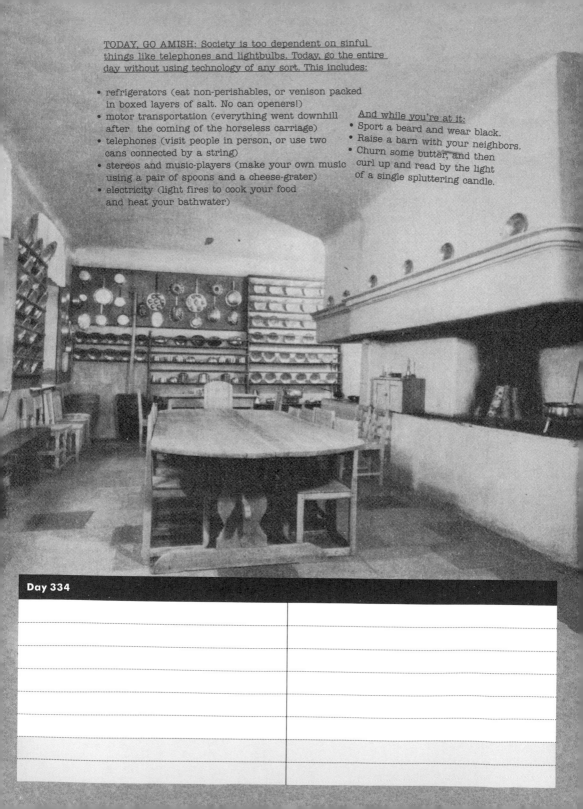

TODAY, GO AMISH: Society is too dependent on sinful things like telephones and lightbulbs. Today, go the entire day without using technology of any sort. This includes:

- refrigerators (eat non-perishables, or venison packed in boxed layers of salt. No can openers!)
- motor transportation (everything went downhill after the coming of the horseless carriage)
- telephones (visit people in person, or use two cans connected by a string)
- stereos and music-players (make your own music using a pair of spoons and a cheese-grater)
- electricity (light fires to cook your food and heat your bathwater)

And while you're at it:
- Sport a beard and wear black.
- Raise a barn with your neighbors.
- Churn some butter, and then curl up and read by the light of a single spluttering candle.

Day 334

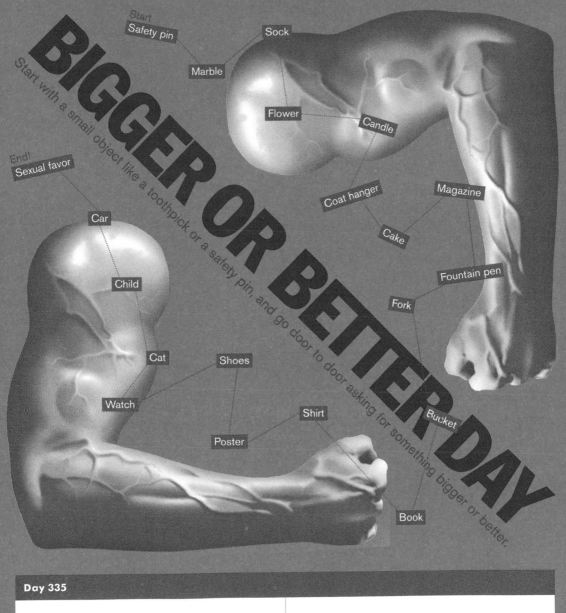

BIGGER OR BETTER DAY

Start with a small object like a toothpick or a safety pin, and go door to door asking for something bigger or better.

Start
Safety pin

Sock

Marble

Flower

Candle

Coat hanger

Magazine

Cake

Fountain pen

Fork

End!
Sexual favor

Car

Child

Cat

Shoes

Watch

Shirt

Bucket

Poster

Book

Day 335

Today, confuse a large corporation

Ever felt helpless in the face of a corporate behemoth? Here's your chance to get your own back. Start a dialogue with a utility about a fictitious meter. Claim you have recently moved and wish them to take over supply on this meter, which until now has been supplied by another utility. Ask the corporation to get in touch with their competitor and arrange a transfer. Make up a credible-looking meter number (455 987), give them a reading (5674.76), get a case reference number, and there you go: you have sparked off months if not years of fruitless correspondence.

Transgas TeleTel PowerWeb CentraFuels Electrica

Directelectric plc Hydroline GloboFuel NorthernGas FuelSource

Metrix WestComms PacificBoard MagnoGen SLAMDUNK

Can't get service? Complain to *60 Minutes*: (212) 975 3247

Day 336

Today work out how many seconds you have left to live Formula

Now plan for each one of them.

987761208
735556478
901739999
092687 sec

1 sec

2 sec

3 sec

Day 337

Time is running out, my friend!

Homeless Day

Today, leave your home and possessions and try to survive on the streets. Could you survive the cold, the hunger, the looks? Experience life on the other side of the begging bowl, and by tomorrow morning, you'll never look down on the homeless again.

What you may take

Your past attitude to begging dictates your level of discomfort.

If you give to beggars every day:	You may take a sleeping bag, comfortable walking shoes and $5.
If you give to beggars once in a while:	You may take a blanket, a pair of woolen gloves, and a toothbrush.
If you never give to beggars:	You may take some foreign coins, a broken umbrella, and a flea-ridden sheet.

HEAVEN $1

SAVING FOR SEX CHANGE

Hungry

Used to be a taecher

Day 338

Arrive three quarters of an hour late for everything today

As Oscar Wilde pointed out, punctuality is the thief of time. Sabotage everyone's attempts at it today by running late for any meetings, thus setting off a chain reaction that will undermine the very basis of technocratic capitalist society. Example of chain reaction:

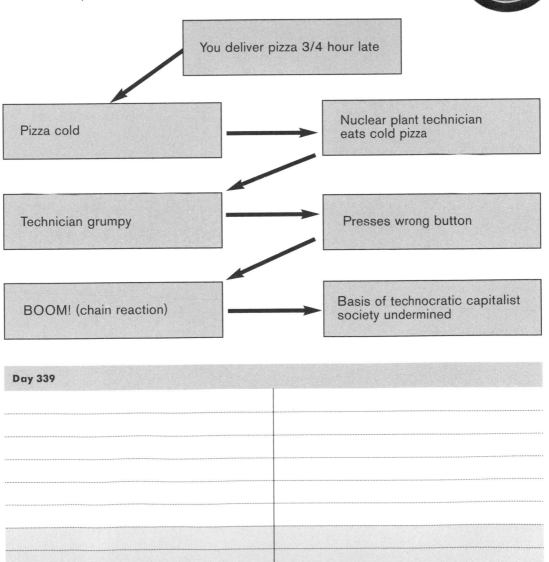

| You deliver pizza 3/4 hour late |
| Pizza cold |
| Nuclear plant technician eats cold pizza |
| Technician grumpy |
| Presses wrong button |
| BOOM! (chain reaction) |
| Basis of technocratic capitalist society undermined |

Day 339

Today dress out of character

Don't be a prisoner of your wardrobe: wear clothes that contradict people's perception of you.

I AM YOUNG AND INSECURE SO I NEED TO SHOW WHAT TRIBE I BELONG TO THROUGH THE PRINT ON MY T-SHIRT.

(HARD) Life is like a nut, but i'm known 2 B a bit of a nutcracker!!!

Autumn is approaching... as usual in my heart...

HELIX

My parents went to Italy and all I got was this lousy t-shirt wich really shows me what a shallow relationship I have to them.

"THEY" SAY LOVE IS WONDERFUL...

Life is like mustard in the ass of a cat – You run 'cause it hurts.

I want to be your friend but you probably don't want to be my friend... Do you?

www.benrik.co.uk. A website with a difference!

I SLEPT WITH PARIS HILTON AND SHE LOVED IT AND SCREAMED FOR MORE.

IF YOU'RE A TEACHER: FUCK OFF! DON'T TRY TO TEACH ME ANY BULLSHIT!

Bach is the Quentin Tarrantino of classical music.

Day 340

Conspiracy Day

There's a potential conspiracy everywhere you look. Today find one in your everyday life!

My neighbor has been poisoning my cat with anthrax pellets! My cat is a different animal. He used to be cuddly but now he growls like a dog. Whenever he comes back from the next door garden, his saliva is greenish and frothing. My neighbor works for a chemical company. She keeps odd hours. I am afraid for myself and my cat.

I am the subject of a snuff reality TV show! There are cameras everywhere in my house. There have been since my birth. I even know which channel the show is on, channel 9 because they have "broken" that button on my TV. My life fascinates millions daily. But it will end with my being impaled to death live on prime time. Help me escape!

My children are the vanguard of an alien invasion! They are not like other kids. They don't go out. They don't play. They just do their homework and eat their greens. Since my wife was abducted (the so-called divorce was just for show), they stare out of the window waiting for the signal from the mothership.

My computer is bugged by the CIA! They are aware of my subversive potential. Every time I sit down to write my exposé of our crypto-world government, they zap my brain with alpha waves to cause writer's block! But I will fight back you evil bastards! What happens if I pour wate<ds5z++…,'√ɔfi√‹.‚ς,∂≈†

Elvis is living in my shed! There's worse: he's using my tools. The other day, my staple gun was on next to the drill, when I 100% remember leaving it next to the saw! I dunno what he's making but it's a big job! He's working flat out all hours of the night. I know this cos I can hear him crooning to cover up the noise.

My cleaner is a communist! She leaves hammer and sickle signs in the dust. And last week, my books must have been rearranged, because the first letters of the titles of five of them spelt Lenin backwards. I fear she is using my toilet pan to leave messages for her Comintern handler, whom I suspect is the plumber. That damn toilet always blocks!

Day 341

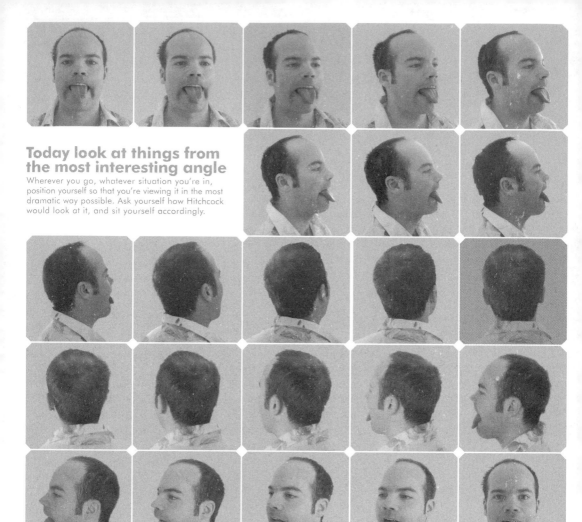

Today look at things from the most interesting angle

Wherever you go, whatever situation you're in, position yourself so that you're viewing it in the most dramatic way possible. Ask yourself how Hitchcock would look at it, and sit yourself accordingly.

Buy your own grain of sand in the Bahamas!

Today purchase a small piece of paradise. Benrik Limited have arranged an exclusive real estate deal whereby our readers may acquire their very own parcel of land on the glamorous tropical island of Great Exuma. One grain of sand can be yours in perpetuity for as little as $1. For your money you will receive: a certificate of part-ownership of Exuma, a photograph of your grain of sand, a map showing its exact location (within 1cm²), and a 20¢ voucher towards a cocktail of your choice at the Big Eddie's Exuma Beachbum Bar. You may transfer your money to us by international banker's draft (IBAN Code: GB21NWBK 60145 58167032). Enjoy your bit of Caribbean beach.

A grain of sand!

Grain of sand near the beach toilets **$1**

Grain of sand under the palm tree **$2**

PRICE RANGE

Grain of sand in the sun **$5**

Grain of sand near the bar **$4**

Day 343

ENTER THE NOBEL PEACE PRIZE

THE NOBEL PEACE PRIZE IS ONE OF THE WORLD'S MOST PRESTIGIOUS AWARDS. UNLIKE THE MORE SPECIALIZED NOBEL PRIZES THE PEACE PRIZE CAN GO TO ANYONE. ALL THEY NEED IS TO HAVE "DONE THE MOST OR THE BEST WORK FOR FRATERNITY BETWEEN NATIONS. FOR THE ABOLITION OR REDUCTION OF STANDING ARMIES AND FOR THE HOLDING AND PROMOTION OF PEACE CONGRESSES." NOMINATIONS CLOSE ON FEBRUARY 1. SO GET YOURS IN QUICK!

TIMELINE: FEBRUARY: NOMINATIONS CLOSE. OCTOBER: COMMITTEE RECOMMENDATIONS. NOVEMBER: PRIZE-AWARDING DECISION. DECEMBER: AWARD CEREMONY (KEEP IT FREE)

NOMINATION FORM

WHAT HAVE YOU DONE TO FURTHER PEACE IN THE LAST YEAR? (MAX. 200 WORDS. SIGN ON BACK)

....
....
....
....
....

I CONFIRM THAT I AM COMPETENT TO SUBMIT THIS NOMINATION IN MY CAPACITY AS MEMBER OF A NATIONAL ASSEMBLY/GOVERNMENT OF STATE; A MEMBER OF AN INTERNATIONAL COURT; A UNIVERSITY RECTOR; A PROFESSOR OF SOCIAL SCIENCES, HISTORY, PHILOSOPHY OR THEOLOGY; A DIRECTOR OF PEACE RESEARCH/FOREIGN POLICY INSTITUTE; A PREVIOUS NOBEL PEACE PRIZE WINNER; A BOARD MEMBER OF AN ORGANIZATION THAT HAS BEEN AWARDED THE NOBEL PEACE PRIZE; AN ACTIVE OR FORMER MEMBER OF THE NORWEGIAN NOBEL COMMITTEE; A FORMER ADVISER APPOINTED BY THE NORWEGIAN NOBEL INSTITUTE; OTHER

SUBMIT TO: THE NOBEL FOUNDATION STUREGATAN 14. BOX 5232. SE-102 45 STOCKHOLM. SWEDEN!

SOME PAST LAUREATES

2003: SHIRIN EBADI
2002: JIMMY CARTER
2001: UNITED NATIONS (KOFI ANNAN)
2000: KIM DAE-JUNG
1999: MEDECINS SANS FRONTIERES
1998: JOHN HUME. DAVID TRIMBLE
1997: BENRIK LIMITED HOLDING COMPANY
1994: YASSER ARAFAT. SHIMON PERES. YITZHAK RABIN
1993: NELSON MANDELA. F.W. DE KLERK
1991: AUNG SAN SUU KYI 1990: MIKHAIL GORBACHEV

ALFRED NOBEL: 1833-1896

IT IS IRONIC THAT ALFRED NOBEL SHOULD BE ASSOCIATED WITH PEACE. IN HIS DAY HE WAS MOSTLY KNOWN AS AN ARMS MERCHANT. BORN IN SWEDEN TO THE INVENTOR OF THE FIRST SEA MINES, ALFRED EVENTUALLY OUTSHONE HIS FATHER BY INVENTING DYNAMITE IN 1866. BY THE TIME HE DIED, HIS BUSINESS EMPIRE STRETCHED AROUND THE WORLD THOUGH HE ALSO FOUND TIME TO WRITE POETRY. YET EVEN IN THE LAST DECADES OF HIS LIFE, WHEN HE BECAME INTERESTED IN PROMOTING PEACE, HE NEVER SAW THE CONFLICT WITH HIS MILITARY WORK. INDEED HE CAN PERHAPS BE CREDITED WITH INVENTING THE CONCEPT OF DETERRENCE: HE SUGGESTED THAT "ON THE DAY THAT TWO ARMY CORPS CAN MUTUALLY ANNIHILATE EACH OTHER IN A SECOND, ALL CIVILIZED NATIONS WILL SURELY RECOIL WITH HORROR AND DISBAND THEIR TROOPS".

Day 344

Invade people's personal space today

We are all surrounded by an invisible barrier which others cross at their peril. However this varies enormously according to degree of intimacy, culture and personality. Today measure how close you have to get to violate the personal space of those you meet.

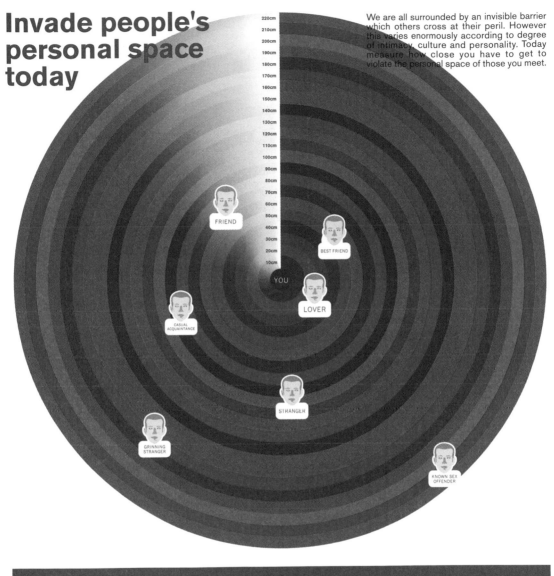

Day 345

Today think aloud all day

"Say what you think" is a common injunction in our mealy-mouthed society. Today put it into practice and let others benefit from your brain's running commentary on events.

No don't beat me, Mr. Badger!!! Huh?! Oh it's the alarm clock. Must speak to a shrink about those dreams. What's that horrible noise? Tony snoring. God, he's really put on weight, will you look at that lump of white blubber. I'd dump him if I had the time to find someone else. Need the loo. Is it me or does my pee smell funny? Could be that asparagus stir-fry. Or cystitis God I hope it's not cystitis. He probably gave it to me. I bet he's sleeping around. As if. Not even a hooker would go near him. Shower. Hmmmmm. Soapy bubbles... I quite fancy a drink actually. Another thing to discuss with shrink. Don't forget to soap cystitis away. OK, what am I going to wear? That white top again? No, boring. Oh, fuck it. Hope no one can see that stain. Is that Tony getting out of bed? I don't want to talk to him. Let's have kids soon so we don't have to talk anymore. Might just get him drunk, easy enough. Let's skip breakfast, I'll get coffee at work. Bye Tony, you lazy blob. Yes yes don't kiss me I'm closing the door now. Maybe I'd be happier with a dog. Less smelly. Is it going to rain? It is. It isn't. It is. It isn't. Is it? It better not. Made it! This bus shelter is full of losers. It always is. You're a loser. And so are you. Everyone is except me. And maybe that girl over there. I wonder what she does? She was on the bus yesterday. Have I seen her on TV in an advert? Maybe maybe not. Who cares? Think about something more interesting. Me! Is this my bus? Yes. Let's get in first. That old lady was there before me. Fuck her. She shouldn't take the rush hour bus. There's a seat. Don't you dare take it, you scum. Got it! Yes!!! I rock! You can look at me all you want but I'm going to stick my nose in the paper of the man next to me. What an ugly head he has! I can't even look or I'll be sick. If I'd had breakfast I'd throw it up. What's in his paper? The sports pages. Boring! Turn to the horoscope. Turn to the horoscope. Turn to the horoscope damn you! I suppose I should read my book. Only I can't be bothered. This bus is slow. Schoolkids. I hope they don't get on my bus. Except that one, he's cute. He's about 15 though. Shit, my stop's next. That old lady's in the way. I'll offer her my seat now and people will think I'm well brought-up. There you go. Buy chocolate. I'm late. I'm late. I'm late. Where's that lift? God it stinks in here, Rita from accounts must be in already. Yippee! Another day at work. Coffee. I can smell it. I need it now! Maybe with some brandy in it. No! Unhelpful thinking. Gosh! Murray's there. He's such a dish. I could lick him like a lollipop right here right now. What would he say if I did? Lick his cute little ears. Yums! Ok behave. Social interaction mode. Hi Murray can I lick your ear? Yadda yadda morning yadda report yadda yadda two sugars thanks. Here's desk. Here's boss what a cow. Your lips are moving but nothing's coming out. Yes I would mind typing this up actually I could do your job in my sleep. Anyway where's that...

THOUGHT

PROCESSING CENTRE FOR REFINING THOUGHTS INTO SPOKEN OR WRITTEN LANGUAGE.

Day 346

Claim your own barcode today

Although mostly used for commercial products, the barcode system was originally also configured to deal with personal identification (as with most technologies, its origins are military...) Anyone can obtain their very own barcode. Today, claim yours and have it tattooed on your wrist in anticipation of the totalitarian society of tomorrow.

How does it work?

Barcodes are assigned by the Uniform Code Council. A certain category of prefix is reserved for individuals: barcodes beginning in 199 to 212. Then comes your day, month, and year of birth (e.g. 130274), and finally your name, which you compress by adding it up (A=1, B=2, C=3 etc). So a typical barcode might read:

2 110110 799862 >   Ben Carey

2 162162 010055 >   Henrik Delehag

To claim yours, simply write to the UCC, 1009 Lenox Drive, Lawrenceville, NJ 08648

Celebrity barcodes:

2 110255 709862   Michael Jackson

2 162025 010255   Newt Gingrich

2 120255 709862   George Soros

2 162070 010256   Yoko Ono

2 120255 709855   Tom Hanks

2 122601 010255   Helmut Kohl

2 120259 707055   Pamela Anderson

2 122226 210255   Jacques Chirac

2 125857 989855   Salman Rushdie

2 112001 010255   Celine Dion

2 127057 989855   Oprah Winfrey

2 012001 010266   Elton John

Day 347

Coincidence Day

Today walk around our small world looking for serendipitous encounters. If your mind is receptive, you'll find that fate's hand can be forced.

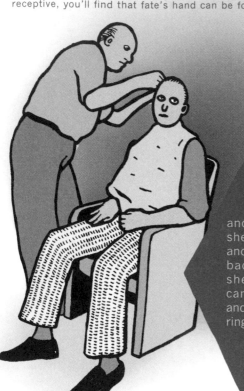

This man has misunderstood today's task. He has just asked the hairdresser to cut his hair for the third time in two hours and he's wearing his nicest trousers (Prada) and his fine shoes (Prada too) that he keeps only for special occasions. The reason is Mary. At some point he knows Mary will walk by because it's Tuesday and Mary does her shopping on Tuesdays. He met Mary on the bus when he helped her with her shopping two months ago and he said "Hi," and she replied to him. His plan is now to sit here until she goes by, and just like in the films he will run out (obviously looking the part – hair and all) and say to her face: "Hey, what a surprise – I happened to see you through the window there and remembered that's that woman I helped with the shopping, how are you?" His plan continues in two parts, depending on Mary's first reaction and if she recognizes him from the bus. 1) If she doesn't recognize him he will apologize and say "sorry, I must be mistaken" and go back quickly to the hairdresser, or 2) If she recognizes him he will ask her if he can help her with her shopping bags again and when they part he will give her the golden ring that he has in his inside pocket.

"Casual meetings are apt to be just the opposite... people who make dates are the same kind who need lines on their writing paper, or who always squeeze up from the bottom on a tube of toothpaste." (J.Cortazar, *Hopscotch*)

Day 348

Today tell someone something they will never forget

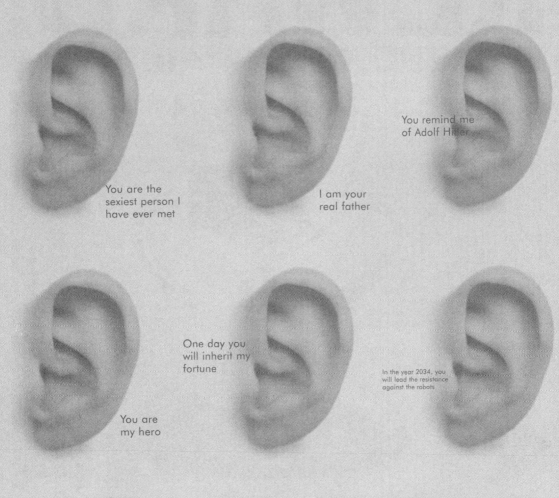

You are the sexiest person I have ever met

I am your real father

You remind me of Adolf Hitler

You are my hero

One day you will inherit my fortune

In the year 2034, you will lead the resistance against the robots

Day 349

REWARD!
FIND THE HOLY GRAIL TODAY

The last known sighting of the Holy Grail was in 1953 in an attic in the French town of Rennes-le-Chateau, where the secretive remnants of the Knights Templar eventually left it in the hands of a parish priest to look after during World War I. His illiterate housekeeper Marie Dernaud didn't appreciate its importance, and thus it was confined to the attic until her death. Her nephew Francois Boulon sold it to an old curiosity shop along with the rest of her possessions, before seeing Rossetti's painting of it a year later and realizing what he'd thrown away. By then the shop owner had mysteriously left Rennes, and according to local accounts, moved to the USA. Today, scour your local charity shops and seek out the Grail! (If you find it don't let them hike the price.)

REWARD:
$300!
For the authentic Holy Grail in full working order

THE HOLY GRAIL
The grail is the bowl from which Christ ate and drank at the Last Supper. After his arrest, it was rescued by Joseph of Arimathea, who took it to the crucifixion and used it to collect Christ's blood after soldiers lanced him. It is endowed with miraculous properties: the hero who finds it is guaranteed eternal life and nourishment. Most accounts differ as to its shape, but the credible ones see it as a cup-shaped vessel, with some fine plastic ornamentation just below the rim.

Je mendierai ma vie
Sur les routes de France
De Bretagne en Provence
Et je crierai aux gens:
Refusez d'obéir
Refusez de la faire
N'allez pas à la guerre
Refusez de partir
S'il faut donner son sang
Allez donner le vôtre
Vous êtes bon apôtre
Monsieur le Président
Si vous me poursuivez
Prévenez vos gendarmes
Que je n'aurai pas d'armes
Et qu'ils pourront tirer

REWARD!
TO THOSE WHO CAPTURE THAT FRENCH WOMAN WHO THREW AWAY A RELIC FOR GENERATIONS TO RELISH SO WE CAN PUNISH HER FOR IT! HEY, IS THAT HER?

Day 350

HAVE A BABY

Yes! It's nine months to the day since you conceived:

TIME FOR YOU TO POP!

Head for your nearest hospital and demand to see the midwife. Then while the father enjoys a soothing cigar in the waiting room, the mother should proceed to break water, begin contractions, feel immense pain and generally start screaming for an epidural. Fifteen hours later, hey presto, a new life is born! Congratulations from everyone at Benrik.

REMEMBER?

Is it a boy or a girl? How to tell:

Boy's eyes are wider and the back of their head is slightly more curved.

Girls often look pinker and their toes twitch when tickled.

What will you name your baby?
- [ ] Benrik
- [ ] Other:.............

How can things go better next time? Ask your baby the following questions while the experience is still fresh in his or her mind. Was your pregnancy satisfactory overall? Was the womb temperature warm enough? Was the placenta a help or a hindrance? Was the amniotic fluid comfortable or on the gooey side? Were you happy with your mother's diet? Were you pleased to emerge into the world? Were you surprised at the post-birth environment? Would you describe your birth as traumatic? Would you return to the womb if you could? Do you think your mommy's pretty? What about your daddy then?

Day 351

Recover your umbilical cord today

Anyone who has a baby these days is going to want to hang on to its umbilical cord, full of stem cells that promise a cure for many previously untreatable diseases. Today call the hospital where YOU were born to try and locate your umbilical cord. Perhaps it was just chucked in a drawer, or a cupboard. Speak to the midwife who delivered you and ask if she remembers where they put it. Check that your mom didn't keep it for luck. Found it? Then call a cryopreservation company and arrange an immediate pick-up.

Day 352

Investigate a news story yourself

Don't accept what the media says at face value. Today do some fact-checking of your own on a suspicious story.

Check spelt right?

Unlikely

Cleaner employed by multinational corporation?

FBI Helpline 08086549753

Reference to cocaine?

Criminal antecedents?

Interview?

Hush money?

Satanic number

Find pencils.

THE POST

POLICE IN MURDER CORRUPTION PROBE

The entire police department of the town of Stanton, Illinois, has been suspended pending the outcome of an FBI investigation. A disgruntled former cleaner, Gertrude Trump, has alleged that the department's officers concealed evidence in the case of contract killer Harold Mason, who was acquitted of six murders in early November 2002. According to Trump, sheriff Rick Lund accepted $100,000 from Mason's attorney in exchange for helping him evade the charges. Trump alleges she saw the money being distributed between Lund and three other officers while she was "cleaning the corridor". Mason was accused of murdering six people in cold blood for interfering in mob business. The local press dubbed him "The Pencil Sharpener", a reference to the weapon he used to despatch his victims by jamming it up their nostril. Gertrude Trump is 38.

Day 353

Overdose Day

Today, have too much of a good thing:

Caffeine 50 cups
Chocolate 30 bars
Water 20 liters
TV 11 hours
Sex 7 orgasms
Alcohol 17 beers
Sleep 25 hours
Ice cream 19 scoops
Happiness 78 smiles

Day 354

Reverse Brainwashing Day

How many of your thoughts are truly yours? Today cast off
your secondhand opinions and return them to their originators.

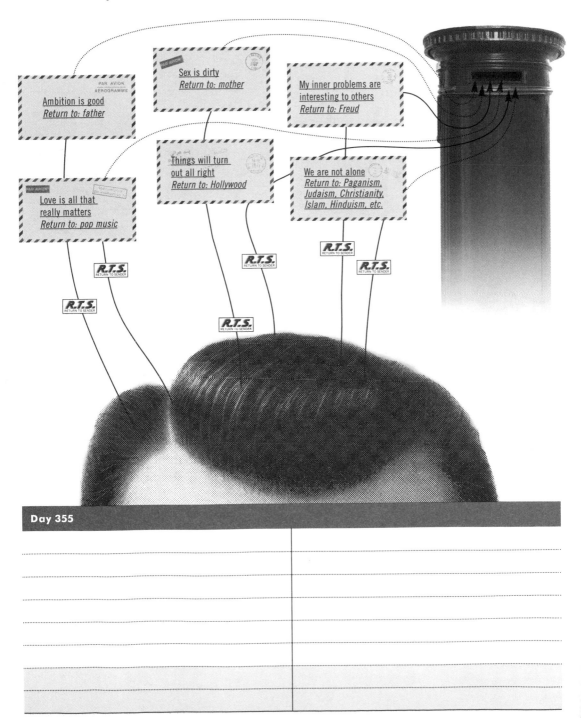

Day 355

Today trust a little...

In the early 90s, the papers in New Zealand were full of horror stories about the crime wave supposedly sweeping the country: things were now so bad that locals had to lock their front doors when out of the house...Today, hark back to a gentler era and trust in your fellow human beings.

Leave your doors and windows unlocked
Don't count your change
Invite the salesman in
Don't check the bill
Leave the engine running
Accept sweets from a stranger

Day 356

Today breach the peace

"Breach of the peace" is defined as "when a person disrupts, or does something which is likely to disrupt, the normal state of society." It is not technically an offense but means you can be bound over to keep the peace. Today challenge this totalitarian statute that shames our supposedly free polity by finding a police officer and doing something that "disrupts the normal state of society" yet harms no one. Bounce on the roof of your car. Stick your tongue out at children. Stare at diners through restaurant windows. Alert passersby to the danger from birds flying overhead. Mimic the officer's every gesture. Argue about the definition of "breach of the peace" as you are bundled off to the nearest police station until you "grow up." Call a lawyer.

Day 357

Parachute!

Make and test your own parachute day

Today test your nerves and your creative talent by making and testing your own parachute.
Finally know what all those lemmings are so hot about!

IMPORTANT

These instructions are foolproof for those who only want to jump ONCE. For everyone else - please use kamikaze potatoes or unwanted D-list celebrities.

1.

2.

3.

4.

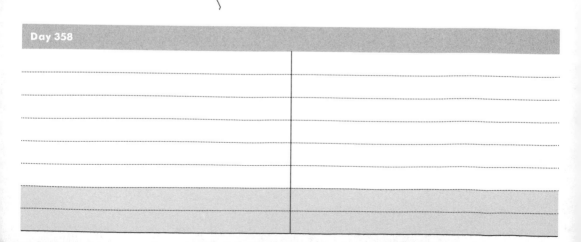

Day 358

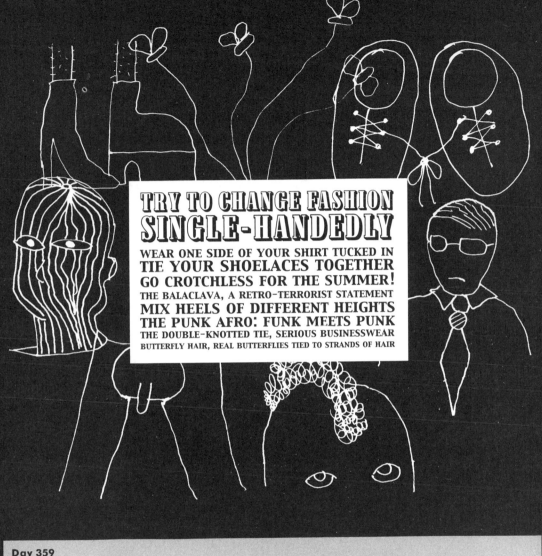

TRY TO CHANGE FASHION
SINGLE-HANDEDLY

WEAR ONE SIDE OF YOUR SHIRT TUCKED IN
TIE YOUR SHOELACES TOGETHER
GO CROTCHLESS FOR THE SUMMER!
THE BALACLAVA, A RETRO-TERRORIST STATEMENT
MIX HEELS OF DIFFERENT HEIGHTS
THE PUNK AFRO: FUNK MEETS PUNK
THE DOUBLE-KNOTTED TIE, SERIOUS BUSINESSWEAR
BUTTERFLY HAIR, REAL BUTTERFLIES TIED TO STRANDS OF HAIR

Day 359

TEST THE NATION DAY Today go somewhere with lots of people, and fall over to see if anyone helps you up.

Today, invent a stereotype

Example of stereotype:

"THE DUTCH ALWAYS TAKE LONG SAYING GOODBYE."

Practical application:
Next time you hear a prolonged goodbye, say "Hey you're just like the Dutch! You take ages to say goodbye."

Example of stereotype:

"SMALL PEOPLE ARE MORE FUN."

Practical application:
At a boring function, suggest "This party could really do with some small people right now."

Example of stereotype:

"Schoolteachers always repeat everything twice."

Practical application:
If someone repeats something to you unnecessarily, "What are you, some damn schoolteacher?"

Example of stereotype:

"Homosexuals love nothing better than pea soup."

Practical application:
When your son tells you he's gay, say "You're my son and I love you, now let's have some pea soup."

Example of stereotype:

"Red-haired girls make good listeners."

Practical application:
When a red-haired girl listens to you, thank her "Wow, you're a good listener, but then I guess I shouldn't be surprised."

Example of stereotype:

"Roman Catholics have superior taste in interior decoration."

Practical application:
When in the shop, ask "Are you a Roman Catholic? May I ask you what you think of this lampshade?"

Example of stereotype:

"THE PEOPLE OF BOLIVIA ARE HUGE EXTROVERTS."

Practical application:
Upon meeting a huge extrovert, exclaim "That's amazing, I could have sworn you were Bolivian."

Example of stereotype:

"CAT-OWNERS WERE ALL BITTEN BY DOGS IN CHILDHOOD."

Practical application:
When confronted by a dog, say "Get that dog away from my child, I don't want her turning into some cat-owner."

Day 361

MINI-PROSTITUTION DAY: SELL A VERY MINOR SEXUAL FAVOR

It's the oldest job in the world, yet most people never even consider it. There's no reason why you have to jump in at the deep end with full-blown sex with strangers. Find out if prostitution is for you by starting small: offer someone a kiss on the cheek for $1 perhaps; caress a neighbor's hand for $3; let the checkout girl squeeze your bottom for $10. Who knows, you may discover your true vocation.

Day 362

DEDICATE TODAY TO
THE GOD THOR.
MAKE SURE THAT EVERY
SINGLE ONE OF YOUR
ACTIONS TODAY IS
DEDICATED TO THE
MIGHTY THOR IN THE
HOPE OF PLEASING HIM.
AND IF YOUR DAY GOES
PARTICULARLY WELL,
WHY NOT MAKE A
HABIT OF IT?

Today greet everyone you cross in the street as if they were a long-lost friend & see if they claim to remember you

Billy Moffat-we used to go fishing together!

Sandy T?-my first kiss...

Matt Clark: one of the gang!

Frank-we started at Datacorp on the same day

Juliet Stern: flatmate at 11 Rosslyn Hill in '86

The Davidson brothers: Harry and...

Day 364

All Or Nothing Day: today gamble everything you have

DON'T LET THE AMERICAN DREAM SLIP AWAY! TODAY, SELL YOUR HOUSE, PAWN THE TV, MAX OUT YOUR CREDIT CARDS, AND ROLL THE DICE ON YOUR CASH! NO RISK, NO REWARD...

Day 365

Congratulations!
You have completed the year! But: how well have you really done? Award yourself 3 points if you completed a day successfully, 2 points if you tried but failed, 1 point if you read it but came up with a lame excuse not to do it, and zero points if you don't even remember the day. Bonus: if you got arrested, award yourself an extra 5 points. If your total is under 700, you must go back to day 1 and start all over again!

1. Warm-up Day
2. Claim you're Jesus Day
3. Promote the Book Day
4. Obedience Day
5. Cannibalism day: eat part of a loved one
6. Marry Jonas Day!
7. Today emigrate to New Zealand
8. Write a bestseller today
9. Today buy a stranger flowers
10. Boycott what's never been boycotted
11. Today apply to an orgy
12. Mainstream Day
13. Amateur Day 1 (Kate Hicks)
14. Family Day: never leave their side
15. Dump your partner for the day
16. Test a proverb today
17. Today review this Book
18. Free someone today!
19. Today test the power of prayer
20. Feast Day
21. Invent your own traffic rule and obey it
22. Today single out one of your toes
23. Record the next generation of canned laughter
24. Speak as if you were a corporation
25. Find your self today
26. Today, live at night
27. Today download and spread a computer virus
28. Today speak only Esperanto
29. Today eat only one color
30. Today prepare your panic room
31. Parasite Day
32. Pretend to be pregnant today
33. Children's Life Change Day!
34. Today learn to hypnotize yourself
35. Today count down to everything
36. Today threaten a foreign country
37. Public Ridicule Day
38. Anti-Consumerism Day
39. Year of the Rooster Day
40. Borrow something from your neighbor
41. "Break gym etiquette" Day
42. Today get psychoanalyzed
43. Lonely Hearts Day
44. Run for President
45. World Domination Day
46. Today eat this book
47. Enforce the "customer is always right" rule
48. Today become schizophrenic
49. Today get rained on
50. Today apologize on behalf of your ancestors
51. Denounce someone to the government
52. Redistribute wealth today!
53. Today answer spam e-mails
54. Amnesia Day
55. Today gatecrash a funeral
56. Today rage against the machine!
57. Tonight patrol a bridge against suicide
58. Lend your cellphone to a tramp
59. Today investigate your early years
60. Today breakfast at someone else's place
61. Emergency Alarm Day
62. Today insure your best feature
63. Self-portrait day
64. Today work out which side you are on
65. Today wreak havoc on a microscopic scale
66. Today mother your mother
67. Today do as you are told
68. Release a dove for peace

69. Madeleine Day: recover a childhood memory
70. Dig for oil today
71. Amateur Day 2 (Joel Moss Levinson)
72. Gender-Bending Day
73. Today use graphology to manipulate others
74. Today reconnect with the outside world
75. Apply to Madame Tussaud's today
76. Today track down the people behind dogshit
77. Today get back at someone
78. Today, make a baby
79. Apply for job you have no chance of getting
80. Today act like a teenager
81. Déjà Vu Day
82. Join the Benrik T-shirt Club
83. Treasure Hunt Day!
84. Sing Wagner in the shower today
85. Amateur Day 3 (Jonas Jansson)
86. Give Ada Peach her 15 minutes of fame
87. Today smile inappropriately
88. Today infect someone
89. Today act like you're over 75 years old
90. Today spark off a huge traffic jam
91. Buddhist Fundamentalism Day
92. Today recover your earliest best friend
93. Imaginary Friend Day
94. Commit all seven sins today
95. Alien Abduction Day
96. Today, fast
97. Today give back what you borrowed
98. Today drive the Devil out of a loved one
99. Visit someone in hospital today
100. Become a hermit today
101. Hyperactivity Day
102. Radical Spring Clean Day
103. Today help destroy an ugly building
104. Self-medicating Day
105. Start a relationship with a fellow Benrikian
106. Today commit treason
107. Today stalk an animal
108. Today act suspiciously
109. Today spaz!
110. Insist on speaking to the media today
111. Today tip abnormally
112. Pilgrimage Day
113. Today pour cocaine down an anthill
114. Naturism Day
115. Today you are a cowboy
116. Petition Day
117. Enter a trailer trash competition today
118. Today put yourself forward for cloning
119. Iconoclasm day: deface a powerful image
120. Visit Benrikland today
121. Today record a suspicious greeting
122. Zombie Day
123. Six Degrees of Separation Day
124. Plagiarism Day
125. Amateur Day 4 (Tracy Shiraishi)
126. Today be a Good Spouse
127. Today be a virtual exhibitionist
128. Today become a movie extra
129. Tonight watch the sun set
130. Win $$$ if this is your DNA sequence!
131. Flashmob Day
132. Today impress your librarian
133. Mess up your kids so they turn into Picasso
134. Plant weed outside a government building
135. Hunter-gatherer day
REVOLUTION WEEK!

136. IDEOLOGY Revive communism
137. UNDERGROUND Print your own samizdat
138. EXILE Foment unrest away from home
139. PROPAGANDA Your revolutionary brand
140. REVOLUTION Hijack a train to your coup
141. NEW DAWN Impose your new society
142. PURGE Liquidate everyone you've met
143. Today confuse future archaeologists
144. Slapstick Day
145. Today be a model consumer
146. Hold hands all day today
147. Muzak Day
148. Adult Material Day
149. Amateur Day 5 (Alex Nicholson)
150. Hospitality Day
151. Make a shrine to a stranger
152. Sue for your share of Beethoven
153. Today return all unwanted gifts
154. Tonight go to sleep with a bedtime story
155. Dream analysis Day
156. Send a children's letter to someone today
157. Listen to a loved one's inner workings
158. Judgement Day
159. Today rearrange your local supermarket
160. Imagine you have the lifespan of a beetle
161. Make people believe you're a cyborg
162. Sing everything today
163. Today let the color orange dictate your life
164. Mouth something obscene to a stranger
165. Today leave a trail behind you everywhere
166. Mass Cheating Day
167. Become a superhero today
168. Write and thank your most influential teacher
169. Benrik Father's Day
170. Bite animals back today
171. Help Frankie choose his tattoo
172. Downshifting Day
173. Use your remote control for evil purposes
174. Amateur Day 6 (Tim Footman)
175. "Unusual Sporting Achievement" Day
176. Benrik Stamp Day
177. Help cobbler Piotr save his business today
178. Today hijack a public performance
179. Today presell your memoirs
180. Have all your food tasted for poison today
181. Today cause an international security alert
182. Make people believe in ghosts today
183. Today audition for Broadway
184. Prepare your own death today
185. Spend today up a tree
186. Today follow the crowd
187. Hidden Promise Day
188. Land Grab Day
189. Today write a letter to your future self
190. Today speak the unspeakable
191. Today, go halfway around the world
192. Sell your sperm or eggs today
193. Today impulse-buy
194. Today invoke an evil spirit
195. Hands free day
196. Today stare into people's homes
197. Today speedread a masterpiece
198. Today do everything in slow motion
199. Amateur Day 7 (Fiona Carey)
200. Attempt to be noticed from space today
201. Dumbing Down Day
202. Today mislead a tourist
203. Today become an Internet Minister

How are we doing?
At Benrik Limited, we are always looking for ways to improve the quality of our offering. Please help us serve you better by completing this suggestion card and sending it in to Benrik Ltd, PO Box 43D55, Houston. We want to give you what you want, so don't be shy: tell us what you think, however stupid it may seem.

	GREAT	GOOD	OK	MEDIOCRE	GHASTLY
How do you rate:					
Did you follow This Book Will Change Your Life?					
The cover	☐	☐	☐	☐	☐
How much did your life change out of 10?............./10					
The pictures	☐	☐	☐	☐	☐
Did it change for the better ☐ for the worse ☐					
The jokes	☐	☐	☐	☐	☐

Where did you buy This Book Will Change Your Life, Again?...
Who gave you This Book Will Change Your Life, Again?...
How did you meet them?...
What do you think Benrik Limited does particularly well?...
....
....
....
....
....
....
....

What do you think Benrik Limited does not so well?...
What areas do you think could be improved upon?...
What would you like Benrik Limited to add to the Book?...

If there is anything you want to discuss with us personally, contact our customer complaints department on www.thiswebsitewillchangeyourlife.com.

ALSO FROM BENRIK!

CHAIRMEN'S LETTER

Dear Shareholder: Benrik Ltd has delivered sustained progress over the fiscal year 2004/5, with inroads being made across the whole Benrik portfolio of companies, notwithstanding the negative impact of the weakening dollar/sterling exchange rate. The sharply fluctuating nature of geopolitical conditions, whilst regrettable in many respects, has enabled us to increase most of our activities, and we remain confident that the Benrik group is poised to take similar advantage of any further deterioration in international relations in the next few years on behalf of our shareholders. May we take this opportunity to thank the 13,400

Benrik employees across the globe. Their effort and sacrifices have made all this possible, and indeed they will be pleased to hear we have increased the "Benrik Widows Benefit Fund" as a result of an upward spike in fatalities this year. Overall it has been an excellent year though, and the board are therefore happy to report an increase in dividends to 34¢ a share. Roll on 2006†

Henrik Delehag

Ben Carey

Benrik Limited Accounts

Profit/loss reconciliation adjusted

$million

	2005				2004			
	Reported profit	Amortization	Special items	Pro forma result adjusted for special items	Reported profit	Amortization	Special items	Pro forma result adjusted for special items
Benrik Petroleum	**3,308**	**177**	**60**	**3,545**	**2,878**	**159**	**50**	**3,387**
Exploration (a)	1257	136	12	1,405	1,178	101	-	1,279
Drilling	213	-	36	249	208	-	-	208
Pumping	156	41	-	197	317	58	11	386
Refining (b)	1,682	-	12	1,694	1,475	-	39	1,514
Benrik Investments	**7,979**	**451**	**1,061**	**9,521**	**7,767**	**244**	**1,014**	**9,025**
Benrik Offshore (1)	2,431	251	1,010	3,692	3,104	129	982	4,215
Banque Benrik de Monaco	152	-	-	152	131	-	-	131
Benrik Global Assets	982	-	11	993	985	-	21	1,006
Benrik Corp ™(junk bonds)	651	45	28	724	413	32	11	456
BK Gold Bullion Reserves	718	32	-	750	719	5	-	724
Benrik Emerging Markets Fund (4)	2,610	153	-	2,763	2,415	78	-	2,493
Benrik al-Bandar (5)	435	-	12	447	-	-	-	-
Benrik Genetix ™ (d)	**732**	**218**	**-**	**950**	**511**	**198**	**-**	**709**
Benrik Operations	**2,264**	**243**	**21**	**2,528**	**1,591**	**31**	**-**	**1,652**
Weapons Systems (6b)	1,182	15	-	1,197	705	23	-	728
Airport Construction +	990	211	19	1,220	817	-	-	817
Performance art	11	-	-	11	39	3	-	42
Subliminal advertising	83	17	2	102	61	5	-	66
Books, TV, films, graphic design	(2)	-	-	(2)	(1)	-	-	(1)
Operating profit	**14,283**	**1,089**	**1,142**	**16,514**	**13,077**	**602**	**1,064**	**14,773**
Taxation	562				611			
Non-governmental taxation (e)	1,218				577			
Replacement cost profit	**13,503**				**11,889**			
Benrik Limited profit	**13,503**				**11,889**			

Notes: (a) Benrik's exploration and production activities were hampered in Iraq for local reasons this year, but we have more than made up the difference with a substantial yet discreet increase in output in new fields in Alaska. (b) Includes out-of-court settlement of $527,000,000 to the islanders of Nauru for the 'Project Vortex' incident. (1) Breakdown confidential: board directors eyes only. (4) New labour and human rights legislation means the following countries are no longer considered viable investing grounds for Benrik Emerging Markets: Bangladesh, Laos, Angola. (5) New division formed to pitch for post-Iraq US governmental contracts (cf also Remuneration Committee report on welcome hiring package for Edward Muskie Sr, ex-CEO of Houston Oil Inc.) (d) Includes one-off compensation to the 'Parents Of The Volcluj Nineteen' association. (6b) In response to dramatic increase in demand, Benrik Weapons System is to subdivide into two in 2006, Conventional and Non-Conventional. (e) In many countries where Benrik Ltd operates, it is customary to pay unofficial 'taxation' to governmental and non-governmental agents to facilitate transactions and ensure the security of Benrik staff. In 2005 the sums spent rose significantly as a result in particular of Benrik Genetix ™ research and development activities in Romania, and of our continuing interest in the TransCaspian pipeline project in central Asia.

* Caution: Benrik's Accounts 2004–2005 contain some forward-looking projections, particularly concerning cashflow and asset appreciation. By their nature, these projections involve risk and uncertainty because they relate to events that may or may not occur in the future. Benrik Limited have attempted to base them on reasonable assumptions, but cannot rule out they may prove incorrect. Additionally they are subject to change due to outside factors including world demand, currency fluctuations, political stability, legal developments, economic growth, new technology, wars and acts of terrorism or sabotage. Investors should take these into account before investing in Benrik Limited and/or any sister companies of the Benrik Limited group.

Benrik could not have created this Book without the help and support of the following individuals.

WE MENTION THEIR NAMES HERE IN LIEU OF ANY ACTUAL PAYMENT. THANK YOU TO:

Kathy Peach, Lana & Anton Delehag, Trena Keating, Jake Klisivitch, Emily Haynes, Fabiana Leme, Melissa Jacoby, Brant Janeway, Norina Frabotta, Clare Ferraro, Elizabeth Ives and all at Plume, Simon & Jack Trewin, Claire Gill, Scott Waxman, Juliet Brightmore, Shailesh Gor, Mark Cole, Jonas Jansson, Julie, Emil Lanne, Andy Moreno, Stuart, Robert Saville, Mark Waites, Matt Clark, Piers North, Jens Grede, Erik Torstensson, Sola, Katie, Nic and Beth at Saturday, Tom, Nick, Iain and all at Poke, Dom Loehnis, Trevor Franklin, Marc Valli & Lachlan at Magma, Hannah Sherman, Ben Ruddy, Kim Green, Kim's friend George, Julie & Michelle at Household, Eric Kearley, Jim Perry, Simon Kallgard, Naomi Hanlan, Rolf Fantom, Heming Welde Thorbjørnsen, Agneau Belanyek, Tim Owen, Gavan Fantom, Eli, Kate "Camel Shoes" Hicks, Joel Moss Levinson, Tracy Shiraishi, William Tiernan, Audrey Hantla, Elspeth Cloake, Billy Wagar, Fiona Carey, Alex Nicholson, Tim Footman, Tatiana Piatanova, David Shrigley, Myxo, the people of Swaziland and specifically Kaphunga, Richard Prue Alex & Elizabeth Carey, Aunt, Katy Follain, Antony Topping, Stefanie & Charlotte Drews, Gaby Vinader, Sarah & Aubrey Woodruff, Veronique Voiret, Clelia Uhart, Joel & Camille Chovet, Andy Cutbill, Jan Lyness, Sally Evans, Alan Payne, Rebecca Bland, Bernard Sue John & Ada Peach, Kenneth & Anna-Lena & Lovisa & Hjalmar & Elin Delehag, hela slakten, Rasmus & Maria & Joel, alla som jag velat ringa samt traffa men inte hunnit: kram!

www.thiswebsitewillchangeyourlife.com

All illustrations, photography, design and typography by Benrik, except as follows.

Where the work is not property and copyright of the authors, all attempts have been made by the authors to contact correct copyright holders. The authors would like to gratefully thank for permission to include the following within this edition:

Day 222 © David Shrigley; collage and various protected under the terms of the "copyleft" GNU Free Documentation License, thank you to the Marxists Internet Archive (www.marxists.org); day 3 model Stuart Campbell thanks Stuart; day 6 photography © Jonas Jansson; day 12 photography © Jens Mortenssen; illustration day 69 © Lana Delehag; photography day 73 Mark Cole; day 98 thank you to the true Catholic Church; day 131 illustration © Emil Lanne; day 171 photography © Jim Perry; day 204 illustration © Kim Green; day 208 photography © Philippe Halsman/Magnum Photos; day 216 photography © Jens Gustafsson & Magnus Engstrom; day 282 illustrations © Rasmus Nilsson; day 284 quote © Marinetti; day 348 quote © Julio Cortazar; day 356 photography © Jens Gustafsson & Magnus Engstrom; day 356 logo © Jonas Jansson; photography day 273 © Justin Newitter; days 16, 52, 70, 98, 100, 106, 110, 129, 157, 161, 177, 188, 205, 229, 239, 258, 265, 269, 283, 287, 292, 306, 309, 315, 322, 328, 353 photography & illustration © Getty Images; day 13 © Kate Hicks; day 29 © Beki Hill; day 32 © Mog Hunter; day 71 © Joel Moss Levinson; days 79 and 89 © Dave "Fierce Pancake" Beattie; day 85 © Jonas Jansson; day 87 © Katherine "incompletia" Calvert; day 93 © Astrid "sven_and_the_sexy_meats" Person; day 125 © Tracy Shiraishi; day 149 © Alex Nicholson; day 151 © Adam "Oscar" Radford; day 164 © Samantha Block; day 174 © Tim Footman; day 199 © Fiona Carey; day 203 © Jack "Bring_your_own_poison" Casey; day 212 Ian "Peregrin" Ferguson; day 224 © William Tiernan; day 262 © Audrey Hantla; day 272 © Zachary Krueger; day 273 © Jake Lindsey; day 275 © Rob "SpoonyBard" Hall; day 290 © Billy Wagar; day 301 © Joshua Hanshaw; day 302 © Samuel "Irn Bru" Wedge; day 303 © Gene "Shadowy" Sweeney; day 318 © Tatiana Piatanova; day 334 © Jessica "Mai-Mae" Wilson; day 335 © Ariel "Ariellyn" Lyn; day 358 © Elspeth Cloake; day 360 © Katy "Twiztedmuffin" Henderson; day 361 © Clare "stick_on_stars" Hobbs; day 363 © Chris "the_Farwall" Mannion. If there is further enquiry, please contact the authors c/o PFD, Drury House, 34-43 Russell St, London WC2B 5HA, UK.

PLUME, Published by the Penguin Group

Penguin Group (USA) Inc., 375 Hudson Street, New York, New York 10014, U.S.A.
Penguin Group (Canada), 10 Alcorn Avenue, Toronto, Ontario, Canada M4V 3B2 (a division of Pearson Penguin Canada Inc.)
Penguin Books Ltd, 80 Strand, London WC2R 0RL, England
Penguin Ireland, 25 St Stephen's Green, Dublin 2, Ireland (a division of Penguin Books Ltd)
Penguin Group (Australia), 250 Camberwell Road, Camberwell, Victoria 3124, Australia (a division of Pearson Australia Group Pty Ltd)
Penguin Books India Pvt Ltd, 11 Community Centre, Panchsheel Park, New Delhi – 110 017, India
Penguin Books (NZ), Cnr Airborne and Rosedale Roads, Albany, Auckland, New Zealand (a division of Pearson New Zealand Ltd)
Penguin Books (South Africa) (Pty) Ltd, 24 Sturdee Avenue, Rosebank, Johannesburg 2196, South Africa
Penguin Books Ltd, Registered Offices: 80 Strand, London WC2R 0RL, England

Published by Plume, a member of Penguin Group (USA) Inc. Originally published in slightly different form by Hodder and Stoughton, a division of Hodder Headline. First Plume Printing, November 2005

10 9 8 7 6 5 4 3 2 1

THIS
BOOK
HAS CHANGED
YOUR LIFE
AGAIN